Deat
the Small Screen

Death on the Small Screen

The Psychology of Viewing Violent Television

JONATHAN F. BASSETT

McFarland & Company, Inc., Publishers

Jefferson, North Carolina

This book has undergone peer review.

ISBN (print) 978-1-4766-8801-5
ISBN (ebook) 978-1-4766-4804-0

LIBRARY OF CONGRESS AND BRITISH LIBRARY
CATALOGUING DATA ARE AVAILABLE

Library of Congress Control Number 2022042949

Front cover images © 2022 Shutterstock

Printed in the United States of America

McFarland & Company, Inc., Publishers
Box 611, Jefferson, North Carolina 28640
www.mcfarlandpub.com

Acknowledgments

I would like to thank Dr. Lucas McMillan, dean of the College of Behavioral and Social Sciences at Lander University, and Dr. Richard Cosentino, president of Lander University, for their support in providing me with a sabbatical in the spring semester of 2020 to work on this book. Earlier versions of the material appearing in Chapters 3, 4, 5, 6, and 8 were presented as papers at annual meetings of the Popular Culture Association in the South. An earlier version of Chapter 7 was published in *PSYART: A Hyperlink Journal for the Psychological Study of the Arts* (Bassett, 2014).

I would like to thank my twin brother, Michael Bassett, for being my earliest television watching companion and for always being a sounding board for my ideas and analysis. I am grateful to my father, Fred Bassett, for being my first and best teacher and for introducing me to the writings of Ernest Becker. I thank Angela Tenga for her insightful comments on earlier versions of parts of this manuscript. I appreciate the useful feedback provided by two anonymous readers, and the helpfulness of Layla Milholen and the rest of the editorial staff at McFarland.

Lastly, I would like to thank my wife, Lori Bassett, for her patience, love, and support throughout the long process of researching and writing this book.

Table of Contents

Preface

Since childhood, I have been drawn to fictional violence. Growing up, I enjoyed watching professional wrestling; television shows and movies featuring ninjas, kung fu and other martial arts; the lethal exploits of swordsmen, barbarians, and the monstrous creatures they fought in low-budget fantasy films; and action shoot-em-ups with extreme body counts starring the likes of Chuck Norris and Arnold Schwarzenegger. I have also had a longstanding fascination with the topic of death. Even at a young age, I can remember grappling with the epistemic uncertainty and emotional apprehension surrounding the question of potential non-being. As an adolescent, I gravitated towards the death iconographies and themes found in the cover art and lyrics of heavy metal music groups like Iron Maiden.

My casual interest in death became an academic one when, as a teenager, I discovered the writings of cultural anthropologist Ernest Becker, author of *The Denial of Death* (1973), and then later, as a college student, the social psychological perspective known as Terror Management Theory (Greenberg, Pyszczynski, & Solomon, 1986). The central idea, so innovatively expressed in these works, that the awareness of death and the varied individual and cultural reactions to that awareness are essential to understanding human psychology was extremely appealing to me. I have spent the last 20 years as a research psychologist investigating people's attitudes about death. While my consumption of fictional violence continued, I found that my interpretations of these fictions were often colored by theories from existential psychology. I would frequently see the quest for both death denial and transcendence as the motives for the violence committed by fictional characters. Further, I began to question the ways in which these motives might also be shaping my reactions of gratification or discomfort in response to not only the violence depicted in what I was watching but also the co-occurring narratives that sought to justify or condemn that violence. I began to suspect that my longstanding interests in death and fictional violence were not coincidental nor idiosyncratic to

1

my unique personal experience. For the last 12 years, I have been applying insights from the psychology of death and dying to popular culture studies in the form of journal articles and conference presentations analyzing death themes in literature, movies, and television. This book represents the culmination of that work.

The aim of this book is to offer insights into the ways death anxiety and the psychological defenses people use to manage this anxiety shape audience appetites for and reactions to fictional depictions of violence in popular television. It is not my intention to condemn totally nor to exonerate entirely the consumption of fictional violence. Rather, I hope to demonstrate the ways that engagement with violence in television can have both potentially beneficial and harmful psychological consequences as people struggle to find the balance between denying the reality of death to minimize existential anxiety and acknowledging the finiteness of existence to foster an authentic and passionate approach to living. Exposure to images of death in violent television can have a cathartic payoff by bolstering psychological mechanisms that minimize existential anxiety in both direct and indirect ways, thereby making the consumption of fictional violence rewarding. However, any benefit of such exposure must be weighed against the possible negative consequences of watching fictional violence, which include reducing aversive emotional reactions to violence, validating belief systems that condone or promote violence and antipathy toward outgroups, increasing the appeal of social narratives that seek to legitimize injustice and oppression, and the tendency to avoid the confrontation with difficult existential and social issues that while painful are necessary for psychological growth.

In addition to presenting a general account of the role existential anxiety plays in shaping audience appetites for and reactions to television violence, this book also provides an extended and in-depth analysis of five specific television series: *Game of Thrones, The Punisher, Jessica Jones, Sons of Anarchy*, and *Hannibal*. Ideally, readers can take from the analyses of these shows a new appreciation of the ways in which psychological defenses triggered by the awareness of mortality can influence reactions to watching fictional violence. These insights might lead readers to new ways of interpreting and ascribing meaning to the programs they watch but might also cause them to interrogate their viewing habits more mindfully.

Introduction

The goal of this book is to present a psychological analysis of fictional depictions of lethal violence in popular culture. Unlike much work by social scientists in this area, my main focus is not on what role violence in media and entertainment plays in promoting and contributing to actual acts of aggression. Rather, I will explore the ways in which the paramount human psychological struggle to come to terms with mortality drives the appeal of fictional violence and influences consumers' reactions to fictional depictions of violent death. My approach is grounded in a perspective from empirical social psychology known as Terror Management Theory (TMT; Solomon, Greenberg, & Pyszczynski, 2015), which asserts that the awareness of death is the primary psychological force that plays a critical role in influencing people's thoughts, feelings, and actions at the individual and cultural levels.

Applying this perspective to the analysis of fictional violence offers (1) insights into how the motives of fictional killers reveal important truths about the motives underlying real-life violence, (2) an understanding that part of the appeal of fictional violence is rooted in the need to manage existential terror, (3) a description of the various ways in which consumption of violent entertainment can buttress psychological defenses that minimize the conscious experience of death anxiety, and (4) an expanded set of criteria for weighing the potential positive and negative consequences of exposure to fictional violence. Understanding how humans deal with the awareness of death in general is essential to understanding why people seek out images and stories of fictional killing and what effects such exposure has on them and their beliefs about the world.

The Psychological Problem of Mortality Awareness

Death is a universal and unwavering constant in the experience of all living things, but mortality plays an especially important role in defining

3

human nature because people not only must die but are also fully aware that finitude is a hallmark of their existential predicament. The awareness of death is both a bane and a boon. The bane is that it can potentially generate dread about the extinction of the self, the annihilation of consciousness and identity, and the permanent deprivation of desired interactions and experiences. The boon is that it can potentially imbue existence with beauty and meaning that maximizes an appreciation for the transient and motivates a sense of urgency to accomplish prioritized goals in a limited time span. The paramount psychological struggle is to find the right balance between unwavering awareness and total denial of death. A chronic and undisguised contemplation of the full reality of the precarious and fleeting nature of human existence would likely be overwhelming. Conversely, a totally sheltered outlook that completely denies the reality of death would lead to a dull existence devoid of passion and urgency. So people must seek the middle ground between a deer paralyzed in the headlights of inevitable doom and an oblivious ostrich with its head buried in the sands of denial.

Two prevalent human responses to the awareness of death have been (1) to attempt to avoid acknowledging personal vulnerability to death through suppression, repression, and denial and (2) to create cultural narratives that articulate human activities as more meaningful and enduring than those of other living organisms and describe means of transcending the death of the individual physical body in the form of either a literal religious afterlife or a symbolic merger with a concept or collective that offers hope to the living that their life has some impact that will continue to matter posthumously. Each approach can be effective at minimizing existential anxiety but does so at a potential cost. The comfort afforded by denial must be balanced against the potential costs of guilt over a life not fully lived, as the lack of anxiety may deprive people of the catalyst which energizes the authentic pursuits of intrinsic goals and dreams. Cultural belief systems reduce the sting of death awareness but often at the costs of increasing animosity and hostility towards those with incompatible beliefs systems who undermine the consensual validation needed to maintain unwavering confidence in the hope for immortality.

The psychological importance of death awareness is illustrated by the historical fascination with the topic evident in the earliest forms of storytelling, literature, art, mythology, and drama. Not only is the theme of death ubiquitous in cultural artifacts across human history, but the preponderance of treatments and depictions of death have also focused on violent death. Think, for example, of the violent deaths in ancient works such as the tragic plays of Sophocles or the epic poetry of Homer. The focus on violent death is not by accident but stems in part from the fact that cultural depictions of violence can both give expression to existential concerns about death while simultaneously reinforcing psychological defenses against those concerns.

For example, in the Gilgamesh epic, perhaps the oldest example of human literature, it is violence that makes Gilgamesh and his companion Enkidu feel invincible, as their strength and courage in battle allow them to slay the demon Humbaba and the Bull of Heaven. It is this perception, that the ability to conquer others implies that death itself can be conquered, which underlies the appeal of violent heroes. However, this illusion is challenged when Enkidu is cursed by the gods to die. The privileged King Gilgamesh must not only face the inevitable reality of the painful loss of others but also his own mortality. This confrontation with mortality motivates him to seek the secrets of literal immortality, and only when that fails, to strive for symbolic immortality through the fame of great deeds and the legacy of his kingdom.

The argument advanced in this book is that an important psychological motive behind the appeal of violent entertainment in modern mass media is the same one that has influenced the popularity of all historical cultural depictions of violence—namely a means of grappling with and potentially managing existential anxiety stemming from the human awareness of death.

How Can Exposure to Fictional Violence Lessen Existential Anxiety?

It may seem counterintuitive to suggest that choosing to seek out images of violent death would be a means of lessening anxiety about death because this strategy would appear to be intentionally forcing attention on the source of anxiety when avoidance of the unsettling subject matter would seem a better option. Suppression and avoidance are certainly prevalent ways that people try to deal with the anxiety potentially generated by the awareness of the inevitability of death. Ultimately, however, these strategies can never be fully effective by themselves because the reality of death cannot always be ignored, and even when not the focus of conscious attention, death anxiety rumbles below the surface lurking in the subconscious. Further, making a topic taboo increases its power over us in two ways. First, the mystery of the unknown makes it seem more frightening and intolerable. Second, forbidden topics become alluring and a source of morbid curiosity. Like the mythological victims of Medusa, we want to sneak a peek at the Gorgon's appearance not just in spite of it, but because we believe it is horrifying. There are several ways in which fictional depictions of violent death can potentially offer a balm against death anxiety. Some of these ways are enumerated below, but this should not be considered an exhaustive list.

First, fictional violence serves as a distraction that shifts attention away from the self and the existential problems arising from self-awareness and allows viewers a voyeuristic escape. The first and foremost defense against death anxiety is denial and suppression, and even though images of death are being presented, they are *Other* focused. By focusing on the violent deaths of fictional characters, viewers can avoid thinking about their own personal vulnerability to more likely causes of mortality. Second, the unrealism of fictional violence allows for a safer psychological distance from which people can confront the topic of mortality without feeling its full emotional impact. This is especially important in cultures and times where the topic is more taboo and where repression is the more dominant means of defense. Third, fictional depictions of killing allow for a sense of mastery over death by allowing viewers to identify with the perpetrators of killing, thereby fostering the illusion that death is something that happens to others and not the self. Killing involves asserting power and authority over life and death. Consequently, identifying with those who inflict death on others transfers a vicarious sense of power over death.

Fourth, focus on violent death facilitates the perspective that death is something that can be avoided through proper vigilance and right living. Viewers can imagine ways in which the fictional victims of violent death deserved their fate for moral, strategic, or intellectual failings and can imagine themselves as immune to the same fate as long as they avoid making the same mistakes. Fictional violence is frequently presented in the context of narrative structures that propagate palliative cultural messages and reinforce comforting worldviews, such as notions of fairness and belief in a just world where the immoral or foolish are victims of violence and the wicked are punished via retributive violence that neutralizes threat and restores justice. Fifth, the narrative structures accompanying presentations of fictional violence can present pathways to symbolic immortality where the successful use of violence is a means to heroism and results in being honored and venerated in this life and posthumously. Further, violence is often presented as a successful way of defending the literal safety and ideological integrity of collectives with which identity is merged, such as family, tribe, or nation. Violence against outgroup members is not only often presented as necessary to protect the physical well-being of the in-group but also as a way of transmitting the cultural values and beliefs that make up the death-denying ideology of that group. Violence is a means of dealing with the symbolic threat posed by *the Others* with their competing and contradictory ideologies and values. Violence eliminates the threat of *the Other* via their forceful conversion or their annihilation. Thus, the fictional depiction of the violent purgation of the evil *Others* assures consumers of the correctness of their cultural belief system and bolsters confidence in the immortality it promises.

Powers and Perils of Exposure to Fictional Depictions of Violent Death

This book explores how exposure to fictional depictions of violent death can have both good and bad consequences. Most examinations of the effects of exposure to fictional violence focus on three negative consequences: (1) the possibility that fictional violence promotes actual aggression, (2) the possibility described in the Cultivation Theory of television (Gerbner, 1969a) that exposure to fictional violence warps viewers' conceptions of the real world such that they come to overestimate the rates of actual violence and come to perceive the world as more dangerous than it objectively is, and (3) the possibility that fictional violence makes people callous and insensitive to the suffering of victims of real-world violence. The first of these consequences is not the primary focus of this book but is briefly considered here in order to put the later arguments in context.

Social scientists have long been interested in the degree to which exposure to media violence has deleterious effects. The most frequently investigated question is whether media violence increases actual aggression. Despite the copious quantities of research on the topic, there is still controversy and contention regarding the issue. The preponderance of the evidence suggests that exposure to media violence does have some impact on increasing aggression (Anderson et al., 2003; Bushman & Huesmann, 2006; Krahe, 2012). However, these effects tend to be small in magnitude and are more robustly substantiated for outcomes focused on aggressive thoughts, hostile feelings, and laboratory simulations of violence (e.g., participants think they are blasting another person with a loud noise or administering them an electric shock) than for outcomes focused on actual violent behaviors in the real world outside the laboratory. Media is just one of hundreds of variables affecting aggression, and there are numerous moderating and attenuating factors. Consequently, the number of consumers of violent media who will be driven to mimic in the real world the fictional violence they see on screen is likely very small. Even so, it is still fair to conclude that violent entertainment does contribute to hostile thoughts and feelings and potentially, at least for some consumers, may increase the likelihood of aggressive behaviors.

Other commonly investigated negative consequences of fictional violence are how it shapes people's worldviews. These consequences have been most extensively studied in relation to violence on television. Violent television can contribute to overestimating actual levels of violence, thereby promoting belief in a mean world, such that people perceive others as more menacing and the world as more dangerous than is actually the case (Appel, 2008; Gerbner & Gross, 1976; Shrum, 2001). In addition, exposure to increasingly graphic and extreme forms of fictional violence may desensitize viewers to real life violence. The principle of habituation states that constant exposure to the same amount of a stimulus produces a diminishing response. Thus, a heavy dose of violent television might numb people, such that they are less bothered by incidences of actual violence and consequently perhaps less motivated to take action or support efforts to curtail it.

The position advanced in the pages that follow is that beyond the potential consequences articulated above, there are additional positive and negative effects of fictional violence related to the human need to grapple with issues of mortality. Fictional violence serves the important psychological function of helping people deal with existential anxiety stemming from the awareness of death. Some degree of denial is necessary in order to mitigate death anxiety to the point where it does not impair the ability to function effectively; however, too much denial is stultifying in that it prevents authentic and full engagement with life. So, while fictional depictions of violent death may be palliative towards death anxiety, they may also prevent the type of constructive grappling with existential issues that leads to psychological growth.

In addition to denial, another way people deal with the problem of mortality is by looking for ways to symbolize how they can participate in and contribute to something that will exist and matter beyond the scope of their physical body. One of the main functions of cultural belief systems is to allay fears of mortality by articulating pathways to immortality. The depiction of death or the threat of possible death prevalent in violent entertainment makes mortality salient to consumers of such fictional violence, thereby intensifying the appeal of comforting belief systems. The content of the cultural messages and ideological beliefs presented in the narrative context of fictional violence become more persuasive to consumers of these narratives because of the existential concerns raised by the violence displayed. Belief systems can vary not just in terms of the degree to which they dampen existential anxiety but also in the extent to which they infringe upon the rights of others and promote aggression and hostility towards those who fail to agree fully with all aspects of the belief system or who endorse alternative beliefs. Rigid, dogmatic, and authoritarian worldviews tend to be the most comforting in terms of the certainty with which they provide their adherents with assurances of transcendence and immortality. However, these worldviews also tend to be the most restrictive of individual autonomy and the most intolerant of differences, in that they insist on unwavering and unquestioned support from adherents and promote hostility and aggression against those who reject, deviate from, or support alternative beliefs.

Reminders of the reality of our mortality can be an opportunity for self-evaluation and psychological growth but more often trigger reflexive and habitual psychological defenses that can be stultifying to the self and can potentially promote animosity and hostility towards others. The nature of our responses to reminders of mortality depends in large part on our awareness of how such reminders can affect us, our mindfulness in monitoring our reactions, and our willingness to resist knee-jerk reactions to suppress the unpleasant and to allow ourselves at least temporarily to feel and tolerate anxiety. Similarly, fictional depictions of violence can serve as an impetus for reflecting on personal mortality in a positive way that stimulates the authentic prioritization of intrinsic and growth motives and that promotes the contemplation, interrogation, and critique of conventional cultural beliefs and practices. More frequently though, fictional depictions of violence facilitate the denial of the reality of personal death by propagating the belief that death is something that happens to the alien and morally flawed *Other*, not to the self and by reinforcing the idea that violence is a necessary and heroic means of protecting traditional cultural values and conventional ideologies through the sense of death transcendence and symbolic immortality they provide.

It is not my intention to condemn the consumption of fictional violence as unilaterally harmful and thoroughly irredeemable nor to exonerate it totally as merely harmless fun. Rather, it is my contention that, across all modalities of arts and entertainment, fictional depictions of violence are cultural constructions, and as such they must be understood as sometimes serving the same important psychological function served by many aspects of culture—namely helping people deal with the awareness of mortality and helping them to find purpose and meaning in the face of this awareness. Presentations of fictional violence can promote either an excessive suppression or an authentic embrace of the existential reality that is the shared human condition. Similarly, consumption of fictional violence can justify the comforting hopes of transcendence offered by cultural assumptions that justify inequalities and injustices maintained by the status quo or can challenge viewers to question the validity of these assumptions. The exact nature of a given response to fictional violence will differ from person to person and within the same person over time depending on the ways in which violence is presented and the mindset of the consumer.

Anxieties about death are best allayed and concerns about death quickly dispelled by comforting depictions in which characters are presented as unambiguously good or bad, victims are presented as deserving of the violence inflicted upon them, and violence is celebrated as a means of restoring justice, creating opportunities for heroism, and protecting the physical and symbolic aspects of identity invested in the collected in-group to which consumers/viewers belong. While such depictions of violence bolster psychological defenses that mitigate existential terror and prevent the debilitating experience of overwhelming anxiety, they do so at the costs of increasing the acceptance of uses of violence against others in reality and by fostering a reflexive allegiance to conventional worldviews that maintain social injustices and protect the status quo. Fictional presentations of a just world, in which the righteous prevail over the wicked, reduce anxiety by facilitating the belief that because the world is fair, people can transcend and possibly avoid death by adherence to cultural standards of proper conduct. However, such depictions also promote complacency about the suffering of others and a blindness to the injustices experienced by others.

Conversely, heightened existential anxiety can occur in response to watching fictional violence in several circumstances including: when depictions present characters as morally ambiguous, violence equally impacts the wicked and the righteous, characters on both sides of conflicts struggle with moral and ethical reservations about the use of violence and search for non-violent alternatives, the full scope of detrimental consequences of violence are shown affecting the perpetrators of violence and those who cared about their victims, and the motivations of all characters are presented as misguided in unquestioned allegiance to flawed ideologies. If consumers can temporarily tolerate the heightened anxiety experienced in response to such depictions, it can afford an opportunity for thoughtful contemplation of the reality that existence is finite and to a genuine questioning of how best to pursue a meaningful life in a way that least infringes on the rights of others.

Overview of the Subsequent Chapters

Chapter 1 reviews various previous theories regarding the appeal of violent entertainment, including the idea that it allows viewers a chance to exercise evolutionary vestiges of life-or-death responses that are not given adequate expression in the safety of modern life, that it provides a cathartic draining away of inherent aggressive impulses that are constrained by moral injunctions against violence, and that it provides a vicarious form of thrill seeking. Then, the focus shifts to examining the central argument that fictional violence serves as a means of gratifying curiosity about death in a cultural milieu in which the topic is taboo and as a means of managing anxieties about personal mortality. Sociological and historical evidence is presented for how decreasing exposure to actual death, co-varied with increased interest in fictional depictions of death in violent and graphic displays, satisfied fascination about the topic, but in sensationalized ways devoid of emotional context. Evidence from numerous psychodynamic theorists is then presented for the existence of psychological defenses that manage anxiety about death. The effective functioning of these defenses is presented as essential to psychological well-being, and arguments are made for several possible ways that viewing fictional violence could bolster these defenses against death anxiety.

Chapter 2 presents an overview of Terror Management Theory (Pyszczynski, Solomon, & Greenberg, 2015), which is a well validated perspective from empirical psychology that places minimizing the conscious experience of death anxiety as the primary motive for a wide range of human behaviors, many of which may not initially seem obviously related to the problem of mortality. The basic idea behind Terror Management Theory (TMT) is that cultural belief systems help protect people against death anxiety by denying and disguising the reality of death and by describing ways by which people can perceive that their life matters in a way that will leave an enduring impact and legacy. Consequently, TMT extends the ways through which violent media can have cathartic effects on death anxiety beyond those described in Chapter 1. TMT offers valuable insights into the motives underlying the appeal of fictional violence and into different audience reactions to violent entertainment. Further, TMT offers a novel approach that compliments other more traditional approaches to popular culture criticism by providing a modern psychological explanation for the motives of and reactions to fictional characters.

Chapter 2 will focus on articulating the main principles of TMT as a general theory of human psychology and will present a broad overview of the empirical research evidence supporting the various hypotheses derived from the theory. The material in Chapter 2 will provide a better understanding of TMT in general, which in turn will facilitate readers' ability to analyze the application of TMT principles to addressing the appeal of fictional violence and the possible lessons TMT can offer consumers of works of fictional violence regarding a better understanding of the cultural artifacts they consume as well as insights into their own reactions to these artifacts. However, the material in Chapter 2 is not essential to understanding the arguments advanced in the subsequent chapters. Consequently, readers eager to learn more about TMT applications specifically related to fictional violence in the realm of art and entertainment can skip ahead to Chapter 3.

Chapter 3 offers an overview of how psychological defenses against death anxiety shape people's reactions to literature, visual art, television, and film. This chapter presents the results of TMT research showing that reminders of death increase preferences for works that offer orderly and meaningful depictions of reality, facilitate epistemic certainty, promote a sense of fairness and justice, and champion the validity of strongly held cultural beliefs. Next, the chapter explores how fictional characters' motives for violence can be interpreted from the perspective of TMT and how such interpretations mirror the role of TMT defenses in contributing to actual violence. The desire to overcome powerlessness and to achieve a sense of mastery over death by inflicting it on others, the need to bolster confidence in the validity of death-transcending ideologies by annihilating those who challenge or threaten one's cultural worldview, and the quest for symbolic immortality in the form of infamy in which one is remembered for their destructive acts, are all presented as terror management motives for actual violence that can be seen in fictional depictions of killing. The chapter ends with an analysis of the potential positive and negative effects exposure to fictional killing can have on viewers and how these effects can vary based on the characteristics of the content and the consumers.

Chapters 4 through 8 mark a transition from a broad analysis of the general applications of TMT for understanding the appeal and consequences of consuming fictional violence to a more narrow and in-depth analysis of five specific television series: *Game of Thrones* (Chapter 4), *The Punisher* (Chapter 5), *Jessica Jones* (Chapter 6), *Sons of Anarchy* (Chapter 7), and *Hannibal* (Chapter 8). My decision to focus on television was made because there has been less attention in the existing literature to analyzing television from the TMT perspective compared to the more prevalent TMT analysis of film (DeFrain, Landau, & Greenberg, 2019; Greenberg, 2019; McMahon, 2019; Schmitt, Sullivan, & Young, 2019; Sullivan & Greenberg, 2013a; Sullivan, Greenberg, & Landau, 2009).

Furthermore, contemporary television series like the ones selected for analysis here elicit strong levels of engagement from audiences, and it is this type of intense engagement that is likely to promote the type of contemplation of cultural worldviews described in TMT. While television may have previously been thought of as a mindless medium in which viewers passively absorb simplistic and formulaic content, this is no longer the case. For example, television scholars have argued that changing technologies, such as streaming services, which facilitated and promoted binge watching, allowed for a trend of increasing narrative complexity in television. This greater narrative complexity fosters intense audience engagement as it requires high levels of investment from viewers in terms of effortful and attentive viewing and also in terms of time and willingness to re-watch previous episodes in light of new revelations (Mittell, 2006). Similarly, the success of television programs in the era of smaller and more fragmented audiences depends on the ability of programs to generate audience engagement not merely in the form of viewing but also by engaging with content related to and inspired by the show in multiple online platforms and outlets (Askwith, 2007).

The five television series selected for analysis all share the characteristics of being recent enough to still be culturally relevant (the last episodes aired between 2014 and 2019), being impactful in terms of widespread viewership, critical acclaim or both, and containing high levels of violence (oftentimes graphic and extreme violence). It is my hope that the analysis of each series from the TMT perspective will enhance fans' appreciation and complement and expand existing scholarly dialogues. In addition, each series serves as a case study for illustrating the ways in which lethal violence on the small screen can both challenge and augment psychological defenses against death anxiety. Some of the series are more palliative against death anxiety than others, and they also vary in the extent of their potential negative impact based on the types of cultural messages presented. However, all the shows are treated as complex amalgams having the dual potential to anesthetize and stimulate viewers. It is my hope that readers might glean from these case studies a better understanding of audience reactions to violent television in general but also, perhaps, insight into the ways TMT processes might influence their own preferences and responses to television. Even more boldly, I hope that readers might gain from an analysis of the defenses of the characters in these engaging fictions some wisdom for how to find balance in their personal confrontations with difficult existential questions.

Chapter 4 considers the numerous ways in which the gruesome violence and high death toll in the hit HBO series *Game of Thrones* actually dampens viewers' concerns about personal mortality by bolstering psychological defenses against death anxiety. The series tends to glorify violence as a means of retributive justice and encourages viewers to celebrate the deaths of those characters who were responsible for the vilest of violent misdeeds. These glorifications of violence exist simultaneously alongside cautionary tales about the evils of blind devotion to ideologies that rationalize violence as a necessary means of making the world a better place. The chapter also explores the ways TMT defenses activated in response to prevalent imagery of death can potentially facilitate acceptance of sexism and misogyny in some viewers while prompting resistance to these messages in others.

Chapter 5 and Chapter 6 examine two series on Netflix inspired by Marvel comics (*The Punisher* and *Jessica Jones*) and the ways in which superheroes can not only alleviate death anxiety but also raise challenging existential questions. Superheroes bolster death denial through the fact that they survive countless violent confrontations with villains and buffer hopes for death transcendence through their religious-like ability to defy the laws of the natural world and their ability to mete out absolute and inerrant justice. However, a trend towards grittier, morally ambiguous heroes who wear the mantle of hero uncomfortably, blur or cross ethical boundaries, and struggle to find meaning and purpose in their heroism, offer less of a balm against existential anxiety than provide characters with whom consumers can more easily identify and relate to in terms of the difficulty they face constructing coherent and comforting worldviews for themselves. Both series raise challenging existential and social issues, but *The Punisher* is more palliative, whereas *Jessica Jones* is more provocative.

Chapter 7 offers an analysis of the interplay between morality and mortality in the dilemmas encountered in the violent lives of members of the SAMCRO motorcycle club in the FX television series *Sons of Anarchy*. *Sons of Anarchy* is neither entirely palliative nor provocative in its depictions of violence but a mixture of both. The prevalence of violence and death iconography in the series serves as a powerful elicitor of mortality salience, but the show also facilitates defenses that assuage death anxiety by inviting identification with members of SAMCRO as instruments of death. Further, by presenting as heroic the members' defense of their club, the show validates viewers' own quest for symbolic immortality by the merger of identify with larger social entities and justifies violence as a necessary means of protecting these immortality projects. Mortality salience increases the desire to uphold the moral principles of cultural worldviews, but this desire is often frustrated by the presentation of extreme moral dilemmas in which multiple moral principles come into conflict.

Chapter 8 uses insights from TMT to explain the fear but more importantly the fascination elicited by the aesthete murderer and gourmet cannibal Dr. Hannibal Lecter in the NBC series *Hannibal*. The character of Hannibal Lecter is captivating and even alluring in that he not only raises viewers' concerns about mortality and corporeality but also simultaneously buttresses psychological defenses against these concerns. The series can potentially comfort viewers with a sense of normalcy in comparison to the deviance of Lecter. Alternatively, it might challenge viewers into the unsettling realization that the same death-denying motives underlying Hannibal's justifications for his peculiar violence are potentially at work in their own minds promoting the acceptance and condoning of more mundane types of violence.

The concluding summary offered in the final thoughts section explores the possible ways to weigh the potential value of violent television in mitigating existential anxiety against the potential harms. The exact nature of the response evoked will depend on several viewer characteristics including their cultural, political, and moral dispositions, their ability to tolerate anxiety and ambiguity, the relative strength of their growth versus defensive orientation, as well as their mindfulness and their ability and willingness to monitor and reflect on their viewing choices and reactions. An awareness of the ways psychological motives shape viewing preferences and reactions can empower savvy consumers to be intentional about their own choices of what to watch and to interrogate what their reactions to violent television reveal about their own struggles with or avoidance of existential issues.

1

Dying to Watch

The Role of Death Anxiety in the Appeal of Fictional Violence

There seems to be an insatiable appetite for violent entertainment. Death, torture, and mayhem compete for onscreen attention in images of zombies, serial killers, gunslingers, knights, gangs, vigilantes, and innumerable other forms. While there are certainly many popular non-violent viewing options and many people who prefer these other options over the consumption of fictional violence, it is safe to say that violence and violent death are a longstanding mainstay of television and cinema. Further, the consistent interest in violent entertainment warrants the claim that the widespread viewing of such entertainment says something about the culture producing and consuming fictional violence. As Desilet (2014) noted,

> The ubiquitous presence and consistent popularity of antagonal screen violence confections in the entertainment marketplace confirm a broad obsession and fascination, not just with violence in general, but with violence of the kind associated with justice and celebration. The broad appeal of this kind of entertain-ment, with its increasing extremes of shocking intensity, offers compelling proof in itself of the existence of a culture of violence [p. 20].

Likewise, Zillmann (1998) observed that "there can be no doubt that fictional superviolence is an enormous attraction" (p. 180). The fascination with violence is not new, is not merely a product of contemporary technologies, and has been a focal point of human narrative long before modern media. Shaw (2004) made the point that television and cinema did not create the appetite for fictional violence but rather cater to, reinforce, and amplify it, stating that "the overwhelming historical presence of violence in folklore, mythical legends, nursery rhymes, lullabies, literature, theatre and film suggests that violence which is experienced receptively through a dramatized medium has some kind of allure" (pp. 131–132). While television may not have been responsible for people's appetites for violence, it certainly facilitated the ability to feed that appetite on a grand scale. Felson (1996) observed that "technological advances have dramatically increased the availability of violent entertainment" and "the introduction of television was critical, particularly in making violent entertainment more available" (p. 237).

Concerns about the levels of violence in television have been around for decades. As early as 1972, the U.S. Surgeon General's Scientific Advisory Committee in Television and Social Behavior was expressing concerns about the levels of television violence, in statements such as this:

> Studies of media content show that violence is and has been a prominent component of all mass media in the United States. Television is no exception, and there can be no doubt that violence figures prominently in television entertainment. People are probably exposed to violence by television entertainment more than they are exposed by other media because they use television so much more [p. 3].

One of the earliest and most influential attempts to quantify the extent and nature of violence on television occurred in the late 1960s with the Cultural Indicators Project (Gerbner, 1969b). This project examined the entire content of dramatic programing (excluding newscasts and documentaries) aired during primetime and Saturday morning viewing hours on network television for a one-week period in October of 1967 and again in 1968. The examination of more than 120 hours of aired content revealed a substantial amount of violence, with 1215 individual acts of violence being depicted at a rate of about five per program or seven per hour. Further, of the 183 programs broadcast, 149 contained at least some violence. The results indicated that serious and frequently lethal violence was commonplace in television and that it was presented predominantly in the context of clear-cut conflict between monolithic good and evil factions (typically defined along national or ethnic lines) and often as a means of achieving a satisfying outcome with little or no negative repercussions to the perpetrators of violence.

An additional large-scale effort attempting to quantify the prevalence of television violence was done in the 1990s. The National Television Violence Study (Wilson et al., 1997, 1998) monitored 23 channels from 6:00 a.m. to 11:00 p.m. daily for 20 weeks and repeated this process each year for three years from 1994 to 1997. The results indicated that 61 percent of programs contained at least some violence. Based on estimates of averages of violent television content and typical patterns of viewership, it has been estimated that by 18 years of age, the average young person will have viewed an estimated 200,000 acts of violence on television alone (Huston et al., 1992).

In preparation for this book, I did my own informal analysis. I looked at the top 100 most watched television programs in the 2018–2019 season based on Nielsen viewership ratings and the level of violence and gore described for each program on the IMDB parent guide. I found that seven of the 100 most viewed programs had severe ratings for violence and gore, and an additional 17 had moderate ratings. Next, I looked at the shows rated as the most violent on IMDB. The average quality rating of the 23 shows that made the list of most violent was 8.0 on a 10-point scale. Although certainly not comprehensive, these findings indicate that violent television shows are not only popular in terms of viewership but also that viewers rate them as being of high quality. Paxton (2015) made a similar observation, noting that many of the shows with the most violent content also tended to be "the most astonishingly artistic and interesting shows on television."

What are we to make of the broad appeal of fictional violence in entertainment? There is no theoretical consensus, but rather several speculative suggestions in regard to addressing this question. The answer that I will advance throughout this book is that the main motivation underlying the consumption of fictional violence is that such consumption helps people manage anxieties about death. Before articulating the arguments for how viewing violent media serves the function of lessening death anxiety, I will review several other competing theories about the appeal of violence.

Competing Theories Attempting to Explain the Appeal of Violence

Several theories focus on the importance of violence in the ancestral past and posit an evolutionary influence in shaping appetites for violence. One version of this evolutionary argument posits that fascination with violence and gore in entertainment is an artifact of a neurological reward system shaped in an evolutionary past when hunting was essential and in which pain, blood, and death signaled the availability of food and consequently came to be associated with pleasure (Nell, 2006).

An alternative version of the evolutionary argument focuses on the idea that we do not so much find imagery of violence rewarding or enjoyable but rather that we find it captivating. From this perspective, we evolved to pay attention to violence because it had life and death consequences, and consequently, we find it highly salient and arousing. Our minds were shaped in an evolutionary past where life and death situations mandating fight or flight responses were common. We now live in a sterilized, safe, and sanitary environment where we do not get the same level of stimulation, so we seek out vicarious stimulation. Therefore, fictional violence provides needed stimulation and relief from boredom by creating vicarious excitement in unexciting times (Elias & Dunning, 1970). The powerful emotions potentially elicited by images of violence are a substitute for the lack of real-life thrills due to the absence of the fight or flight eliciting types of confrontations that may have characterized our ancestors' struggles for daily survival in less civilized times. This *need for stimulation* argument has been summarized as follows:

> It has only been in relatively recent times that the dangers of the world have been significantly reduced. Sure, you can get hit by a car, struck by lightning, or fall off a ladder, but the odds of getting picked off by a lion or ambushed by a marauding band of enemies are relatively rare.... Enter vicarious sensation seeking: the kinds of experiences when we can elevate our arousal levels by pretending that we are in danger [Kottler, 2011, pp. 182–283].

Support for the vicarious stimulation argument comes from research showing that individual differences on the personality trait of sensation seeking are predictive of preferences for frightening and violent media such as horror movies (Hoffner & Levine, 2005). Sensation seeking is defined as "the seeking of varied, novel, complex, and intense sensations and experiences, and the willingness to take physical, social, legal, and financial risks for the sake of such experience" (Zuckerman, 1994). Higher levels of sensation seeking are associated with higher scores on the Curiosity about Morbid Events Scale, which measures enjoyment of violent media including horror as well as fascination with true crime, news coverage of murder, and violent spectacles (Zuckerman & Litle, 1986).

A third explanation for the appeal of fictional violence is rooted in the attraction to those who possess the dominance to inflict violence on others. Humans, like other primates, are social animals with dominance hierarchies. In the past, men's status was more strongly tied to their physical strength and aggression as these would have facilitated their skills as hunters and warriors. As a consequence, aggression would have been linked to greater access to resources and more social influence. Success in hunting and warfare conveyed not only survival benefits but also reproductive benefits, as intra-sexual competition between men for status, leadership positions, and access to mates was also likely tied to physical dominance. As part of the gender socialization process, cultures would promote male aggression as a value to be cultivated. From this perspective, there is a vestige of this tendency to value aggression and physical dominance in our veneration of athletes in violent sports like boxing and MMA and also in the appeal of the violent action hero.

Proponents of this position have argued that gender role socialization explains the enjoyment of violent and frightening media such as watching horror films. In the past and today in many hunter gatherer societies, males must undergo a rite of passage to evidence their bravery and stoicism before being deemed a man and ready to take on the adult responsibilities of hunting and warfare. In modern post-industrial societies, such rites of passage are lacking, but there is still a vestige of gender socialization that expects men to be brave and tough. Watching frightening and disgusting images of violence without showing strong emotional reactions is the modern version of trial by fire through which adolescent males demonstrated their bravery and masculinity (Zillmann & Gibson, 1996).

Another type of argument for the appeal of fictional violence is underpinned by psychodynamic ideas in addition to evolutionary theorizing and focuses on the idea of catharsis. Catharsis has been characterized as the idea that consumption of fictional violence serves to "draw out negative emotions, such as fear, rage, and disgust, to render the mind more healthy and to protect the social order by providing a safe outlet for 'unsafe' emotions" (McCauley, 1998, p. 147). It is important to note that there are two distinctive variants of the catharsis argument that differ in terms of claims about what exactly is being purged. The first way to think about catharsis is as a means of draining aggressive impulses. This approach assumes people are inherently violent by their nature, and yet because of societal constraints, people turn to fictional violence for the vicarious satisfaction of their own aggressive impulses in fantasy that are denied them in reality. This perspective assumes (1) people have an intrinsic drive towards violence, (2) fictional violence is rewarding because it somehow satisfies this drive, and (3) the gratification of the aggressive drive-in fantasy reduces the need to act on it in reality by perpetrating real-world aggression. A second way to think about catharsis is as a means of alleviating fear and anxiety. From this perspective, fictional depictions of violence allow viewers to gain a sense of mastery and control over their own fears. It is this second meaning of catharsis that is most relevant to the arguments I wish to advance in this book. Before turning our attention to the fear aspect of catharsis, let us briefly consider the proposition that fictional violence purges aggressive impulses and some of the problems with this argument.

One possibility is that the appeal of violent entertainment is an indictment of the baser aspect of human nature—a testimonial to the intractable bloodlust inherent in the human condition. The violence inherent in human nature and the appeal of guilt free outlets for its expression was examined by the empirical philosopher Alford (1997) in his study of evil. Alford described the classic Milgram (1963, 1974) obedience studies to both a group of prison inmates convicted of violent crimes and a control community sample and asked for their insights into the behavior of the participants in these experiments. In Milgram's (1963, 1974) infamous studies, participants were instructed to give incrementally increasing voltages of shocks to another person in the context of an investigation of how punishment affects learning. In reality, the other person was not getting shocked, and the true purpose of the study was to determine at what point the participants would disobey the experimenter and refuse to administer any more shocks. The majority of participants in the Milgram studies never refused to obey and administered the full scope of shocks up to the highest possible voltage.

In Alford's (1997) study, the community sample offered the traditional social science explanations about how the Milgram studies reveal that even good people can be coerced into harming others by succumbing to powerful conformity pressures. In contrast, the inmates viewed the experiments as revealing the inherent evil of people. They were convinced that the teachers wanted to hurt the learner and enjoyed delivering the shocks. The inmates focused not on how the participants must have caved to authority but on how the authority figure gave them an excuse, a guilt-free means to satisfy their natural violent impulses. One inmate responded, "People love to watch violence, and they love to do violence. They just don't want to admit it. So, here this dude tells them to do it, and they must love it … a chance to do their violence and pretend it's all in a good cause" (p. 28).

If people do inherently crave violence, then the volume of consumption of violent entertainment can be conceptualized as a good thing to the extent that it is viewed as cathartic in the purgation of these aggressive impulses in fantasy such that they may be less likely to give rise to real-world violence. This argument is epitomized by the speculations of horror writer Stephen King (1981) who asserted that "the potential lyncher is in almost all of us (excluding saints, past and present; but then, most saints have been crazy in their own ways), and every now and then, he has to be let loose to scream and roll around in the grass" (p. 526). King further described viewing horror as "lifting a trap door in the civilized forebrain and throwing a basket of raw meat to the hungry alligators swimming around in that subterranean river beneath" and suggested that the benefit of watching horror is that it feeds the alligators and keeps repressed violent urges from entering conscious awareness where they might be acted upon (p. 527).

Kottler (2011) offered a scholarly argument for the innate human capacity for violence, suggesting that "we each hold within us the capacity to respond violently and swiftly to any threat or problem that confronts us" (p.23). He further asserted that this universal human propensity for violence was a product of an ancestral environment where aggressive responses were often necessary to deal with dangers such as those posed by predators. From this perspective, in a modern environment where such threats are less frequently encountered, our retained predilection for violence that was ingrained by evolution is now rechanneled into a captivation with fictional violence. Further, Kottler defended the cathartic effect of vicarious exposure to violence, claiming that "among the reasons why there is such a fascination for violence as a form of entertainment is that it provides a kind of vicarious gratification that can actually prevent destructive or antisocial behavior" (p. 36).

Zillmann (1998) is skeptical of catharsis theories, which assert that consumption of violent media is driven by the need to quell some aversive state such as fear and is thereby negatively reinforced as viewing fictional violence purges the undesired emotion, increasing the likelihood of future consumption. Zillmann is critical of these approaches and views them as lacking in empirical support of the assumed underlying fear and incompatible with existing evidence that watching violent media increase rather than decreased negative emotions. Zillmann describes two fundamental problems confronting catharsis explanations: "first, the existence of the presumed anxieties and ill emotions from which relief is sought is by no means established; and second, the presumed power of violent expositions to provide relief from the anxieties and ill emotions is very much in doubt" (p. 185).

The "feeding the gators" version of catharsis exemplified earlier in King's (1981) writings, in which the goal of violent entertainment is to pacify viewer's own aggressive urges, does not fare well when evaluated on either of these fundamental issues. First, while the assumption that there is a persistent and universal human predilection towards violence would account for the current popularity of violent entertainment, it does not explain why the apparent increase in the prevalence and appeal of fictional violence was preceded by a decrease in actual violence. Second, the preponderance of evidence indicates that consumption of violent media is associated with an increase in hostile feelings, thoughts, and intentions. Let us address each of these issues in more detail.

If violent entertainment is a gratification of inherent violent impulses that would give rise to actual aggression if not satisfied in fantasy, then audience demand for it should increase as individuals within a society become increasingly aggressive in their sensibilities. In contrast to this expectation, people seem to be becoming more empathic and less cruel in their real-life sensibilities. For example, political scientists James Payne (2004) has argued that the human appetite for violence and killing has decreased over time and that one of the causes underlying this change is the increasing value placed on human life. As new technologies extended life expectancies and improved the quality of life, perceptions of one's own life became more valuable, and therefore, a greater respect for the life of others and aversion to inflicting suffering on others also emerged. When life expectancy is short and death due to illness or violence is pervasive and suffering is ubiquitous, then life seems a cheap commodity, and people have fewer concerns about taking life and are less reticent to act violently.

Pinker (2011) offered a more extensive elaboration showing that we have seen a humanitarian revolution in which increasing levels of regard for the value of human life and expanding levels of empathy for others has resulted in declines in many forms of violence and cruelty such as superstitious killings, torture, capital punishment, and slavery. Pinker noted that there has been a recent and rapid decline in the longstanding patterns of human cruelty: "the killing of witches, the torture of prisoners, the persecution of heretics, the execution of nonconformists, and the enslavement of foreigners—all carried out with stomach turning cruelty—quickly passed from unexceptional to the unthinkable" (p. 168). Consequently, the increased frequency and intensity of violence in television and other forms of entertainment should not be interpreted as a response to an underlying increase in human cruelty or callousness. Pinker highlighted the implausibility of such a claim by observing that "Hollywood movies are bloodier than ever, unlimited pornography is a mouse-click away, and an entirely new form of violent entertainment, video games, has become a major pastime. Yet as these signs of decadence proliferated in the culture, violence went down in real life" (p. 128). Although concerns about the levels of violence in fictional entertainment such as film and television are sometimes presented as evidence of cultural decline, such arguments neglect the fact that levels of actual violence have been declining even as depictions of violence in media have become more graphic and more frequent. The fact that some people's sensibilities are offended by the fictional depictions of violence may actually signify how far we have come in our empathy from times in which there was an appetite for public displays of real violence. Pinker summarizes this possibility nicely when he writes, "Most people today have no desire to watch a cat burn to death, let alone a man or woman. In that regard we are different from our ancestors of a few centuries ago, who approved, carried out, and even savored the infliction of unspeakable agony on other living being" (p. 169).

Additional evidence against catharsis comes from decades of research examining the effects of exposure to violent media. While a full treatment of this topic is beyond the scope of the present work, a few relevant reviews will be briefly mentioned here. In their review of the sizeable body of research looking at the effects of violent media exposure on aggression,

Anderson et al. (2003) concluded that there is compelling evidence across multiple types of research designs that consumption of violent media is a risk factor associated with greater aggressive thoughts, feelings, and behaviors, and the evidence is strongest specifically for the medium of television and film, which have been the most extensively investigated. Additionally, in a meta-analysis, Bushman and Huesman (2006) combined the results from 431 previous studies involving 68,463 participants and conducted statistical analysis on these aggregated data. The results showed that exposure to media violence was associated with more aggressive thoughts, feelings, and behaviors. Further, Krahe (2012) reviewed the evidence from 50 years of research on the effects of violent media exposure on aggression. The evidence includes (1) cross sectional surveys showing that people with higher rates of exposure to violent media were more likely to act aggressively, (2) longitudinal studies showing that violent media exposure levels initially measured in childhood predict the actual aggression levels of the same people assessed as adults, and (3) experimental studies showing that randomly assigning people to watch violent versus non-violent media increases aggressive thoughts, feelings, and behaviors. They concluded that "what is clear is that exposure to media violence is one risk factor for increased aggression in both the short and long run" (p. 340).

McCauley (1998) agrees that the research findings on the effects of watching violence are inconsistent with catharsis theory because they reveal that exposure to violence does not purge but rather increases violent thoughts and impulses. He does however note that there are typically several methodological limitations accompanying such research including (1) the fact that participants are exposed typically to only brief violent clips that are extracted from a film or show instead of the full work, (2) the measures of aggression do not allow for differentiating various types of aggression (for instance instrumental versus impulsive), and (3) the social and interactive context of viewing is eliminated because participants typically watch in isolation rather than as part of a group. It is not my intention here to engage fully the nuance, extent, and mitigating factors related to the causal role of media violence in contributing to real-world aggression. While there is continued debate about the size of the impact violent media has on promoting actual aggression and what the relevant moderating variables are, there is sufficient evidence to cast doubt on the notion that viewing violent entertainment purges aggression.

Thus, it seems clear that the notion that violent entertainment purges people of aggressive urges inherent to their nature that would otherwise demand action on real-world targets is not tenable. There is, however, a more defensible variant of the catharsis approach based on the idea that it is not viewers' violent impulses that need quelling but rather their fears and anxieties.

Arguments That the Appeal of Violence Lies in the Motive to Minimize Death Anxiety

One of the more commonly espoused versions of this modified approach to catharsis theory focuses on human apprehensions about mortality. From this perspective, imagery of violent death or the threat of violent death is alluring because it allows people to confront death from a safe psychological distance and thereby reduces uncertainty and fear surrounding the topic. Piven (2004) asserted that "one cannot assume that our cultural absorption in images of blood-shed, the undead, and forensic mystery is proof of acceptance of death, but rather implicates our relentless unease, anxiety, disgust, and rage" (p. 2). Correspondingly, Kottler (2011) suggested,

> One of the most prevalent ways for desensitizing yourself to apprehensions related to death is to face the fears in controlled doses, on your own terms, and that is exactly one benefit of observing violence, whether in the form of photographs, movies, books, or sports. It is yet another paradoxical aspects of our subject that, whereas encountering violence or association with death in real life are often devastating experiences that produce lasting trauma, watching violence as a spectator is often viewed as interesting if not entertaining [p. 29].

In addition, Goldberg (1998) claimed that "the struggle to come to terms with death is built into the human condition" and that this struggle can be facilitated by consumption of images of violence. He stated that "a terrible need for answers, a deep and implacable denial, and a desperate yearning for mastery buttress our combined fascination, fear, and avoidance of scenes of death" (p. 38). Further, Durkin (2003) posited that "the thanatological themes in U.S. popular culture function as a mechanism that helps Americans to deal with death" (p. 47). Likewise, Pizzato (2005) stated,

> We may avoid thinking about our own deaths, yet we are attracted to the performance of violence by others, involving life-threatening glimpses of death, onstage and onscreen.... Through such spectatorship we experience the fear, suffering and death of others vicariously. We identify with the struggle of the human offering or feel superior to the doomed victim. We explore the potential meanings of our own mortality, our being towards death through the sacrifice of others on screen [pp. 1–2].

Although the idea that fictional violence helps people cope with fears of death is frequently championed, this variant of catharsis should be subjected to the same analysis offered earlier. Is it plausible to assume that humans have a need to pacify existential anxieties about death? Have attitudes about death changed in ways that coincide with the timing of changes in the frequency of depictions of violent death in media? In what ways might the consumption of violent entertainment help people to deal with uncertainties and anxiety about death?

Numerous philosophical and psychological thinkers have argued that death anxiety is a primary concern that motivates human behavior. One of the earliest treatments of the prominence of death anxiety in human affairs occurs in Martin Heidegger's philosophical treatise *Being and Time* (1927/2008). Heidegger argued that mortality was a fundamental part of the human condition and that we are all beings towards death; meaning it is the temporal aspect of existence that defines what it means to be human. He noted however, that the human awareness of this existential predicament resulted in the potential for anxiety and that many people attempted to avoid this anxiety by inauthentically denying the finite nature of life.

Resistance to the importance of death anxiety in human psychology has sometimes been supported by reference to Freud's (1913/1953) claim that fear of death could not be an important motivational force because it did not exist in the unconscious for "in the unconscious every one of us is convinced of his own immortality" (p. 305). Piven (2004) notes that while Freud did at some places in his writings explicitly cast doubts on the role of death anxiety as a primary unconscious motivation, his writing is more nuanced and contradictory than typically presented. Piven argued that there are examples in Freud's writings that "suggest that the fear of death requires vigilant defensive and coping techniques, especially the distortion of reality though defenses and fantasies, so that the organism is not psychologically crippled by overwhelming terror" (p. 220). Piven reframed the psychoanalytic perspective to "demonstrate that all anxiety is essentially the reactive fear of annihilation" (p. 9). The tension between competing claims that death cannot be conceptualized in the unconscious and that death anxiety is a primary unconscious force can be resolved by looking at what philosopher Stephen Cave (2012) describes as the mortality paradox. By the mortality paradox, Cave means that we are simultaneously certain and incredulous about the fact of our own death. At an intuitive level, we are cognitively incapable of simulating what death would be like. We cannot turn off our consciousness and still be able to experience and report back about what the cessation of consciousness caused by death will be like. Consequently, we feel that we are immortal, immune to death, and that death happens to others but will not happen to us. At a rational discursive level, we are aware that all living things, including us, must inevitably die. This awareness of our mortality, when we do not deny and repress it, can yield feelings of anxiety, dread, and terror.

Several psychoanalytic and psychodynamic theorists have argued for the prominent role of death as a source of human anxiety. For example, psychoanalyst Gregory Zilboorg (1943) asserted that all fears and anxieties, no matter how mundane or trivial they appear on the surface, are ultimately manifestations of the deep-seated fear of death. Norman O. Brown (1959) offered further psychoanalytic arguments for the primacy of death as a source of anxiety. According to Brown, awareness of corporeality was the primary anxiety that must be defended against and that corporeality was threatening because it implied fragility and impermanence. Therefore, the conflict in the anal stage of development is not based on thwarted *id* gratification but on the infant's dawning recognition that his/her consciousness, dreams, ambitions, and whole identity is confined to a fragile and transient physical body that produces foul-smelling waste. Brown further posited that the inability to accept death produces a preoccupation with establishing one's cultural identity as a symbolic alternative that is more enduring than the physical self. Similarly, Otto Rank (1941) suggested that human beings' recognition of mortality led them to strive for concrete symbols of their immortality such as religion, art, literature, architecture, or anything else that endures longer than the individual life span. Existential psychotherapists Irving Yalom and Robert Firestone have also advocated for the primacy of death anxiety in shaping human behavior. Yalom (1980) posited that children become anxious about death at a very early age and attempt to defend against this anxiety by developing a sense that they are special and somehow immune from death and by developing a belief in an ultimate rescuer who will protect them against death. Firestone (1993) suggested that psychological defenses emerge in infancy in response to concerns about parental frustration or abandonment, but once children begin to understand that their parents will die and then that they themselves will die, the existing psychological defenses are then conscripted to ward off the new threat of personal mortality.

Perhaps the most extensive and influential argument for the relevance of death anxiety in human psychology comes from cultural anthropologist Ernest Becker, who in his Pulitzer Prize–winning book *The Denial of Death* (1973), concludes that fear of death is the most pressing human concern and that mitigating and controlling that fear is the primary motive behind much of human activity in the cultural and psychological realms. Becker asserts that "of all things that move man, one of the principle ones is his terror of death" (p. 11). Becker prefers the term *terror* over fear or anxiety as a way to express the human reaction to the confrontation with mortality because of the power of the word to "convey how all-consuming it is when we look it full in the face" (p. 15). According to Becker, the powerful need to deny mortality is not merely evident in cultural rituals related to dying and burial but permeates all aspects of culture: "everything man does in his symbolic world is an attempt to deny and overcome his grotesque fate" (p. 27).

Although dealing with the awareness of mortality has been asserted to be a universal aspect of the human existential predicament, in the 20th century much attention has been given by historians and social scientists to the changing attitudes towards death, particularly in Western culture. Sociologists frequently describe contemporary Western culture as death-denying and assert that the development of death as a taboo topic to be denied and suppressed emerged in response to several socio-historical factors. These factors include (1) changes in causes of death from infectious disease to chronic illness, (2) changes in who died from mostly infants and young children to the elderly, (3) increased life expectancy, (4) changes in the place of death from the home to institutional settings like hospitals and nursing homes, (5) advanced medical technologies that resulted in prioritizing efforts to prolonging life over focusing on the quality of death, (6), decreased confidence in religious beliefs offering assurance of an afterlife, (7) an increased sense of individualism and privacy that isolated the bereaved and shifted death from a public to a private event, and (8) the rise of the professional funeral service industry that not only removed family members from having a role in the preparation and disposal of dead bodies but also promoted techniques such as embalming to distort and deny the reality of death (DeSpelder & Strickland, 2015). All of these factors served to decrease people's exposure to and comfort with the actual reality of death.

One of the most influential accounts of the changes in Western societies' attitudes about death was articulated by historian Philippe Aries (1981), who described a transition from a time of tamed death to invisible death. According to Aries, for much of the last thousand years, people were familiar with death because of their frequent exposure to death not only because they witnessed the deaths of their family members in the home but also because of the public place of death and the participation of the community in death rituals. People were also protected from anxieties about death because of the ubiquitous confidence in the meaning of death provided by the widespread and unshakable adherence to the well-established public religious and cultural practices and rituals surrounding the act of dying and burial. In the last few hundred years, changes in the rise of secularism and individualism altered death attitudes, but the most radical transformation occurred in the mid–20th century with the medicalization of death such that it became an enemy to vanquish. Death was no longer seen as an inevitability to be accepted but came to be viewed as a failure of science and medicine to be ignored and denied. Aries writes that death "has now been so obliterated from our culture that it is hard for us to imagine or understand it. The ancient attitude in which death is close and familiar yet diminished and desensitized is too different from our own view, in which it is so terrifying that we no longer dare say its name" (p. 28).

It has also been frequently observed that there is a rough correspondence, although not a perfect one, in the timing of the increasingly taboo attitudes surrounding actual death and the proliferation of images of violent death in media and entertainment. The seminal work in this area is Gorer's 1955 essay *On the Pornography of Death*. Gorer differentiated obscenity from pornography. Obscenity, he argues, is a culturally universal (although the exact circumstances vary extensively from culture to culture), shared, and social phenomenon involving situational taboo violation that typically evokes a unique type of laughter. In contrast pornography, he suggested, is unique to literate societies and involves a private gratification in fantasy achieved through the consumption of material deemed unacceptable to mention in public. He defined prudery as "some aspect of human experience" that is "treated as inherently shameful or abhorrent, so that it can never be discussed or referred to openly, and experience of it tends to be clandestine and accompanied by feelings of guilt and unworthiness" (p. 50). He asserted that the prevalence of pornography increases in step with levels of societal prudery. Stated differently, the more a society tries to repress or deny the reality of some aspect of the human condition, the more people are driven to seek encounters with it in secretive and private ways. Gorer argued that the focus of prudery (the taboo topic of human experience that must be avoided) has shifted from sex to death: "In the 20th century, however, there seems to have been a shift in prudery; whereas copulation has become more and more 'mentionable,' particular in Anglo-Saxon societies, death has become more and more 'unmentionable' as a *natural process*" (p. 50).

Gorer speculated that the increased prudery around death was a function of decreasing confidence in traditional Christian religious beliefs such as the immortality of the soul or the resurrection of the body that might offer some solace that death was not the complete destruction of the self. He also mentioned changing medical technologies as a causal factor because as death in childhood became less frequent, people were less likely to be exposed to the death of siblings in the home. Just as the societal taboos around sex in the 19th century led to a desire for gratification in the form of illicit images of sex, so too did prudery around death give rise to a pornography of death in the 20th century: "While natural death became more and more smothered in prudery, violent death has played an ever-growing part in the fantasies offered to mass audiences—detective stories, thrillers, Westerns, war stories, spy stories, science fiction, and eventually horror comics" (p. 51). Gorer drew further parallels between the pornography of sex and death in that in both cases fantasy gratifications sought by people during times of prudery divorce the natural human act from the context of meaning and emotion and focus on the vivid and graphic imagery of the mechanics. Gorer (1955) writes, "There seem to be a number of parallels between the fantasies that titillate our curiosities about the mystery of sex, and those which titillate our curiosity about the mystery of death. In both types of fantasy, the emotions which are typically concomitant of the acts—love or grief—are paid little or no attention" (p. 51). In both cases, he argued that the fullness of the person is replaced by a reduction to just the reproductive organs or to the corpse (p. 52).

Goldberg (1998) agreed that there was a connection between the declining exposure to actual death and the increasing depictions of fictional death as a way to satisfy people's curiosity about the topic. In describing the period of invisible death ushered in around the 1950s, Goldberg wrote,

> For a while there was a peculiar fantasy that maybe we had it beat, and there was a tacit social compact not to discuss it, not even quite to believe it. But of course it does not work that way, and we need to know, or think we need to know, what it is, how it looks, what it does to us, what we can do about it. Images step up and offer their services [p. 51].

He further claims that as "as actual death was toned down by every means available, depicted death swaggered violently onto the stage, and new means and forms were found to keep it before the public eye" (p. 40). But Goldberg asserts that the process in which depictions of death increased in response to declining familiarity with actual death began in the early 19th century, far before the 20th century when Gore wrote about the pornography of death. Goldberg describes how the predecessors of television violence can be found in the depictions of violent crimes and grisly executions of prisoners in wax museums, in the melodramatic stage productions of criminal trials and executions, and in the illustrations of murder that proliferated in cheap newspapers and journals of the mid to late 1800s. The tendency for vivid details and graphic depiction was limited to coverage of violent death. Papers in the 1800s did not show the same sensationalism in their coverage of death due to outbreaks of infectious disease. However, these earlier images of violent death share with modern entertainment violence an underlying motive of increased fascination with a forbidden topic and a desire to frame death as a more manageable and avoidable phe-nomenon: "The popularity of images of violent death, then as now, con-ceivably has something to do with its relative rarity in real life: it is 'safer' to fantasize about something unlikely to occur than about death from can-cer or Parkinson's" (Goldberg, 1998, p. 43).

Foltyn (2008) updated Gorer's analysis of the pornography of death by claiming that "in societies oversaturated with images of sex, death is the new sex" (p. 153) and suggested that with the increasing public appe-tite for media depictions of the details about the bodies of deceased celeb-rities and the explosion in the popularity of television shows focused on murder investigations and forensic science, such as the numerous instan-tiations of *CSI*, "the corpse has become pop culture's latest porn star, the new body voyeuristically explored" (p. 167). She noted, however, that even as the displays of fictional corpses have become more graphic and detailed, there remains a sensational quality to the depictions:

> The new pornography of death is as grief-gutted as the old but dazzles the audience with its shocking corpses, flashy forensic science, and exotic causes of death that are far removed from most people's experiences. There is an unre-ality as well as reality about corpse shows in which people die from asphyx-iation in tar, stomachs burst from overeating, accidental decapitation, being sucked into a tree shredder, or being eaten alive by insects. Even if the viewer learns something about death, dying, decay, and dissection, this is death at its most ghastly [p. 164].

Foltyn (2008) shares the assessment that media and entertainment depictions of death are pornographic, not merely in their pandering to a fascination with a culturally forbidden topic, but also in their focus on the corporeality of a physical reality divorced from any emotional and cul-tural contextualization. She highlights how, as with the sexualized body of the porn star, the new porn star of the television corpse also focuses "on the close-up, the exploration of every nook and cranny of the body, which is prodded, poked, penetrated, and presented as an outrageous sight. Both luxuriate in body fluids. Socially appropriate emotion is absent from both. Love from sex porn. Grief, reflection, and discussion of the preciousness of life from corpse porn, which also divorces the dead body from the spiri-tual or other moral lessons such as compassion" (p. 167).

Based on the preceding arguments, there seems to be a plausible case that managing concern about personal mortality is an important human motive and that changes in the popularity of violent entertainment have at least co-varied with changes in attitudes about death. But there still remains the question of why people would seek out violent entertain-ment as a means of dealing with such existential concerns. If there exists a psychological motivation to avoid unsettling thoughts of death that remind people of their vulnerability to premature demise and the inevitability of their eventual extinction, then why would people be drawn to media depictions of violence that would seem to make such thoughts more salient?

Becker (1973) described "defiant Promethianism" as an alternative reaction to the more common approach of simply avoiding and repressing thoughts of death. This reaction is still motivated by "modern man's defiance of accident, evil, and death," but it involves an attempt to symbolically conquer death through displays of wealth or power, and these symbolic displays can often involve violence (p. 85). In her analysis of Mary Shelley's novel *Frankenstein* and the 1931 movie directed by James Whale, Jennifer McMahon (2008) draws on Becker's distinction between different types of defensive reactions to death. In describing the character of Victor Frankenstein, who became obsessed with death, she asserts that he is driven by hopes of overcoming it.

> Rather than using the conventional technique of repressing anxiety about death by avoiding the thought of it, the individual who is fascinated with death attempts to inoculate himself against anxiety by conjuring the hope that death can be controlled, even conquered.... Simply put the Promethean type's objective is still the denial of death. He simply takes the offensive approach as opposed to the defensive [McMahon, pp. 76–77].

If the viewing of violent media can be conceptualized as a Promethean type of defense against death anxiety, then the question remains. Through what routes or mechanisms is the catharsis of death terror accomplished? What is the psychological payoff in terms of addressing curiosity or anxiety regarding death?

Durkin (2003) noted the paradox that at the same time Americans were becoming increasingly uncomfortable and avoidant of issues regarding real life death and dying, they seemed to be developing an increasing fascination with death in popular culture and that death, particularly violent death, was becoming a mainstay of popular television. Durkin speculated about three potential explanations of this paradox. His first explanation focused on the idea of the allure of the forbidden. Because the topic of death is repressed, people crave information and are curious about the topic, and because there is a scarcity of opportunities to address the topic in realistic ways, they seek out sensational depictions of death in popular culture. His second explanation focused on the idea of reducing fear through gradual exposure. Frequent depictions of death might desensitize people to it, making it less disturbing over time with increasing exposure. His third explanation focused on a cognitive reframing or relabeling of the experience. Perhaps the popular cultural presentations of death in the guise of entertainment is a means of trivializing death and making it less frightening. Depictions of death in popular culture might ameliorate anxiety about the topic by recasting it as entertaining, humorous, or captivating. Each of these three possibilities will be briefly discussed before moving on to additional explanations.

The idea that people are drawn to forbidden topics is certainly compatible with conventional wisdom. For example, adolescents may find movies more appealing if they have an R rating or are deemed by moral pundits as unsuitable for young viewers and may be more drawn to music with parental advisory labels. The theory of psychological reactance states that people are motivated to maintain a sense of personal freedom and perceived attempts to limit that freedom are met with reactions to reestablish it (Brehm, 1966; Rosenberg & Siegel, 2018). For example, when a driver being tailgated slows down or a shopper returning to their vehicle fumbles a few more moments because they notice a car waiting for their parking spot, they are reacting against perceived attempts to limit their freedom. Similarly, parental advisory warnings or otherwise labeling media as taboo may increase the appeal of these media. Perhaps the more strongly cultural messages that death is a forbidden topic are communicated the more alluring the topic becomes. This is certainly consistent with the pornography of death accounts offered by Gorer (1955) and Foltyn (2008) and is articulated nicely in the following quote by Goldstein (1998): "violent imagery may be attractive to humans in general because we, alone among creatures, know that we will die but, except in rare cases, we do not know when or how. Hence, we may be motivated by morbid curiosity. Violent images may be compelling in part because we are tantalized by images of mortality" (p. 224).

Durkin (2003) claimed that "we may be more accepting of death, dying, and the dead because of our frequent exposure to these phenomena through our popular culture" (p. 48). The idea that exposure to fictional death is motivated by a fear of mortality may seem initially counterintuitive but does potentially have some merit. This is consistent with the general idea of habituation, which asserts that repeated exposure to the same stimulus elicits responses of diminishing intensity. Further, the most common psychological treatment for phobias involves gradual exposure to the feared stimulus for increasing durations in controlled settings. Foltyn (2008) also seems to endorse this idea when observing that "many people living in North America and Western Europe today have never seen an actual dead person or witnessed a real death; they have only seen pop cultural representations of both" and that these representations serve a function of "desensitizing and normalizing death through mass exposure to dead bodies" (p. 164). Depicting death by reducing it to a created artifice or symbol gives the person a sense of control over it. The person can decide when and how to respond to it and whether to look at it at all. Goldberg (1998) advanced this position asserting that "there is also a ritual aspect to repetitive viewing of moving pictures. Knowing when the violence and death will turn up allows a certain monitoring of one's emotions" (p. 39).

A variation of this argument focuses not just on exposure but on a reframing or relabeling of the emotion as the important ingredient for reducing fear. Whereas heights and falling are potentially frightening, experiencing them in a controlled environment and relabeling them as entertainment (e.g., bungee jumping or riding a roller coaster) allows the same physiological experience of a pounding pulse to be reframed as fun rather than terrifying. As Durkin (2003) put it, "The treatment of death as entertainment and humor is simply an extension of, or another configuration of, death denial. By rendering death into humor and entertainment, we effectively neutralize it; it becomes innocuous, and thus less threatening, through its conversion and ephemerality in the media" (p. 47).

A similar argument for the ability of humor to tame societal fears was advanced by Harvey Greenberg (2001) who described a "heimlich" maneuver in which the object of horror, something unheimlich or uncanny in the terms of Freud's (1919/1959) analysis of horror, is transformed into something "heimlich," familiar and comfortable. He traced this tendency back to myth and folklore such as tales in which a protagonist outsmarts death or the devil. These tales reduce anxiety by making the feared character the butt of the joke. Greenberg sees more modern variants of this theme in the tendency to recast monstrous characters that were once frightening in farcical or slapstick roles. For example, the Universal Studios' monsters that horrified viewers in the 1930s become sources of lighthearted frivolity in films such as *Abbott and Costello Meet Frankenstein* (1948), *Young Frankenstein* (1974), *Love at First Bite* (1979), and *Dracula: Dead and Loving It* (1995).

Although not mentioned by Greenberg, a similar example of the notion that humor can be used to collapse the power of a potential threat was illustrated in the first episode of season four of the television series *Magnum, P.I.* "Home from Sea." When Magnum finds himself stranded at sea in shark-infested waters, he attempts to calm his fears by naming the circling shark Herman (a trick viewers see in a flashback that he learned from his father who taught him to master his fears by giving the things he was scared of, such as imagined monsters lurking in the closet, silly-sounding names). This phenomenon was also given popular depiction in the movie *Harry Potter and the Prisoner of Azkaban* (2004), in which Professor Remus Lupin (David Thewlis) teaches the students in his defense against the dark arts class how to deal with a Boggart (a creature that takes on the appearance of a person's greatest fear) by using the spell *Riddikulus*, which transforms the Boggart into something so silly as to induce laughter rather than terror, such as a spider wearing roller-skates or an intimidating professor dressed in old ladies' clothes.

In addition to the allure of the forbidden, desensitization, and reframing as fun or humorous explanations reviewed above, there are some additional possibilities for the psychological mechanisms by which viewing violent entertainment might offer catharsis in the form of reducing uncertainties and anxieties about death. One such mechanism focuses on gaining a sense of perceived mastery and control over fear of death in which viewers hope to learn vicariously from the victims of fictional violence thereby contributing to an enhanced sense of safety and confidence in the ability to avoid premature death in real life. Another such mechanism focuses on symbolic attempts to perceive the self as immune to death by identifying with the perpetrators of violence and thereby conceptualizing death as something that happens to others.

Although death is a biological inevitability that cannot be avoided, the fear of death, especially the fear of premature death, can be managed by fostering a sense of self-efficacy through which people conceptualize themselves as being able to ensure their own safety through proper vigilance. From an evolutionary perspective, it would be adaptive to pay attention to the behaviors that led others to suffer aversive consequences such as death or injury in the hopes of vicariously learning from the mistakes of those others and thereby potentially avoiding those same mistakes in one's own actions. From this perspective, interest in fictional violence is motivated out of an adaptive attention to potential threats. Although not a proponent of this approach, Zillmann (1998) summarized it as follows: "on the premise that monitoring the environment for danger, for potentially threatening violent events in particular, proved adaptive over millennia, and that a deep-seated inclination for such monitoring persists, it can be projected that violent incidents still draw strong attention" (p. 194). He further observed that "protective vigilance is not limited to screening for immediate dangers. It extends to the circumstances of victimization, conceivably to provide additional information about a particular danger. It might prove useful, for instance, to know how a serial killer stalks his victims" (p. 195).

A similar argument was made by Clasen (2012) who suggested that fictional violence, specifically horror, allows people a means of learning about potential dangers in the environment and rehearsing ways to avoid those dangers. From an evolutionary perspective, the opportunity to hone the ability to detect danger and to develop well practiced responses to dangers would be adaptive. In this sense, Clasen views horror as serving a function similar to playing chase in that it allows people to practice ways of avoiding real-world danger in a safe environment. Clasen claims that "the modern horror story is a kind of supernormal stimulus, a hypertrophied variation on chase play" which allows "for learning about danger and to calibrate our responses to danger" (p. 227). He further asserts that "consuming horror fiction could thus be adaptive. It has all the benefits of learning about danger and one's own response to danger, but without the risk of actual harm" (p. 227).

Consistent with this perspective, in his exploration of the reasons high school students reported for watching slasher horror films, Johnston (1995) identified one of the motives as independent watching, which involved a tendency to identify with the victim, to feel a sense of mastery over fear, and to report positive emotional reactions. For the independent watcher, the enjoyment of horror is not in the violence or the experience of fear but rather in thinking about the ways they might avoid the types of dangers depicted in the film and thereby feeling a sense of self-efficacy in their perceived ability to keep themselves safe. Likewise, in his analysis of different motives people express for watching violent entertainment, Kottler (2011) described the prevalence of a curious self-protective theme such that people are fascinated with true crime and serial killers because they think by learning as much as they can about these topics, they can keep themselves safe and avoid becoming victims.

The mastery argument is also consistent with the fact that fictional depictions of violent death in television and movies are much more prevalent and popular than depictions of death due to old age or chronic disease (in spite of the fact that the former is much less common than the latter in real life). The importance of death being presented as due to violent causes is that this implies that it is avoidable. Goldberg (1998) argued that it is safer to fantasize about something unlikely to occur than about death from more statistically feasible causes such as illness and asserted that the appeal of watching the death of others due to violent causes is that it facilitates a temporary denial of one's own vulnerability to death. He describes a viewer's reaction to fictional violent death as involving the thought that "this was not me; for this moment at least I have been saved from the particular fate I have just witnessed" (p. 43).

Freud (1913/1953) asserted that the inability to think about the reality of personal death drew people to fictional representations of death because watching others kill and die in fiction helped perpetuate the natural mental sense that our own death is impossible. Just as we continue to exist as a spectator to the deaths of others in fiction, our consciousness continues to exist as a spectator when we try to imagine or own death, thereby facilitating the conviction that death is something that happens only to others.

As described in the previous paragraphs, the conviction that death is the fate of others and not the self can be achieved by focusing on the victims of fictional violence (how one is different from them or can avoid the mistakes made by them), but fears of personal vulnerability to death can also be allayed by the focus on and perhaps identification with the perpetrators of fictional violence.

Otto Rank (1941) claimed that "the death fear of the ego is lessened by the killing, the sacrifice, of the other; through the death of the other, one buys oneself free from the penalty of dying, of being killed" (p. 130). Becker (1975) affirms this point in his description of the appeal of sacrifice and gladiatorial blood sport, writing, "The longer people looked at the death of someone else, the more pleasure they could have in sensing the security and good fortune of their own survival" (p. 110). By extending this analysis to the appeal of fictional violence, if we accept the thesis that viewing death in popular media is motivated in part by a need to thwart death anxiety, then it stands to reason that by identifying with the perpetrators of fictional violence viewers can project death onto the other and symbolically hope to avoid it.

Several psychodynamic theorists have described the origin of violent impulses aimed at asserting power as rooted in the experience of childhood trauma and feelings of helplessness. For example, Firestone, Firestone, and Catlett (2013) argue that even the experience of normal levels of childhood neglect, deprivation, and vulnerability give rise to maladaptive psychological defenses that are later deployed in adulthood to ameliorate existential anxiety but that the severity of these defenses is proportionate to the level of trauma. They suggest that even the best of parents sometimes express anger towards their children, which children view as life threatening. It is too unbearable for children to accept that the person on whom their survival depends has hostile and violent impulses towards them even if those impulses are often controlled or kept under the surface. Rather than feeling helpless to the capricious anger of a parent, the child identifies with the punishing parent and not with themselves as the one being punished. Fonagy, Gergely, Jurist, and Traget (2002) give a similar account of how childhood identification with the punishing parent gives rise to an alien or other sense of self that is activated in response to later painful events, writing, "Later experiences of trauma in the family or peer group force the child to dissociate from pain by using the alien self to identify with the aggressor. Hence the vacuous self comes to be colonized by the image of the aggressor, and the child comes to experience himself as evil and monstrous" (p. 198).

In his philosophical analysis of evil, Alford (1997) draws on object-relations theory to suggest that evil stems from dread at our powerlessness against suffering and death. He writes, "This, though, may be what evil is really about, the fantasy that the misfortunes of old age and death can be inflicted on others to save ourselves" (p. 51) and posits that "evil inflicts pain, abandonment, and helplessness on others, so that the evildoer will not have to experience them himself" (p. 52). Becker (1975) makes a similar claim, asserting that "men spill blood because it makes their hearts glad and fills out their organisms with a sense of vital power; ceremoniously killing captives is a way of affirming power over life, and therefore over death" (p. 102).

The idea that killers seek to become an instrument of death as a means of symbolically denying their vulnerability to it is given voice in depictions of fictional serial killers. For example, in FX television series *American Horror Story Asylum* Episode 8 "Unholy Night," we meet Leigh Emerson (Ian McShane), an inmate at Briarcliff psychiatric facility, who is deemed criminally insane for dressing as Santa Claus and killing 18 people on Christmas Eve. Emerson has been locked in solitary confinement for the last year by Sister Jude (Jessica Lange) because he savagely attacked another inmate at the previous year's Christmas party. Sister Mary Eunice (Lily Rabe), possessed by some demonic spirit, offers Emerson a chance to leave solitary confinement and to put his Santa suit back on if he will help her deal with a guard who has become suspicious of the nefarious activities at Briarcliff. In response to Sister Mary Eunice's offer and the presentation of the suit, Emerson objects that she does not understand what Christmas means to him. This objection leads to the exchange below, in which Mary Eunice reveals preternatural insight into how Emerson's abuse and desire to avoid feelings of powerlessness are responsible for his murderous behavior.

> SISTER MARY EUNICE: "I know you were a petty criminal thrown into jail for shoplifting a loaf of bread and while you were in there the jailors went caroling in the cell block and five men held you down and took your virginity. The first one did. The others took your dignity, your self-esteem, and most importantly your Christmas spirit. But then you found the suit and it gave you everything you were missing"
> LEIGH EMERSON: "You see I knew who deserved to live and who deserved to die, who was naughty and who was nice."
> SISTER MARY EUNICE: "And you had the power, Leigh. You can have it again. Who do you want to be, the victim or the victor?"

Like the fictional Emerson, perhaps some real-life viewers feel a symbolic victory over death as watching it befall others on the television screen solidifies the fantasy that it will not happen to them.

We have now reviewed a number of plausible explanations for mechanisms through which viewing fictional violence could be cathartic in the form of alleviating anxieties about death. Despite the fact that these are all interesting and perhaps even logically compelling, they still suffer from the same criticism Zillmann (1998) lobbed at all catharsis approaches in that they are speculative and lacking in empirical support. There is, however, a well-established theoretical perspective in psychology that is substantially supported by empirical evidence that documents mitigating the experience of death anxiety as a paramount human motive.

2

The Paramount Place of Death in Human Psychology

An Overview of Terror Management Theory

Terror Management Theory (TMT; Greenberg, Pyszczynski, & Solomon, 1986; Pyszczynski, Greenberg, & Solomon, 1997; Solomon, Greenberg, & Pyszczynski, 2004; Pyszczynski, Solomon, & Greenberg, 2015) is an ambitious theory generated in answer to the question—why do people do what they do when they do it. The broad scope of TMT is a departure from contemporary trends in the social sciences towards compartmentalization characterized by focus on small, specific, and localized aspects of human behavior. TMT represents a comprehensive theory of human motivation, which is based on the writings of Ernest Becker (1962, 1973, & 1975), and views the uniquely human experience of death anxiety as a profound force driving human affairs. TMT builds on the work of Becker by expanding his ideas into the parlance of modern social psychology, generating testable and falsifiable hypotheses, and amassing a substantial body of supporting empirical evidence. From the perspective of TMT, a single motivational system can be applied to a wide range of human activity. TMT is based on the principle that much of human behavior is defensive and irrational, and that these psychological defenses are aimed at protecting the self from the conscious experience of death anxiety, which if left unchecked, could disrupt the pursuit of goal directed behavior to the point of being debilitating.

The first main proposition of TMT is that the highly evolved human brain confers an ambivalent intensity to our psychological experience that is unique in the animal kingdom, offering both a marvelous richness of experience exemplified in the ability to wonder about the cosmos and our place in it but also a terrible capacity for penetrating anxiety exemplified in the ability to imagine the myriad perils that pose unpredictable and uncontrollable threats to continued existence. Human beings share with all other animals a drive for self-preservation. This drive motivates the avoidance of possibly life-threatening dangers, as when the perception of a potential predator initiates a fight-or-flight reaction. But what makes humans different from other animals is the emergence of higher order cognitive capacities that conferred an evolutionary advantage by leaving us less reliant on instinctive reactions to danger.

One such advantageous mental capacity is the ability to engage in counterfactual thinking. People can observe and remember what happened in the past but more importantly can also imagine how things might have played out differently in myriad ways by running hypothetical simulations involving multiple variables. Consequently, a human observer can learn vicariously from the misfortunes of others and plan to avoid making the same mistakes if ever in a similar position. Further, people can also plan out alternative, more effective strategies via mental rehearsal without having to learn through the painful consequences of mistakes. Perhaps even more remarkable is how the ability of imagination allows us to anticipate and plan for events never experienced or even observed.

Whereas humans' ability to imagine future events is likely in large part responsible for our success in spreading across diverse ecological niches, it carried an unfortunate side effect. Even after escaping from danger, humans can continue to ruminate about the close call and can imagine the horrible consequences had things transpired even slightly differently. Even worse, they can become fixated on the potential of future dangers not yet encountered. While an antelope might feel fear when being chased by a cheetah, once safe, it does not feel anxiety about the prospect of what would have happened if it had not escaped, nor does it feel dread at the thought of the gapping jaws inevitably lurking in the future. The title of the television show *1000 Ways to Die*, which aired on Spike TV from 2008 to 2012, is a gross underestimate. The human capacity to imagine all the ways our existence could possibly end prematurely due to accident, illness, predation, homicide, war, terrorism, nuclear annihilation, and etc., gives rise to a potentially overwhelming sense of existential terror.

To make matters worse, the human capacity for reason and logical-analytical thought yields the awareness that personal death is an inevitable and unavoidable eventuality. Encounters with the remains of deceased animals and people coupled with the observation of the death of others (both young and old via natural and violent causes) results in the irrefutable conclusion to the syllogism—all living things die, I am a living thing, therefore I will die. It may be true that at an intuitive level people feel as if their conscious experience is permanent because they are unable to mentally simulate its cessation (Bering, 2002). This is what Freud (1913/1953) meant when he claimed that "in the unconscious every one of us is convinced of his own immortality" (p. 305). Even so, at a rational and discursive level, people recognize the inevitability of the death of the physical body as an empirical and logical fact. This recognition puts humans in the unenviable existential position of being driven by a goal for self-preservation while saddled with the knowledge that this goal is doomed.

The second main proposition of TMT is that human identity is dualistic involving both corporeal and symbolic aspects. We are embodied beings, and our physical bodies are certainly an essential aspect of what we claim makes us a distinct entity separate from others. The face we see in the mirror is a key component of who we say we are, and we are certainly motivated to seek pleasurable and avoid painful sensation derived from the activities of the body. Unlike other biological organisms, however, humans extend their identity beyond the limits of the physical body and are highly invested in extra-somatic entities that we come to think of as representing us in meaningful ways. We think of ourselves as our names, our bank accounts, our reputation, our accomplishments, our social media profiles, our resumes (or curriculum vitae if we are academics). We invest as much if not more time and energy in the pursuit of these symbolic aspects of identity as we do in the maintenance and satisfaction of the body and its needs. Several years of informally surveying students in my university classes has revealed that the overwhelming majority of them report that they would rather suffer physical pain than embarrassment via social media.

In his *Essay on Man,* Alexander Pope (1734) described the ambivalence people feel regarding their dualistic nature: "In doubt to deem himself a God, or beast; In doubt his mind or body to prefer." From a terror management perspective, however, it is clear that people favor the mind over the body. While the belief in a non-material soul and the focus on the symbolic aspects of human identity may facilitate hopes for death transcendence, it is the physical aspects of existence and human corporeality that undermine these hopes because empirical observation makes clear that the body dies and deteriorates. Corporeality carries with it the threat of creatureliness. If humans are made of the same biological materials as other animals, then perhaps we are no more special, significant, or enduring than any other form of life and not only will we eventually die and inevitably decompose, but also the scope of human activity may be no more meaningful in the cosmic scheme of the universe than the Darwinian quest for survival and reproduction pursued by all living things. Consequently, biological processes such as eating, excretion, and procreation are sources of ambivalence for human beings. Although these are necessary for survival, they undermine our death-denying cultural illusions, reveal our physicality, and therefore our finitude. The idea that the discomfort of human similarity to animals is rooted in fear of extinction and insignificance is given ancient expression in the Biblical lament: "surely the fate of human beings is like that of the animals; the same fate awaits them both: As one dies, so dies the other. All have the same breath; humans have no advantage over animals. Everything is meaningless" (Ecclesiastes 3:19; NIV). This sentiment was more recently summarized by TMT co-originator Sheldon Solomon, who in the 2005 documentary film *Flight from Death: The Quest for Immortality* quipped, "The explicit awareness that you're a breathing piece of defecating meat destined to die and ultimately no more significant than let's say a lizard or a potato is not especially uplifting."

The third main proposition of TMT is that most people most of the time are protected from the conscious experience of death anxiety because of the effective deployment of a complex set of psychological defenses. Comedian Mitch Hedberg once joked, "I had a stick of carefree gum, but it didn't work. I felt pretty good while I was blowing that bubble, but as soon as the gum lost its flavor, I was back to pondering my mortality."

TMT does not claim that people are constantly worried about the prospect of death with only the occasional sugary treat to distract them with moments of temporary solace. Quite the contrary, TMT asserts that most people are able to function quite well in day-to-day life unbothered by the reality of their existential predicament. This point is illustrated by the musing of Jack Gladney, a fictional character in Don DeLillo's 1985 novel *White Noise*, who wonders, "How strange it is. We have these deep terrible lingering fears about ourselves and the people we love. Yet we walk around, talk to people, eat and drink. We manage to function. The feelings are deep and real. Shouldn't they paralyze us" (p. 198).

From the perspective of TMT, the awareness of personal mortality has the potential to elicit terror but rarely does so because it is so effectively managed by the buffering mechanisms of self-esteem and cultural worldview. The fact that most people are able to function in their day-to-day lives with little concern about death is a testament to how well terror is managed.

TMT theorists differentiate between proximal/direct and distal/symbolic defenses as two distinctive psychological systems that protect against death anxiety (Pyszczynski, Greenberg, & Solomon, 1999). The first line of protection is what they labeled as proximal or direct defenses. These types of defenses are initiated when thoughts of death become the focus of conscious attention and involve rationalizing away the threat of premature death by focusing on it as a distant event that need not be worried about for a long time. This can be accomplished by exaggerating one's likely longevity, by thinking about or professing intentions to adopt healthier lifestyle changes that might make premature death by accident or illness less likely, or simply by suppressing thoughts of death and trying to block the topics from one's mind. For example, when a person learns of the recent death of a peer or friend of about the same age, they might highlight differences (he was a smoker and I am not), search for examples offering hope for genetic protection (I had a great uncle who lived to be 100), or promise to make behavioral changes to increase their projected longevity (I will definitely start to exercise more and to watch my diet—soon).

Reminders of death occur with surprising regularity, as when one drives past a cemetery, hears the latest mortality rates from COVID-19 on the news, or hears ambulance sirens in the distance. During such regular occurrences, the reality of one's mortality will become an unwelcome intruder into daily existence. William James (1917) commented on this phenomenon, "Let sanguine healthy-mindedness do its best with its strange power of living in the moment and ignoring and forgetting, still the evil background is really there to be thought of, and the skull will grin in at the banquet" (p. 138). At this point the best way to maintain psychological equanimity is simply to suppress these unwanted thoughts and try to focus on more pleasant distractions. These direct defenses involving suppression and exaggerated longevity are important and effective in a limited way but in and of themselves would be insufficient to adequately abate death terror.

The direct defenses are insufficient in and of themselves to ameliorate fully existential anxiety for two important reasons. First, while people are able to control the contents of their thoughts for a short time, long-term mental control is untenable as efforts to suppress unwanted thoughts eventually fail. As the extensive body of research on thought suppression reveals, attempts to block unwanted thoughts not only fail but also have the ironic effect of making such thoughts more prevalent following delay or distraction (Wegner, Schneider, Carter, & White, 1987; Wegner, 1994). For example, think back on previous efforts made by you or someone you know to avoid thinking about: palatable foods (e.g., chocolate cake) while dieting, cigarettes when attempting to quit smoking, a secret in the presence of the person who cannot know, or a forbidden/unavailable yet highly attractive potential romantic partner. These efforts may succeed for a few minutes or even hours but will eventually come back with a vengeance as a deluge of the thoughts to be avoided come rushing to mind with greater frequency and urgency than when the initial attempts at suppression were enacted. Similarly, thoughts of mortality cannot be permanently suppressed without the addition of some other mechanisms that causes them to dissipate. The second problem with direct defenses that involve focusing on health and longevity is that while they can abate anxiety about the prospect of premature death, they do not address concerns about the inevitability of death. No matter the ripe old age reached by one's relatives, no matter how frequently one exercises, no matter how one restricts the consumption of red meat, no matter the quantity of antioxidants ingested, death like taxes is certain.

Direct or proximal defenses are augmented by a second type of defense labeled distal or symbolic defenses. These defenses occur after a delay or distraction from reminders of death, when thoughts of death are highly accessible but not the focus of attention. They are not necessarily logically or obviously related to death and involve attempts to conceptualize how individual existence matters in an important and enduring way on a cosmic scale and how personal identity and legacy will endure beyond the span of the corporeal self.

If the problem of death cannot be conquered physically, it can be managed symbolically by conceiving of the self as a valuable contributor to some meaningful and enduring legacy. Symbolic defenses are made possible by a psychological buffer composed of cultural worldview and self-esteem that protect people against the potential terror stemming from the awareness of personal mortality. Cultural worldviews are the shared socially constructed interpretations of reality that allow people to make sense of existence and their place in it. A cultural worldview represents the system of beliefs that while shaped by acculturation in a particular time and place, must be individually accepted and internalized. Cultural worldviews offer protection against the threat of premature death, the threat of inevitable death, and the joint threat of corporeality and insignificance which imply that human activity is no more meaningful or enduring than the wriggling, writhing, and oozing gyrations of other animals striving for survival and reproduction.

Cultural worldviews attenuate concerns about premature death by allowing individuals to perceive the world as an orderly, stable, predictable, and manageable place where premature death can be avoided through proper vigilance and adherence to societal prescriptions for proper conduct and right living. Cultural worldviews also ameliorate concerns about the inevitability of death by describing pathways to literal and symbolic immortality. Religious beliefs offer adherents hope that death is not the annihilation of the self and provide assurances of a post death continuity in terms of consciousness, identity, and continued enjoyable experiences, whether this be in the form of a recurrent cycle of reincarnation or in a permanent existence via bodily resurrection or as a disembodied spirit in heaven. Symbolic immortality does not literally prevent death but allows for the transcendence of death by conceptualizing a way in which one's existence mattered and left some lingering impact that will outlast one's physical body. This can take the form of merging one's identity with a larger entity such as a political party, country, school, company, or even sport's team that will presumably last for longer than the span of an individual life. Additionally, one can symbolize a continuity of existence through perceived impact on the world through accomplishments, influence on future generations, or the genetic legacy of children and grandchildren.

Cultural worldviews also offer protection against the threat of our animal nature. Although the exact nature of the cultural trappings may vary across time and place, people deal with the threat of corporeality by imposing regulations on the appropriate ways in which biological functions can be discussed and enacted. Consider the extensive dietary rules and sexual taboos described in the Biblical book of Leviticus. Note also the numerous euphemisms for talking about sex and *bathroom functions* and the shame and embarrassment surrounding these topics. Humans' discomfort with these topics stems from the fact that corporeality implies death. The threat of corporeality is lessened by imbuing these activities with cultural significance that makes the way humans do them different from, and therefore presumably more meaningful than, the way similar activities are engaged in by other animals. Rather than a bestial act of physical gratification in the services of a biologically imposed drive for procreation, sex can be conceptualized as a romantic expression of a uniquely human emotional and perhaps even spiritual connection between two people in love.

Confidence in the veridicality of a particular cultural worldview is necessary but insufficient in and of itself to assuage concerns about the inevitability of death. The palliative effects of religious beliefs about literal immortality in the afterlife are dependent on the concurrent perception that one is living up to the often demanding moral and ethical requirements asserted as requirements for becoming eligible to enjoy such posthumous pleasantries. Convictions about the reality of a religious afterlife do not abate fear of death unless one also views themselves as adequately adhering to religious teachings posited as eligibility requirements. Similarly, embracing a culturally defined sense of the important accomplishments that must be accrued while living in order to leave any memorable legacy will only dampen fears of extinction with insignificance to the extent that one believes they are meeting those standards. For example, a prevalent message of symbolic immortality, which is widely conveyed in Western secular culture is that in order to be a person of worth, that is in order to matter, one must be attractive (often narrowly defined by fashionable images reflecting biases for thinness and Eurocentric features), famous, and wealthy. Obviously, a very small percentage of people can feel valuable based on these criteria.

An effective terror management system requires two components: (1) a cultural worldview that defines the standards of meaning and (2) a sense of self-esteem derived from the perception that one is living up to those standards. Self-esteem can be defined as the overall evaluation of one's worth as a person. High self-esteem presumably attenuates death anxiety by assuring one that in comparison to similar others, they are living up to the tenets of their worldview, thereby affording them literal and/ or symbolic immortality. Of course, a sense of self-esteem does not in any direct or rational way abate conscious concerns about death. Reflecting on a list of one's positive traits, abilities, and accomplishments would do little to lessen a hiker's fear in response to a charging grizzly bear or a pedestrian's fear in response to a rapidly approaching truck.

TMT theorists trace the roots of the link between feeling good about one's self and feeling safe back to the developmental process of socialization (Solomon, Greenberg, & Pyszczynski, 1991). The human infant is a very vulnerable creature whose survival is entirely dependent upon the beneficence of caregivers. The infant is aware of his/her utter dependence on parental care and consequently is very sensitive to cues indicating parental approval or disapproval. The childrearing process involves expressing approval when culturally sanctioned behaviors are emitted (parents give the child praise for eating applesauce) and expressing disapproval for culturally prohibited actions (parents admonish the child for smearing applesauce on draperies). Children feel good about themselves when they have been praised for behaving in appropriate ways, but they also feel safe. Because children recognize that their survival is dependent on parental care, any parental disapproval evokes anxiety. Over time, this process results in a habitual association, such that feeling bad about the self also means feeling anxious.

This anxiety is initially interpersonal in nature because what is feared is parental abandonment or parental failure to meet adequately the child's basic needs. The child learns that if parents are pleased with their behavior, there is no need to fear abandonment or neglect. It is during this process that the infant equates feeling good about the self with feeling safe. As cognitive capacities develop with age, children become aware of their parents' mortality and limitations. Parents, previously viewed as omnipotent, are now seen as unable to offer adequate protection from all potential threats. Somewhere between the ages of 10 and 12, children develop a mature understanding of death as a permanent and irreversible event that happens to all life forms including the self (Speece & Brent, 1992). At this point, death anxiety becomes the primary source of concern that must be protected against, but the well-learned pattern persists, such that any anxiety evoking threat produces the need to enhance self-esteem. However, the source of self-esteem has now also shifted from parents to larger social structures. Parental approval no longer ensures adequate protection, so one must obtain approval from larger social institutions such as church or country. The lack of any logical connection between self-esteem and safety from death does not undermine the assumption of TMT that self-esteem serves as a buffer against death anxiety because the defenses against death anxiety are habitual, irrational, and forged early in development.

To summarize, the basic assumption of TMT is that human awareness of creatureliness, the possibility of premature death, and the inevitability of personal mortality give rise to the potential to experience existential terror, but this terror is rarely consciously felt because of a psychological buffer composed of cultural worldview and self-esteem, which allow people to believe that they are making a valuable contribution to a meaningful existence that will be enduring and significant. Three testable hypotheses, each of which has garnered substantial empirical support, have been derived from this basic assumption: (1) the mortality salience hypothesis, (2) the death anxiety buffer hypothesis, and (3) the death thought accessibility hypothesis.

The Mortality Salience Hypothesis

The mortality salience hypothesis states that if psychological defenses are aimed at protecting people against death anxiety, then reminders of death should result in the initiation and more intense utilization of these defenses. In this paradigm, participants are primed to think about death and then their reactions are measured. In the terminology of scientific experiments, the independent variable that is manipulated is whether participants have been forced to think about death or some other topic, and the dependent variable that is measured is how they respond to those thoughts. Mortality salience has been experimentally induced in several different ways, such as interviewing people in varying proximity to a funeral home or cemetery or by subliminally flashing the word "death" or "pain" very quickly on a computer screen. However, the most common means for manipulating mortality salience has been the use of a writing prompt, in which people spend a few minutes answering open-ended questions about what will happen to their body as they physically die and the emotions that thinking about their personal death arouse in them. In this type of research, participants are randomly assigned to write about either death or a control topic. The control topic is sometimes innocuous (e.g., listening to the radio) but more often involves thinking about something unpleasant (e.g., pain, failure, or isolation).

Several studies using this paradigm have demonstrated that people use direct or proximal defenses immediately after reminders of mortality when thoughts of death are still the focus of conscious attention. For example, mortality salience inductions have been shown to increase: suppression of thoughts of death (Greenberg, Pyszczynski, Solomon, Simon, & Breus, 1994), expression of desires and intentions to engage in healthier behaviors such as getting more exercise (Arndt, Schimel, & Goldenberg, 2003) or to use safer products such as higher SPF sunscreen (Routledge, Arndt, & Goldenberg, 2004), and exaggeration of their longevity by expressing more traits and characteristics shown by medical research to predict longer life (Greenberg et al., 1993).

Numerous studies also support the use of symbolic or distal defenses by showing that reminders of death increase strivings for self-esteem, symbolic immortality, and literal immortality, but that these effects only occur following delay or distraction when thoughts of death are no longer the focus of conscious attention. Research on these proximal defenses involves the inclusion of a delay/distraction task in which participants do a word-search puzzle, read a boring passage of text, or fill out an innocuous questionnaire for a few minutes after the mortality salience induction prior to measuring the response of interest. Reminders of death create a delayed increase in attempts to bolster self-esteem, as evidenced by (1) taking more credit for success and blaming external factors for failure (Mikulincer & Florian, 2002), (2) people who were pleased with the appearance of their body more strongly identifying with their bodies (Goldenberg, McCoy, Pyszczynski, & Solomon, 2000), and (3) people who valued being physically strong actually squeezing harder on a device that measures grip strength (Peters, Greenberg, Williams, & Schneider, 2005).

In addition, mortality salience has also been documented to augment people's desire for literal immorality as evidenced by greater reported agreement with statements about the reality of heaven (Conn, Schrader, Wann, & Mruz, 1996) and increased belief in the existence of God (Norenzayan & Hansen, 2006; Vail, Arndt, & Abdollahi, 2012). Further, mortality salience has been shown to increase the appeal of symbolic immortality as evidenced by greater appeal of materialistic success such as higher salary (Kasser, & Sheldon, 2000), increased interest in fame (Greenberg, Kosloff, Solomon, Cohen, & Landau, 2010), and a greater desire for legacy through children (Fritsche et al., 2007; Wisman & Goldenberg, 2005).

The responses to mortality salience described above all represent attempts to transcend death symbolically by enhancing the perception that one is a person of worth making a valuable contribution to the world that will afford them either literal or symbolic immorality. There is, however, a more insidious aspect of the mortality salience hypothesis regarding reactions to different Others. The most extensively studied and well replicated finding in the mortality salience literature is that reminders of death lead to praise of similar others and derogation of dissimilar Others, a phenomenon labeled cultural worldview defense. Although most people likely consider their perception of the world as a reflection of absolute reality, it is better thought of as an ephemeral personal construction that depends on the validation of others. Because there are many ambiguous stimuli in life, groups with a shared culture use each other to solidify their perception of the world. Because cultural worldviews are social constructions, the presence of Other people with differing worldviews is threatening because it implies implicitly or explicitly that one's own worldview is invalid. Pyszczynski, Solomon, and Greenberg (2003) have argued that "all isms are schisms." By this they mean that any creed, ideology, or other means of classification that binds together group members into a cohesive identity of "us" is divisive and leads inevitably to conflict because it provides a means of distinguishing "them" as those who do not belong to the group.

From the perspective of TMT, individuals should like others with similar beliefs because these others strengthen the confidence that the individual has adopted the correct worldview. Conversely, individuals should dislike dissimilar Others because they call into question the validity of the individual's cultural worldview. If the attitudes and beliefs of the out-group cannot be altered, then the out-group must be maligned, demeaned, and derogated in order to discredit the threat their contradictory beliefs imply. Research consistently shows that mortality salience intensifies preference for similar over dissimilar Others on dimensions of nationalism (Arndt, Greenberg, Pyszczynski, & Solomon, 1997), political affiliation (Greenberg, Simon, Pyszczynski, Solomon, & Chatel, 1992), and religious identity (Greenberg et al., 1990).

Not only does mortality salience intensify dislike of out-group members, but it may also lead to aggression against those who threaten cultural worldview. If out-group members cannot be converted, then attempts to eradicate them altogether may be enacted as an extreme form of eliminating the threat they pose to cultural worldview. Consistent with this hypothesis, McGregor et al. (1998) found that subtle reminders of personal mortality led to increased aggression against those with different political attitudes. Participants were pre-screened as to their political attitudes. Next, they completed either a mortality salience manipulation or non-death related material and then observed someone expressing political views in stark opposition to their own. Later, participants were given the opportunity to allocate the amount of hot sauce to put on food that was presumably to be eaten by the person who had expressed political views dissimilar to their own. Aggression was measured as the amount of hot sauce allocated (because participants were told that the politically dissimilar person who must eat the food did not like spicy food). Participants in the mortality salience condition spiked the dissimilar Other's food with substantially more hot sauce than did participants in the control condition.

The Death Anxiety Buffer Hypothesis

The anxiety buffer hypothesis is conceptually similar to the mortality salience hypothesis but reverses the direction of the tested relationship between psychological defenses and death anxiety. According to the anxiety buffer hypothesis, if psychological defenses such as cultural worldview and self-esteem operate to mitigate death anxiety, then weakening or undermining the integrity of these defenses should leave people more prone to death anxiety, whereas augmenting or enhancing these defenses ought to leave people less vulnerable to death anxiety. In experiments designed to test this hypothesis, the strength of the psychological defense system is the independent variable manipulated by researchers and death anxiety is the dependent variable measured by researchers. Support for the anxiety buffer hypothesis comes from the finding that threatening valued aspects of cultural worldview by having participants read an essay arguing that marriage (a valued cultural institution) is an outdated and untenable practice increased their implicit levels of death anxiety as measured by a task called the Implicit Association Test that assesses the speed with which people can respond when pairing words about death or about life with words about the self or other people (Bassett, 2005). Inversely, bolstering people's self-esteem has been demonstrated to lower death anxiety (Greenberg et al., 1992). Greenberg et al. reported that participants who received positive feedback on a purported personality test, and therefore had enhanced levels of self-esteem, reported less anxiety (and showed less physiological evidence of anxiety as measured by heart rate) when watching a video depicting graphic death imagery, such as an autopsy.

A variation on tests of the anxiety buffer hypothesis uses the reduced need for additional defenses as the index of augmented protection against death anxiety. In these types of experiments, researchers manipulate self-esteem or confidence in cultural worldview prior to exposing participants to reminders of mortality and then measure their defensive reactions. In these studies, participants who have had their psychological buffer against anxiety strengthened via enhanced self-esteem or increased confidence in their cultural worldview show no defensive reactions to reminders of mortality. For example, affirming people's sense of self-worth by having them think about a way in which they had lived up to an important value reduced the need to engage in cultural worldview defense by derogating dissimilar Others following mortality salience (Schmeichel & Martens, 2005). Further, having people read information presenting evidence from near-death experiences that supposedly offered unequivocal scientific proof that life continues after death, negated the otherwise observed effects of mortality salience on increased self-esteem striving and cultural worldview defense, thereby providing further support for the claim that these defenses are activated specifically to prevent death anxiety (Dechesne et al., 2003).

The Death Thought Accessibility Hypothesis

The death thought accessibility hypothesis asserts that weakening the psychological structures (self-esteem and cultural worldview) that operate to protect against death anxiety will reduce people's vulnerability to experiencing potentially unsettling death related cognitions. This hypothesis was derived from theoretical refinements recognizing that it is the potential to experience death anxiety that must be managed because, by the time one is consciously experiencing anxiety about death, the terror management system has already failed (Arndt, Cook, & Routledge, 2004).

For a psychological system to optimally manage death terror, symbolic defenses need to be activated when thoughts of death are accumulating in the preconscious mind on the periphery of awareness but before a person is actively ruminating about their mortality. The activation of these defenses should then result in the dissipation of the unwanted death thoughts, making them less likely to enter awareness, and thereby averting the potential experience of anxiety. If self-esteem and cultural worldview help avert death anxiety by keeping people from consciously thinking about death, then the disruption of these terror management defenses should result in an increased accessibility of death-related thoughts. The difficulty here is in the need for a way to measure what people may be likely to think about in the near future before they are actually thinking about it. Obviously, self-reported introspection is of no value here because by the time one can report on their thoughts, they are already aware of what they are thinking. How then do researchers measure thoughts that exist outside of consciousness that are what people may be likely to think about soon but are not currently thinking?

The most common approach to this problem has been to use a word fragment completion task. In this task, participants are given a string of letters with some blank spaces. They are asked to write in letters in the blanks to make a meaningful word. Example items on this task might be: coff_ _, sk_ ll, and de_ _. The important aspect of these fragments is that they can be completed in multiple ways. Some participants might respond with the words *coffee, skill,* and *dear,* indicating that they have low levels of death thought accessibility and are not likely to start thinking about mortality in the near future. In contrast, other participants might respond with the words *coffin, skull,* and *dead,* indicating that they had high levels of death thought accessibility and that these death-related thoughts were just waiting to enter into their conscious mind and become the topic they were thinking about.

Research using these word-fragment completion measures has consistently shown that disruptions to the terror management defenses increase death thought accessibility. For example, priming creatureliness in the form of highlighting the similarities of humans to other animals (Cox, Goldenberg, Pyszczynski, & Weise, 2007), threatening self-esteem in the form of feedback suggesting that one is ill-suited for a desired occupation (Hayes, Schimel, Faucher, & Williams, 2008), and undermining faith in cultural worldview such as pointing out to literal-religious-creationists contradictory details of two different version of the creation story in Genesis (Schimel, Hayes, Williams, & Jahrig, 2007) all resulted in increased prevalence of death-related thoughts.

Now that we have reviewed the basic ideas of TMT and research evidence supporting these ideas, we will turn our attention in Chapter 3 to the ways in which TMT can be applied to analyzing works of art and entertainment and audience reactions to these works. In their recent review of the application of TMT to art, film, and media, Young, Sullivan, and Palitsky (2018) noted that "humans have perennially turned to art as a means for seeking transcendence, however fleeting, of their mortal existence. TMT has made, and stands to continue to make, an important contribution to the extant interdisciplinary scholarship on death, art, and media by highlighting and empirically documenting the significance of this psychological imperative" (p. 553).

3

Applying TMT to Illumine the Motives for and Reactions to Fictional Violence

TMT can be applied to understanding works of artistic creation at three levels of analysis. First, the human need to create art can be motivated by a desire for symbolic immortality, which is itself a defense against death anxiety. Second, death anxiety can be a contributing factor for why people interact with art and media and can affect their reactions to these interactions. Third, the content of the works themselves can be explored in terms of how they allow consumers to engage with the topic of death and in terms of how they augment psychological defenses that suppress death anxiety. The main focus here is on the second and third levels of analysis by showing how TMT offers insights into understanding motives for consuming works of art and for explaining consumers' reactions to different types of art and media. This chapter will highlight some burgeoning research on how reminders of death can influence people's reactions to different types of entertainment in ways consistent with the defenses described by TMT and will also explore the ways in which insights from TMT have been and can be applied to supplement the analysis of the content of artistic and popular cultural creations.

In the introduction to their edited volume on the applications of Terror Management Theory to film, Sullivan and Greenberg (2013a) assert that "human life is characterized by two particularly resonant psychological realities: the fear of death and the desire to overcome it" (p. 1). They further argue that human storytelling has always given a central place to these two psychological realities from ancient times in the *Epic of Gilgamesh* to modern day cinema. The focus on overcoming death extends the scope of potential applications of TMT beyond fiction, in which explicit images of death are prevalent, and beyond those stories that have the dying of central characters as main themes. TMT asserts that cultural worldviews offer people hope of transcending death. Consequently, all forms of entertainment that transmit or reinforce cultural beliefs about the ways in which people can achieve self-esteem or find meaning in life can serve a terror management function by bolstering the structures that form the psychological buffer against death terror. Because TMT "is not necessarily focused on how people understand death per se, nor on people for whom death is a chronically salient cognition (e.g., the elderly and infirm)" it can be utilized to explore how "compensatory strivings for immortality motivate characters in films and scenes that do not explicitly focus on death" (Young, Sullivan, & Palitsky, 2018, p. 540). This same analysis applies to the motives of audiences. Viewers may find satisfaction in consuming entertainment that reinforces and solidifies their existing cultural beliefs systems. Consequently, the appeal of many types of entertainment could be interpreted as serving a terror management function even if images of death or narratives of dying were not prominent elements or defining features of a particular show or film.

Although TMT can be applied to the analysis of audience motives and character motives across the whole spectrum of art, literature, film, and television regardless of the genre or theme, it is particularly well suited to the analysis of fictional violence. Fictional violence helps to augment confidence in a cultural worldview because the protagonist's ability to avoid death and to inflict it on others offers a form of proof to viewers of the correctness of the cultural worldview symbolized by the hero (Young et al., 2018). This idea, that the appeal of violent media lies in its ability to validate belief systems, has a well-established precedent in theorizing outside of TMT.

The appeal of violent media lies not in violence for violence's sake, but rather the ultimate payoff, what is desired by viewers—the enhanced sense of justice that is produced by the violence (Zillmann, 1998). People are capable of empathizing with characters in fiction and, as such, may feel distressed by the suffering of fictional victims of violence. However, presenting victims of violence as deserving of their suffering tends to negate any empathy audiences might otherwise feel towards them. In addition, watching violence against "bad" characters can even be met with enjoyable reactions to the extent that it bolsters viewers' confidence that justice and moral order have been restored. Consequently, viewers' reaction to images of violence (enjoyment or distress) depends on the viewer's attitude toward the character. Dispositional alignment theory asserts that viewers are predisposed to react with empathy or pleasure to the victim's suffering depending on how they evaluate the character's behavior, especially their moral behavior up to the point of the violence. The suffering of liked characters or prosperity of disliked characters will elicit distress whereas the suffering of disliked characters can elicit pleasure (Zillmann, 1998).

Similarly, excitation transfer theory advances the proposition that what audiences enjoy is not so much the violence as it is happening but the sense of relief that occurs when the threat is successfully resolved or even when the unpleasantness is removed by the ending of the film (Zillmann, 1998). According to the excitation transfer theory, the physiological arousal caused by one type of emotion can be transferred to an increase in the intensity of experience of a different emotion, and this transfer can happen across different valences. As applied to violent entertainment, the more upsetting or distressing the violence, the greater the sense of relief or enjoyment once it is over. The distress can be caused by empathic reaction to the suffering of a victim or by the tension and suspense created by the threat of potential violence against a character. The tension can be relieved, and a sense of enjoyment evoked by a satisfying dramatic conclusion in which the threat is eliminated or in which the potential victim escapes harm. Alternatively, the relief may simply come once the film or episode is over.

The dispositional alignment and excitation transfer principles may be combined to explain the appeal of violent media as not residing in bloodlust for the violence itself but in the heightened sense of relief once the violence is over and justice and order have been reestablished. Zillmann (1998) put it this way: "escalations in the portrayal of righteous, enjoyable violence necessitate escalations in the portrayal of morally enraging, evil, and distressing violence" (p. 206). He concludes,

> There can be little doubt, then, that righteous violence, brutal but justified by the ends, will prompt gloriously intense euphoric reactions the more it is proceeded by patently unjust and similarly brutal violence. In other words, displays of monstrous gratuitous slaughter and the distress they evoke are a necessary prelude to the portrayal of righteous maiming and killing that is to spark euphoric reactions. Without such prelude, violence cannot be righteous and, hence, is rendered unenjoyable—at least for nonsadists, which should constitute the vast majority of the drama-consuming public [p. 208].

Zillmann (1998) conceptualized fictional violence as enjoyable only to the extent that it appealed to viewers' sense of justice. He further suggested that the psychological motive underlying the appeal of justified violence was the viewers' need to feel safe. He claimed that it is the need to feel safe that motivates the appeal of violence and particularly violence that is presented as justified and necessary for protecting the safety afforded by the typical social order from the menacing threat of disruption. So, while it is possible that frequent exposure to fictional violence increases viewers' perception that the real world is a dangerous place (Appel, 2008; Gerbner,

Gross, Morgan, & Signorielli, 1986), ironically this same increased concern about real life dangers may increase the appeal of fictional violence to the extent that such violence promotes messages of justice. Such messages convey a sense of safety by comforting viewers that they are safe from violence because ultimately the "good guys" win. To make an argument by analogy, we can imagine that high profile cases of actual gun violence might enhance the appeal of gun ownership for those who believe that owning a gun will keep them safe from violence. Similarly, violent entertainment can both increase people's fear of being victimized by violence while simultaneously ameliorating that fear with a bolstered confidence that the world is just, and that in a just world, they are safe because they are good.

Applying TMT to the existing arguments for the role of belief in a just world as underlying the appeal of fictional violence offers additional insight. The same consumption of violent media that elicits the threat of death can also sure up and buttress the psychological defenses against death anxiety. If the death of others can be presented as just or deserved due to their status as infidels, dehumanized out-group members, moral transgressors, or just foolish careless people, then viewers can increase conviction in the correctness of their worldview and protect themselves against anxiety about their own mortality. Thus, to the extent that the cultural messages that follow violence bolster viewers' sense of meaning, fairness, self-esteem, or group identity, people are receptive to these messages and find them appealing because of the unpleasant emotional reactions and potential anxiety elicited by the violence that preceded them. Sullivan and Greenberg (2013a) made this point in their application of TMT to film analysis:

> The context of death in films raises the interesting possibility that images of death spark a nonconsciously registered potential for anxiety in viewers, which film narratives often subsequently allay by bolstering certain normative aspects of the contemporary worldview.... Imaged death not only accentuates a narrative or provides aesthetic release; it also primes viewers with a fundamental but typically repressed anxiety, making them possibly more receptive to messages that reinforce the cultural defense mechanisms they rely on for protection against death awareness [p. 7].

The TMT distinction between proximal and distal defenses can be applied to explain the timing of different viewer reactions to screen violence (Young et al., 2018). Proximal defenses occur immediately after confronting reminders of mortality when thoughts of death are still the focus of conscious attention. These defenses involve trying to repress thoughts of death or to downplay one's vulnerability to it. Watching fictional depictions of violence and death should make mortality salient to viewers.

Proximal defenses mentioned by Young et al. could involve looking away or focusing on the fact that the images are not real. Distal defenses are symbolic defenses that occur a few minutes after reminders of mortality when thoughts of death are no longer the focus of conscious attention but have faded to the periphery of the mind and are lingering below the threshold of consciousness but still accessible enough to potentially re-enter consciousness. These are symbolic defenses that involve bolstering self-esteem or enhancing conviction in the certainty of one's worldview. Watching on-screen violence might "be more likely to reinforce adherence to cultural worldviews when the violent content is shown before and apart from the primary ideological content" (Young et al., p. 543). From the TMT perspective, fictional violence should be appealing to the extent that it makes thoughts about death and existential anxiety salient and then offers catharsis for those anxieties by strengthening cultural messages that offer viewer's hopes of transcendence via literal or symbolic immortality.

Young et al. (2018) pointed out the relevance of TMT in explaining why people may be drawn to media that elicits unpleasant or aversive emotional reactions. They draw on the distinction between enjoyment (hedonic motives) and appreciation (eudemonic motives), stating, "Many consumers can appreciate (i.e., think highly of or value) a work of art without enjoying it. In fact, art that is hardly enjoyable at all can impact a sense of meaning by conveying values or beliefs that the perceiver holds in high regard, an offering that is particularly valuable when staving off death anxiety" (p. 546). They offer as an example Mel Gibson's *The Passion of The Christ* (2004). While viewers may not have enjoyed watching the graphic torture and crucifixion of Jesus as the events were being depicted during the film, they may have felt a sense of appreciation at the film's conclusion based on the fact that it had confirmed and bolstered their religious beliefs and offered the promise of eternal life. The appreciation of seeing the Christian worldview and its promise of literal immortality visually confirmed was made all the more important because of the graphic reminders of corporeality and death elicited by the explicit violence and gore of the film.

Empirical Evidence for the Role of Terror Management in Reactions to Art and Entertainment

There is a small but growing body of empirical evidence to support the TMT assertion that a motive to minimize existential anxiety underlies preferences for and reactions to different types of art and entertainment. The earliest of these studies examined how inducing people to think about their mortality would affect their reactions to different types of literary passages (Goldenberg, Pyszczynski, Johnson, Greenberg, & Solomon, 1999). Participants who had been primed to think about their mortality had stronger emotional responses to tragic literary passages with themes of death and bereavement than those who had not been primed to think about mortality; however, the two groups did not differ in their reactions to a neutral literary passage. Goldenberg et al. interpreted these findings as indicating that while people typically try to avoid thoughts that elicit existential anxiety, grappling with such issues in a fictional realm where there is greater psychological distance may offer a sense of control and mastery.

Several studies have examined the relationship of death anxiety to preferences in the visual arts. A correlational study revealed that the tendency to fear death (because it implies the annihilation of the self) predicted greater dislike for a photograph that challenged traditional representations of reality compared to one that conformed to expectations (Rubin, 2018). Specifically, the control photo was a fisherman in a boat during stormy seas, whereas the meaning-threatening picture showed a similar scene except that the fisherman had the head of a horse and was holding a cat. The greater preference for the expected image over the unexpected one was associated only with the fear that death meant self-annihilation and not with fears about the uncertainty surrounding death. This is an important finding because some critics of TMT have claimed that uncertainty, and not death, is the paramount threat that activates psychological defenses and that reminders of mortality elicit distal defenses in the form of worldview validation and self-esteem striving simply because death is one of many stimuli that primes epistemic uncertainty (e.g., Uncertainty Management Theory; van den Bos, Poortvliet, Maas, Miedema, & van den Ham, 2005).

A set of experimental studies similarly supported the idea that the motive to mitigate death anxiety gives rise to a preference for order and meaning in works of art (Landau, Greenberg, Solomon, Pyszczynski, & Martens, 2006). In study 1, activating thoughts of mortality decreased liking for non-representative abstract modern art. In study 2, this result was refined by the discovery that mortality salience reduced liking for abstract art only among people high on the trait of personal need for structure (a rigid type of thinking style that does not tolerate ambiguity and uncertainty). In study 3, the effect of mortality salience on disliking abstract art was shown to be due to an increased preference for a structured way of easily interpreting the world in a meaningful way. Providing a title for the abstract artwork that offered a readymade meaningful interpretation decreased people's dislike of it even under conditions when mortality was salient.

The need to manage existential terror can influence reactions to visual art, not just in terms of a preference for order and meaning but also in terms of a preference for messages and themes that validate existing cultural beliefs. For example, Christians preferred Christian art over art depicting secular themes, and this preference was intensified when mortality was salient (Beck, McGregor, Woodrow, Haugen, & Killion, 2010). This study showed that reminders of death increased preference for Christian over secular art among Christian participants even though the secular art was of objectively higher artistic value. The implication of these findings is that art can be a means of strengthening the beliefs of one's cultural worldview and that people may be especially drawn to art that bolsters their belief system under conditions when they have been reminded of existential threat.

A small number of studies have explored the role of terror management in audience preferences for and reactions to different types of film and television. For example, one such study examined how inducing thoughts of death would influence reactions to pleasant (those that elicit only positive emotions), meaningful (those that elicit strong but ambivalent emotions), and informative (documentaries than convey information in a fairly neutral way emotionally) types of film (Reiger et al., 2015). Mortality salience did not affect enjoyment in response to any of the types of film but did have an impact on appreciation, with the highest levels of appreciation being reported by participants who watched the meaningful film under conditions of mortality salience.

Other studies indicate that there may be individual differences in whether or not thoughts of death motivate people to find appreciation in meaningful films. For example, experimentally inducing thoughts of death increased people's appreciation for a film depicting a character's attempt to find meaning in life in the face of her terminal cancer diagnosis (Hofer, 2013). However, this effect only emerged among people who were generally high on the dispositional trait of seeking meaning in life.

Still other studies seem to suggest that offering a potential lesson about meaning is not enough for a film to buffer death anxiety, but rather it must present the survival of the protagonists in order to augment viewer's hopes of transcendence. Movies in which characters were threatened with the prospect of death but survived helped viewers cope with fears of their own death (Rieger & Hofer, 2017). In this study, all participants watched a film about a man diagnosed with cancer who sets out on a long road trip to contemplate the meaning of his existence. Half of the participants watched a version of the film in which he died at the end of the film; whereas the other half watched a version in which he survived. Prior to watching their respective versions of the film, participants were primed to think about death or a neutral topic. There was no difference in liking for the two versions of the film in either the mortality salience or control conditions. There was no difference in appreciation levels of the two versions among participants in the control condition who had not first been primed to think about death. There was, however, a difference in appreciation of the two versions among those in the mortality salience condition who had been reminded of death, with participants reporting greater appreciation for the version where the protagonist survived than the version where he died.

The role of terror management has also been examined in the appeal of television crime dramas emphasizing the rule of law and justice (Taylor, 2012). This investigation was grounded in the TMT assumptions that perceiving the world as just and fair is essential in order for people to manage anxiety about death and that death can be made less threatening by immersing oneself in a cultural worldview that specifies the standards of conduct that afford self-esteem and allow for the perception that one is making a contribution to something more important and permanent than their bodily existence. Taylor emphasized the importance of fairness as the *sine qua non* for any worldview to abate existential dread, because the comfort of adhering to any worldview is nullified if people are not rewarded for living up to its standards and punished for failing to do so. He hypothesized that reminders of personal mortality would increase the appeal of television shows in which symbols of traditional moral order (the legal system and criminal justice system) confirm the principle of fairness by punishing those who have violated the standards of ethical and legal conduct. Many crime dramas not only have a focus on justice but also contain extensive themes and imagery related to violence, murder, and forensic work with dead bodies. Such shows would seem to be powerful reminders of personal mortality. Consequently, it may seem counter-intuitive to claim that it is a motive to deny death that drives the appeal of such shows. Ironically, the death themes in the shows may be essential to promoting the appeal of their message that the world is fair and that humanly created cultural institutions such as the legal system operate effectively in bringing about justice.

In two experiments, college students were assigned to write about either their own death or another aversive topic prior to rating the appeal of various types of television programs. Students who had been assigned to think about death showed an increase in the appeal of law and justice television programs (e.g., *Law and Order, CSI, Criminal Minds, 24*) compared to those who wrote about studying or physical pain. Reminders of death did not increase the appeal of television overall, just the appeal of shows with law and justice themes (Taylor, 2012).

Although not directly involving reactions to film or television, a study by Hayes, Schimel, and Williams (2008) should be noted here because it has profound implications for the possibility that the death of worldview threatening Others can actually reduce the accessibility of death-related concerns. These researchers threatened the worldview of Christian participants by having them read a story describing how the residents of Nazareth (the hometown of Jesus according to the Bible) were now predominantly Muslim. Because people rely on consensual validation to maintain confidence in non-empirically verifiable religious beliefs, the mere existence of Others, with different religious beliefs undermines the credibility of personally held beliefs, and therefore, weakens hopes for literal immortality. Participants in this study who read about the spread of Islam in a place symbolically important to the Christian faith experienced a disruption in their terror management defenses as evidenced by an increase in death-related thoughts making them more vulnerable to death anxiety. Even more interesting, however, was the finding that the researchers were able to nullify this threat by having participants read about a plane crash in which hundreds of Muslims died. Christian participants who read about the prevalence of Islam in Nazareth but then read about a plane crash killing Muslims did not show elevated levels of death-related cognitions.

Ironically, a dramatic reminder of death (reading about victims of a fatal plane crash) that should have made mortality highly salient seemed to have the inverse effect of buffering or protecting people from death related concerns. Hayes et al. interpreted this finding as evidence that the misfortune affecting Muslims actually strengthened Christian participants' convictions in the superiority of their own religious beliefs, thereby strengthening their psychological buffer against death anxiety. If we extrapolate these findings to violent media, we can make an intriguing hypothesis about audience reactions to depictions of fictional killing. To the extent that violence in entertainment is depicted as restoring justice and results in the death of threatening Others who are perceived as immoral or different from viewers, watching such fictional deaths could actually be cathartic to viewers by bolstering their psychological defenses against death and dissipating potentially troubling thoughts of death.

The evidence reviewed above suggests that TMT can offer valuable insights into understanding the appeal of fictional violence and audience reactions to violent entertainment. In addition to this important contribution, TMT can also be applied to the analysis of fictional characters' motives for violence.

Insights from TMT into the Analysis of Fictional Violence

Although it is certainly possible to have pacifistic and altruistic heroic projects, TMT reveals numerous ways through which the quest for death transcendence can be manifested in violence; therefore, these revelations can offer valuable insight into understanding and analyzing motives for aggression depicted in violent entertainment. Inversely, the recognition of motives for fictional violence can be instructive in understanding real-world violence.

The quest for heroism is driven by a need to conquer death symbolically, and one way to define heroism is as the violent conquest of the Other. By projecting the source of the world's problems onto another person or group of people and labeling them as evil, the means to heroism becomes the quest to expunge these evildoers from the planet and purge their vile and corrupting influence through complete annihilation. Becker (1975) put it this way: "All you have to do is to say that your group is pure and good, eligible for a full life and some kind of eternal meaning. But others like Jews or gypsies are the real animals, are spoiling everything for you, contaminating your purity and bringing disease and weakness into your vitality. Then you have a mandate to launch a political plague, a campaign to make the world pure" (p. 93). From this perspective, violence is often ideologically motivated, as the death-denying worldview of one group can be validated through the destruction of those with conflicting and therefore threatening worldviews.

This tendency is illustrated in dark comedic fashion in the movie *The Last Supper* (1996). The movie depicts a group of liberal graduate students who, after killing a menacing drifter in self-defense and covering it up, decide to host a weekly dinner party at which they poison conservative or bigoted thinkers who violate their worldview. What begins as the group's hypothetical musings regarding a thought experiment about the ethicality of preemptively killing Hitler before he could perpetrate the Holocaust is transformed into a serious mission of ideological purification by murder when Luke (Courtney B. Vance) poses an earnest question: "What if you kill someone whose death makes the world a better place?" Initially, their plan is to offer each special guest poisoned wine only after all possible attempts at conversion have failed. Over the course of the film, a series of people who the group considers homophobes, prudes, and book-burners are dispatched in increasingly cursory fashion as the bodies buried in the tomato garden pile up at an alarming rate. The growing callousness of the group is exemplified by Luke, who dismisses the suggestion that they are no longer giving people a chance to repent from their perceived erroneous ideologies before killing them and are not even serving their victims decent cuisine with the retort "The fag-basher got Chinese." Although a comedy, the film offers a sobering reflection on how easily evil can be perpetrated in the name of ideological righteousness.

Another way to abate existential anxiety is through the pursuit of what Robert Jay Lifton (1976) calls symbolic immortality. The sting of corporeal mortality can be made more palatable by the sense that one has left some impact on the world that will endure. One form of seeking symbolic immortality is the hope of becoming famous so that people will remember you after your death. In fact, empirical research has documented that experimentally inducing thoughts of death increased college students' interest in being famous (Greenberg, Kosloff, Solomon, Cohen, & Landau, 2010). Although the quest for symbolic death transcendence can be achieved through pro-social means, such as creative works or the positive influence on the lives of others, it can also be expressed in more insidious forms. Greenberg (2012) suggested that "the most unfortunate version of this fame seeking may manifest itself through committing heinous acts" (p. 25). He goes on to point out that Mark David Chapman (who shot John Lennon) and Seung-Hui Cho (the Virginia Tech shooter) explicitly acknowledged the desire for fame and to be remembered as the goal behind their acts of lethal violence.

Cave (2012) noted that the desire to achieve fame through destructive means is not a modern cultural phenomenon. In support of this claim, he offers the case of Herostratus, who in hopes of becoming famous, perpetrated an act of arson that destroyed the temple of Artemis at Ephesus in 356 BCE. Cave described Herostratus syndrome as referring to intentional nefarious deeds done in hopes of achieving fame. The syndrome is especially likely to affect those who live in a culture that values fame but who lack the skills or abilities to create something memorable. Consequently, they will feel a sense of injustice that the world has denied them the aptitude to achieve the fame they so desperately seek and will feel justified in seeking symbolic immortality through violent means. Cave posited that these requisite circumstances are prevalent in contemporary American culture, writing, "In a society such as ours, obsessed with celebrity, the temptation is high to immortalize one's name through some wicked but dramatic act: assassinating a president or pop star, blowing up a building or gunning down fellow high schools students" (p. 212).

The Herostratus syndrome is certainly present as a motive among fictional killers. For example, Schmid (2005) noted that the John Doe killer (Kevin Spacey) in the movie *Seven* (1995) is motivated by a desire for symbolic immortality, as evidenced by his claim that "what I've done is going to be puzzled over and studied and followed forever." Schmid further argued, "Doe has learned well the lessons of James Dean, Marilyn Monroe, and Bonnie and Clyde. He knows that contemporary American culture reserves its most exalted iconic status for those who refuse to linger and instead go out in a blaze of glory. His death is therefore a perfectly appropriate way of satisfying his desire for immortality" (p. 119).

The frustration of lacking the aptitude to transcend death by achieving fame even through violent means is seen in the character of the son of Bloody Face (Dylan McDermott) on the FX television series *American Horror Story Asylum (2012)*. In the series, Bloody Face was an infamous serial killer who used his medical training to remove his victim's skin with surgical precision. The son of Bloody Face is trying to carry on his father legacy by replicating his *modus operandi*, but he lacks the necessary ability. In Episode 9, "The Coat Hanger," the son of Bloody Face has sought out a psychotherapist based on her ad claiming to help people curb their unwanted impulses. The therapist listens with growing horror as the true nature of his impulses and his identity become evident. He bemoans his inability to live up to his father's notoriety, claiming, "I didn't have the same skills as my father. I didn't get the medical training. I made a mess.... I'll never live up to him."

The above insights into the motives for fictional violence have implications for illuminating audience reactions to this violence and what effects watching such violence has on viewer's own terror management processes.

Is Consumption of Fictional Violence a Productive Way to Manage Terror?

On the question of whether fictional forms of entertainment can actually impact real life psychological processes devoted to dealing with the pressing problem of human mortality, Sullivan and Greenberg (2013b) suggest:

> Film does indeed have the capacity to aid us in our struggle with this problem. In the confines of a film we can safely contemplate death, the ultimate tragedy, and feel our way through both familiar and foreign systems of meaning as we try to come to grips with it but for there to be any real value viewers cannot be passive participants in the act of viewing. Rather, they must actively engage with film on a psychological level [p. 243].

Even if the psychological engagement of viewers with fictional entertainment can potentially provide psychological benefits in helping people deal with existential concerns, when it comes to fictional violence, any potential benefit in the form of catharsis regarding death anxiety must be balanced against concerns about potentially harmful effects of watching violent entertainment. Fictional violence could lead to deleterious effects if the cultural messages presented promoted greater hostility towards outgroups and/or the acceptance of violence against Others.

Desilet (2014) makes a compelling case for potential harmful effects of watching screen violence. Although he does suggest that onscreen violence is a factor increasing the likelihood of real-world aggression (although certainly not the sole or even the main cause), he is more concerned with the capacity for violent entertainment to reinforce prevalent cultural attitudes about violence as an acceptable and perhaps even necessary means of maintaining justice.

He clearly distinguishes that not all media violence is harmful in promoting accepting and favorable attitudes towards real-world violence but rather that such an effect depends on the dramatic structure in which the violence is situated; specifically, the level of moral struggle in character's consideration between violent and nonviolent alternatives.

It is only in the context of what Desilet (2014) calls the antagonal dramatic structure that television and movie violence "serves to promote and amplify the identities, attitudes, and behaviors consistent with a culture of violence" (p. 199). In antagonal conflict "each side appears alien and unnecessary to the other and, therefore, functions as an illegitimate and threatening intrusion. This conflict reflects a tension of differences approaching all or nothing, life or death, the mutually exclusive outcome of a zero-sum game model" (Desilet, p. 12). It is this antagonal type of structure that fails to offer a full sense of conflict between competing moral agents and neglects the tragic consequences of violence in favor of promoting audience revelry in the spectacle of morally righteous retributive violence.

Desilet responds to the argument that the audience demand for screen violence is an unavoidable consequence of a bloodlust endemic to human nature by claiming that as with all appetites, the ways in which they are gratified can vary on a continuum of harmfulness. He suggests that the depiction of "extreme violence carries with it the obligation to show adequate background for the violence in the complexities and details of the characters and circumstances through which the violence arises" (pp. 19–20). Such a responsible use of violence requires depicting villains in nuanced rather than unidimensional ways and fully highlighting the negative consequences of violence enacted by villains and heroes alike in such a way that violence, even when deemed necessary or justified, is never celebrated. In the absence of such responsible depictions of violence "Dramatic designs joining justice and celebration to violence detach violence from tragic emotions and fuel dysfunctional attitudes towards the complexity of conflicts and people in the real world" (p. 19).

Pizzato (2005) similarly contends that it is not the overall level of screen violence that is the issue to be concerned about but rather the manner in which the violence is depicted. Pizzato views complex, tragic depictions of violence, in which characters are shown as having both good and bad characteristics, and in which the negative consequences of violence are fully portrayed, as superior to melodramatic depictions featuring unidimensional characters and presenting simplistic notions of the absolute triumph of good over evil through morally righteous violence. Pizzato sees the broader popularity of melodramatic violence as rooted in its ability to offer viewer's the short-term reduction in fears. He argues that "melodrama's reassertion of metaphysical righteousness, through individual heroism, becomes even more tempting, and perhaps addictive, with the postmodern collapse of universal values" (Pizzato, p. 4). He also notes that this type of cathartic purging is never fully effective and that repeated exposure to melodramatic violence has negative consequences in that it likely increases animosity and perhaps even real-world violence towards the vilified Other.

According to Pizzato, these potentially deleterious effects of melodramatic violence can be attenuated by "more tragic presentation of motives and consequences for violence, along with better education of viewers to watch the dominant melodrama more critically" (p. 180). Complex tragic depictions of violence offer a different type of catharsis, in which viewers' desires, fears and emotions are clarified allowing for a "communal working through of specific, personal and social traumas" (p. 2). Pizzato contends that "rather than repeating violence by blaming and punishing certain villains for the victim's trauma, and thus boosting the hero's ego, a truly cathartic sacrifice reveals tragic errors of judgment and painful consequences for all involved in such righteous vengeance" (p. 15).

Analysis, such as that offered by Desilet (2014) and Pizzato (2005), shows that the types of dramatic depictions of violence most likely to promote a reflexive level of audience enjoyment are also the ones most likely to reinforce viewer's attitudes of acceptance towards actual violence. This point resonates with the TMT premise that the belief systems that offer the greatest protection against death anxiety are also the most prone to promoting hostility and aggression. Pyszczynski, Solomon, and Greenberg (2003) suggested that cultural worldviews need to be evaluated on two dimensions: (1) the extent to which they offer adherents psychological security by quelling anxieties about mortality through the articulation of clear pathways to meaning and value and (2) the extent to which they allow for tolerance and acceptance of Others with differing conceptions of reality. Unfortunately, there is a tension between these two criteria such that it is difficult to maximize both simultaneously. This tension creates a dilemma, such that people find themselves between the rock of unquestioned certainty in death-denying ideology and the hard place of feeling hostility towards those who challenge or undermine that certainty.

Those cultural worldviews that are the most rigid and dogmatic in describing unquestioned assurances of immortality are the most successful in abating death terror, but also the most likely to promote hostility and violence against anyone who does not unwaveringly endorse their narrow doctrine. Inversely, those worldviews that are humbler in their claims about the absolute nature of reality and allow for the types of relativistic, flexible, and nuanced interpretations of existence likely to promote tolerance and acceptance of different beliefs and discourage hostility towards different Others, tend to be the least effective at providing the certain confidence in immortality that ameliorates existential dread. In the same way, violent entertainment that offers the most black and white depictions of justice and the most comforting reinforcement of cultural narratives of immortality likely does so at the cost of promoting hostility towards out-groups and facilitating the acceptability of violence as a legitimate solution to dealing with the psychological threat posed by the different *Other*.

In addition to reinforcing cultural attitudes that tolerate or even venerate actual violence, especially to the extent that it is perceived as reestablishing justice or directed against others perceived as threatening, fictional violence might have an additional harmful effect in that by providing viewers with a means of reducing concerns about death it may also become an obstacle to the type of psychological growth that comes from existential struggle. To the extent that it focuses on more sensational types of death, attraction to violent media might be a hindrance to more realistic confrontations with mortality that occur in more serious dramatic film and television focused on more realistic portrayals of death due to old age and degenerative illness.

Thomas (2000) argued that screen violence may actually prevent people from a fuller contemplation of the reality of death. He speculated that he has seen as many as 100,000 depictions of death in film but only two actual dead bodies in reality and based on anecdotal evidence from conversations with his students over the years, concludes that this is probably quite typical. Further, he notes that the stylized portrayals of death on screen lack the realism and difficulty inherent in actual death. He asserts that "death is so slick in film.... These deaths are not messy or untidy. The attitude is proud, masterful, in love with meticulous detail. Nothing in the sensibility disturbs the remorseless efficiency of vengeance, or departs from managerial pleasure in seeing intricate plans work sweetly" (pp. 91–92). The problem for Thomas is that film offers the chance to "stare at death without honoring pain or loss" (p. 93).

Different depictions of fictional on-screen death may be palliative or provocative when it comes to existential anxiety and may promote either reflexive defenses or more thoughtful reactions. This point was suggested by Greenberg and Ayars (2013), who offered an analysis of four seemingly quite different films (*The Matrix*, *Iron Man 2*, *Life Is Beautiful*, and *Ikiru*) through the lens of TMT and highlighted some interesting similarities in the ways in which all the films focus on the quest for legacy and the desire to transcend death through symbolic immortality. They also highlighted some important differences in the way the films deal with terror management issues. Specifically, the science fiction/fantasy films present death in more violent and less realistic ways and also offer more extreme forms of symbolic immortality through a large-scale heroism beyond the scope achievable by the audience (most viewers will not save the world). In contrast, the more dramatic films offer not only more realistic depictions of death but also more modest and attainable means of transcendence through small scale legacy. Greenberg and Ayars conclude that "TMT analysis suggests that both escapist fantasy films and grimmer films involving tragedy often reinforce modes of terror management. But the more escapist fare does so more through vicarious identification, whereas the more realistic films do so by providing messages that people can more readily apply to their own lives" (p. 35). So, it seems to be the case that fantastic films are more palliative towards death than realistic ones because their less realistic portrayals of death may evoke less anxiety about personal mortality, but realistic films may be more instructive in terms of dealing with the reality of death in that they offer viewers a more feasible balm against death anxiety.

If TMT is correct in the claim that a persistent and unabated rumination about the inevitability of personal demise is likely a hindrance to psychological well-being, then to the extent that consumption of fictional violence provides catharsis through the attenuation of existential dread, such consumption can be conceptualized as beneficial to viewers. However, there is a sound argument to be made for the case that a complete and total denial of the reality of death has deleterious effects on human psychology by promoting a complacent acquiescence to prevalent cultural norms that may stunt or limit peoples' creativity, individualism, and full engagement with the thrills and joys of life. Thus, not only can people suffer from too much anxiety caused by a lack of adequate protection against death anxiety, but they can also be too protected as an excessively defensive approach to existence not only blocks the painful aspects of life but also limits the experience of the good as well. Consequently, forms of entertainment that promote the suppression of death anxiety may ultimately be of less psychological value to viewers than engagement with forms of entertainment that disrupt such psychological defenses in the service of facilitating thoughtful contemplation regarding the meaning of existence and force a reprioritization of values and goals.

The proposition that living fully requires the courage to face mortality has a long philosophical history. For example, Heidegger (1927, 2008) interpreted guilt as a signal that one was not living authentically. To live authentically means to take personal responsibility for constructing one's values and goals rather than living according to values and goals imposed by society. Heidegger viewed awareness of personal death as essential for authenticity. He acknowledged that death was a great source of anxiety but advocated courage to live authentically with that anxiety. Heidegger further distinguished between the everyday mode of existence in which we focus on how things are and the ontological mode of existence in which we marvel that things are. Most of the time we focus on mundane things instead of really experiencing the awe of existence and our small place in it, but realizations of life's finitude can serve as a catalyst for shifting into the ontological mode. Likewise, Martin, Campbell, and Henry (2004), following in the tradition of Heidegger, describe encounters with personal mortality as the "roar of awakening." They argue that people usually grow psychologically following actual near-death experiences. From this perspective, reflecting on personal death can have positive effects because it serves as a call to more authentic living.

Evidence for positive effects of death awareness comes from findings that real life survivors of near-death experiences show a shift from extrinsic to more intrinsic values (Flynn, 1984; Ring, 1984; Sutherland, 1990). One such survivor described his brush with death as analogous to having a cataract removed from his brain, because he saw the world and what was important more clearly (Wren-Lewis, 1988). Additional support for the notion that mortality serves as an impetus for psychological growth comes from laboratory research showing that asking people to imagine a close brush with death resulted in decreased greed and more unselfish behavior (Cozzolinio, Staples, Meyers, & Samboceti, 2004). Similarly, asking people to imagine only having a year to live resulted in a shift towards more intrinsic values and goals (Martin, Campbell, & Henry, 2004).

Firestone and Catlett (2009) are additional vocal advocates of the need to at least periodically and in part face the reality of mortality. They argued that confrontation with death can be an awakening experience that leads to reassessment of priorities and to a focus on what constitutes living a good life. Similarly, Yalom (2009) suggested that there are numerous types of experiences (e.g., death of a loved one, major life decision, school reunions, estate planning, birthdays, and anniversaries) that serve as a reminder of the urgency of a finite existence and act as a wakeup call to shift out of thoughtless emersion in culturally prescribed death-denying ideologies in order to start living more fully with the awareness that our time one Earth is limited.

If fictional violence can potentially serve as a mechanism for helping people contain existential terror at manageable levels, can it also perhaps potentially serve as a roar of awakening providing viewers with a catalyst for post-traumatic growth? Schneider (1993, 2019) suggested that film can break through the safety of conventional conceptualizations of reality, forcing people to struggle with deep existential issues and resulting in valuable personal insights. In his analysis of classic horror film, Schneider (1993) argued that horror can produce a disorienting sense of what he calls the groundlessness of being—meaning the sense of complete loss of identity. This sense of groundlessness can be achieved through narratives and images of two distinctive types: either complete restriction to the point of annihilation (hyper-restrictive horror) or expansion into chaos and infinity (hyper-expansive horror). While both of these types of experience evoke terror, they can also produce a sense of wonder or awe at the vastness and incomprehensible nature of the universe, which can break through people's reliance on habitual and reflexive conceptualization of existence and offer the potential for psychological growth. Schneider notes that although the confrontation in film with groundlessness (which includes, but from his perspective, exceeds death anxiety) can potentially serve as a means for viewers to grapple with big questions of identity and meaning, it does not necessarily evoke this response. The viewer must be willing to avoid the temptation to shrink reflexively from or deny the experience of groundlessness and to work consciously through the trauma evoked by the feeling in order to gain any insight or expansion in their psychological perspective.

In Schneider's (2019) analysis of the films of Lars von Trier, which not only traumatize viewers with severe imagery of death, violence, and corporeality, but also dissolve and explode conventional structures of meaning, he sees a potential benefit to viewers who are able to extract the insights that "the best we human beings can offer is a heartfelt and mindful response to, rather than reaction against, our tragic condition" (p. 224) and that "we cannot know anything for certain, but we can choose our response to events, and that response can be personal, passionate, and far-ranging" (pp. 226).

So, it is at least possible that for some viewers under some circumstance, exposure to violent media might serve as a positive opportunity for growth. This possibility is consistent with some TMT theorizing and research. Rogers, Sanders, and Vess (2019) noted that while the most common reaction to reminders of mortality is to suppress thoughts of death and to engage in terror management defenses unconsciously and reflexively, there are circumstances in which a periodic and brief reflection on the finitude of existence can stimulate a prioritization of goals and values. They write,

> Regrettably, the conditions under which personal growth can spring from mortality awareness, namely, conscious and vivid (but not ruminative) reflections upon death, presumably, are often avoided. However, as terror management and other death-related research attests, when we suspend defensively averting our eyes to our existential reality and consciously reflect, if only briefly, on our transient state, we avail ourselves the opportunity to trivialize that which may deserve it, and grow as we pursue personally meaningful intrinsic projects in an effort toward authentic being [Rogers et al., p. 339].

Just as there are individual differences in the way people respond to reminders of mortality, so too will screen violence impact people differently depending not only on the content and context of the violence but also on the engagement and interpretation of the viewer. For example, Shaw (2004) suggests that each individual interprets the meaning of fictional violence through narrative and that it is important to focus on this phenomenological level of analysis. Likewise, Pizzato (2005) claimed that the effects of screen-violence can be either "positive of negative, ethical or not, in their potential effects on the audience—even though a nearly infinite variety of shows actually occur in different spectators' minds as they watch the same performance together, with each viewer's personal associations, distinctive fantasies, and conscious or unconscious transferences" (p. 14). It seems that screen-violence may serve different functions for different people depending on the meanings to which they ascribe to the violence.

So, whether defense or growth-oriented TMT processes are activated by consumption of violent media will likely depend not only on the level of nuance and moral ambiguity depicted in the fictional narrative but also on individual differences in viewers. There are individual differences in openness to new ideas versus rigid thinking, and these differences moderate reactions to mortality salience. For example, among people who score low on a dimension called personal need for structure (pns), a trait associated with traditional and inflexible ways of thinking, reminders of death actually increased their openness to exploring and learning about unfamiliar cultures and perspectives different from their own (Vess, Routledge, Landau, & Arndt, 2009). Specifically, in one study, Vess et al. found that mortality salience increased low pns participants' interest in watching documentaries about the difficulties faced by immigrant groups in America and the ways in which American foreign policy created dissatisfaction that fueled support for terrorism. In another study, Vess et al. showed that reminders of death led low pns individuals to become more interested in learning about the practices and customs of people in foreign cultures such as Iran. In both of these studies, the information sought out would have been threatening to mainstream American values and would run counter to the nationalistic bias generally observed in response to reminders of death. Extrapolating these findings to reactions to fictional violence, it seems possible that individual differences such as openness versus rigidity in thinking might moderate the types of cultural messages that viewers find more appealing in response to the mortality salience induced by on-screen depictions of violent death. For some viewers, the consumption of fictional violence may enhance the appeal of messages that defend tradition and celebrate conventional values; whereas, for other viewers the same exposure may increase the appeal of counter-cultural messages that challenge and subvert the status quo.

This chapter has explored the ways in which fictional violence has both potentially positive and negative consequences for the ways its consumers deal with the awareness of death. On the positive side, fictional violence can potentially provide a needed means of confronting the topic of death from a safe distance, and at least for some viewers, can serve as a catalyst for rethinking personal values and contemplating more deeply the meaning of life. On the negative side, unrealistic displays of violent death, especially when victims are presented as unambiguously bad and deserving of their fate and when perpetrators are presented as suffering no aversive consequences, can facilitate an excessive suppression of death anxiety that deters a vital engagement with the fullness of life. Violent entertainment has the potential to reinforce both the reflexive embrace of prevalent extrinsic cultural values but also to be a possible impetus for more critical analysis of these cultural messages and perhaps even to motivate a quest for new and different perspectives.

The subsequent chapters represent a move from the general to the specific by offering extended treatments of five popular television series— *Game of Thrones* (Chapter 4), *The Punisher* (Chapter 5), *Jessica Jones* (Chapter 6), *Sons of Anarchy* (Chapter 7), and *Hannibal* (Chapter 8). For each series, the principles of TMT will be applied to offer an understanding of the role that death anxiety plays in fictional characters' motives for killing and an appreciation of the complex reactions consumers have to those killings. These analyses are intended to highlight the benefit of including insights from TMT into the examination of the meanings being conveyed by the series. Further, the potential adverse and beneficial effects of violence on viewers will be articulated for each series. The effects can be palliative or challenging in terms of whether they promote or thwart contemplation of existential issues and stultifying or stimulating in terms of the messages they convey about the necessity and appropriateness of violence as well as in terms of the beliefs about the self, others, and the world that they promote.

4

There Is Only One Thing We Say to Death—Not Today

Battling Existential Terror in HBO's Game of Thrones

The critical acclaim (318 awards and 560 nominations; IMDB) and widespread popular appeal (19.3 million viewers for the series finale; Otterson, 2019) of the HBO series *Game of Thrones* (*GoT*; 2011–2019) is an anomaly in the fantasy genre, a genre historically derided as frivolous escapism, simplistically formulaic, and low brow in its pandering to baser lustful and violent appetites. Reactions to the series are mixed, with advocates lauding it as thought-provoking and challenging, while detractors lament it as offensive and oppressive. *GoT* has been praised for its positive depictions of characters with disabilities (Ellis, 2014) and for its heuristic value as a mechanism for stimulating philosophical contemplation about the strengths and weaknesses of various approaches to government (Walton, 2019). The series has also been heavily criticized for its misogyny, gratuitous female nudity, and sexual objectification of women (Needham, 2017), as well as for its perpetuation of ethnocentric notions of the superiority of Western culture and stereotypes about orientalism that depict people from the East as *Other*—prone to savage cruelty and sexual deviancy. For example, the series displays strong notes of colonialism in presenting the idea that the people of Essos need the governance of their Misa (mother) Daenerys Targaryen (Emilia Clarke), their White maternal savior from the West, to rescue them from their own barbarism (Hardy, 2019).

Many scholarly assessments of the show are ambivalent. For example, Marques (2019) applauds how *GoT* subverts traditional gender roles by replacing the damsel-in-distress trope ubiquitous in fantasy and midlevel literature with a showcase of strong, dominant, and fierce female characters such as Brienne of Tarth (Gwendoline Christie), Arya Stark (Maisie Williams), and Yara Greyjoy (Gemma Whelan). However, Marques also notes that these depictions are not entirely positive in that they reinforce the false dichotomy between femininity and power and perpetuate the sexist Catch-22, in which women must choose between being perceived as capable but not feminine or feminine but not capable. Similar ambivalence was expressed by Ferreday (2015) in her analysis of the potential effects the depictions of rape in *GoT* could have on viewers. She sees potential harms in the perpetuation of rape myths such as the idea that women's refusals are not a genuine lack of consent but merely a faux protest requiring increasing male pressure and persistence and in the seeming validation of current privileged arguments about the need for concerns over how allegations of rape could affect the futures of affluent White men. Both of these concerns are in reference to the scene from season four "Breaker of Chains," in which Ser Jaime Lannister (Nikolaj Coster-Waldau) rapes his sister Cersei Lannister (Lena Headey). However, Ferreday also sees some benefits in that feminist dialogues generated in response to depictions of rape in *GoT* can offer the potential of imagining better future worlds without rape.

Ambivalently conflicted reactions within individuals and contradictory reactions across individuals may be better understood through the insight that there are a variety of different motives for viewing television and that engagement with media can serve different psychological functions for different people. For example, Poscheschnik (2018) noted that "television series, as any other narrative, can fulfil many functions for the individual mind. Among them are entertainment and distraction from unpleasure, the opportunity for a cathartic experience by showing a secret wish as satisfied, providing a moral of the story and offering a model of what is ethical and what is not" (p. 1011).

Many scholars suggest that the most important psychological function served by fictional media is the opportunity to grapple with and come to terms with challenging and complex issues. For example, Ferreday (2015) argued that fantasy is somewhat transgressive in that it allows exploration of taboo topics in ways that are less threatening than realistic temporally and geographically grounded depictions. Similarly, Poscheschnik (2018) posited the main benefit of audience engagement with television as allowing viewers to "work with unconscious material" in a "transitional space which offers the possibility to contain and work through personal and psycho-cultural conflicts" (p. 1011).

According to Poscheschnik's (2018) psychoanalytic perspective, the psychological benefit gained from grappling with threatening material in a safe fictional space operates at two levels. On the conscious level, the manifest content of the series can trigger contemplations about pressing social issues related to gender, race, and politics. On another level, *GoT* gives symbolic expression to unconscious anxieties. For example, Poscheschnik sees the wall that separates the civilized seven kingdoms from the wildness of the North as symbolizing the divide between the conscious and unconscious mind and sees the dangers beyond the wall, in the form of threats posed initially by the wildling tribes and then by the White Walkers, as representing repressed anxieties and infantile beliefs, which, when returned to consciousness, threaten to undermine psychological equanimity. In addition, Poscheschnik contends that the death of King Robert Baratheon (Mark Addy) and the subsequent battles between competing claimants for the iron throne represent concerns about the deterioration of order, powerlessness, and chaos. Further, the fact that Daenerys Targaryen is trapped across the sea in Essos unable to reach Westeros is interpreted as a symbolic manifestation of the vague but persistent hope for a savior who will transform the world into a better place, coupled with uncertainty about the feasibility of such a world or any clear vision of what it would look like.

I agree with Poscheschnik's (2018) position that the most important function of television viewing is the opportunity to work through mental material about topics that are societally taboo and therefore repressed and with his claim that the need for such processing stems from the fact that repression is never fully effective and that "defense never works perfectly, and somehow there is a simultaneous knowing and not-knowing about repression and denial" (p. 1009). I diverge from other psychoanalytic perspectives in my assertion of the nature of the taboo threat. My main thesis is that death is the most salient taboo topic depicted in *GoT*. While it is certainly true that *GoT* gives voice to current social-political issues related to gender and class that are relevant to our specific culture and time, these aspects have been well studied in the literature (Chau & Vanderwees, 2019). I hope to shed light on a less examined area, namely how *GoT* simultaneously offers viewers a means of confronting universal existential concerns, especially those related to fears of personal mortality, while also serving to buttress psychological defenses against those concerns.

GoT would seem to offer a heavy dose of death salience to viewers. The show features graphic violence and high body counts, has a tendency to kill off important and well-liked characters, and offers the frequent refrain in high Valerian *Valar Morghulis* (translated as all men must die). According to one estimate, the series has depicted or implied 6,887 deaths, with a steady increase in the death toll from 59 in season one to 4,548 in season eight (Tan, 2019). Given the ubiquitous nature of violent death in the series, it is perhaps not surprising that many characters claim to accept the inevitability of mortality. For example, in the penultimate episode

"Baelor" from season one, while imprisoned in the dungeons of King's Landing, Lord Eddard "Ned" Stark (Sean Bean) initially rejects advice from Lord Varys (Conleth Hill) suggesting that his life might be spared and he might be allowed to take the black and join the Night's Watch at the wall, if he were to acknowledge Joffrey Baratheon (Jack Gleeson) as the rightful ruler of the seven kingdoms. Ned says, "You think my life is some precious thing to me.... I learned how to die a long time ago."

The *memento mori* theme of the fantasy show is consistent with the historical claim that Western culture in medieval times was more comfortable with the reality of death (Aries, 1981). Sociologists frequently describe an increasing discomfort with death in contemporary Western culture such that, at present, death is a taboo topic to be denied and suppressed (DeSpelder & Strickland, 2015).

Paradoxically, at the same time Americans have little exposure to actual death, they seem to have a fascination with death in popular culture and death, especially violent death, is a mainstay of popular television (Durkin, 2003). One possibility is that there is a direct connection between the lack of familiarity with real death, which created taboos around frank discussion surrounding the topic, and the prevalence and appeal of death in popular culture. It is because the topic of death is repressed, and people crave information about it, that they seek out that information in popular culture.

However, consumption of fictional death is not merely an attraction to the forbidden, but it is also a form of psychological defense in which the viewer tries to manage their fears of mortality. While *GoT* could, for some viewers and in some circumstances, break through the typical defensive denial of death and force people to confront the unpleasant existential reality of death and to process how life can be conceptualized as meaningful in the face of this inevitability, it is more likely that for the majority of viewers it provides a form of reflexive satisfaction through the augmentation of psychological defenses against death that symbolically gratify their wish for immortality. That *GoT* is more palliative than challenging in regard to death is most evident in the fact that almost all of the thousands of deaths depicted are due to violent causes. Very few deaths are depicted as due to natural causes. Some rare exceptions are Maester Aemon (Peter Vaughan), aka Aemon Targaryen of the Night's Watch, and Lord Hoster Tully (Christopher Newman), both of whom die of old age, and Lyanna Stark (Aisling Franciosi) who dies in childbirth. Death from infectious diseases, far and away the most common historical cause of death in medieval times, is entirely absent from *GoT*. The series does present gray scale as a contagious disease that disfigures its victims and drives them to madness. Both Shireen Baratheon (Kerry Ingram) and Ser Jorah Mormont

(Iain Glen) are shown as temporarily afflicted by gray scale, but neither dies from the disease.

The importance of death being presented as due to violent causes is that this implies that it is avoidable. Developmental psychologists point out that young children conceptualize death as something that is due to accident and can therefore be avoided by proper vigilance (Nagy, 1948), and it is not until around the age of 9 or 10 that they realize that death is inevitable, having natural and accidental causes, and universal, happening to everyone including the self (Speece & Brent, 1992). The appeal of violent media is due in part to the defense mechanism of regression in which viewers can revert to an earlier cognitive state in which the hope of avoiding death is given confirmation by visual and narrative elements.

Kottler (2011) asserted that viewing violence in fantasy is not about venting the viewers' repressed aggressive urges, but rather it is about quelling existential anxiety. The appeal of violent death in the media is a product of the audience's need for denial. *GoT* does not just present a message of *Valar Morghulis* but also a message of mastering death and "raging against the dying of the light." For example, Braavosi master swordsman Syrio Forel (Miltos Yerolemou) tells Arya Stark, "There is only one god, and his name is Death, and there is only one thing we say to Death: not today" ("The Pointy End"). Just as the warriors in the series hope to avoid death by the mastery of the physical world through disciplined training in the arts of mortal combat, viewers psychologically attempt to gain a sense of mastery over their fears of death. Kottler (2001) described a "curious self-protective motive" in which people are fascinated with violent death in media because they think by learning as much as they can about it, they can keep themselves safe and avoid becoming its victim.

The themes of the human proneness to violence, what constitutes acceptable killing, and the acceptability of enjoying killing are all explored in *GoT*. In season three's "Walk of Punishment," Ser Jorah Mormont tells Daenerys Targaryen, "There is a beast in every man, and it stirs when you put a sword in his hand." The implication is that warfare provides men with a culturally sanctioned outlet for innate aggressive impulses. War also offers an opportunity for heroism by demonstrating fighting prowess and defeating the evil forces of the enemy. Of course, not all violence is deemed heroic. Violence is admired only when it is a means of self-esteem by showing skill and ability greater than those of most others or when it is culturally sanctioned as just or working for the elimination of evil. We can admire Jaime Lannister or Sandor "The Hound" Clegane (Rory McCann) even if we do not always like them (especially in their less sympathetic depictions in early seasons) because of their abilities as swordsmen. In contrast, it is difficult to admire Joffrey Baratheon. His sadism and malicious pleasure in inflicting suffering on others is likely no greater than that found in The Hound. The difference in our reactions to the characters may lie, not in the extent of their violent natures, but in the targets of their violence, and the skill and courage with which they exercise it.

Individuals are perceived as crossing a moral line when they kill not out of obligation or duty but for enjoyment. The Hound unabashedly professes his enjoyment of killing and insists that others share his sentiments but are disingenuous in disguising the motives for their killing in terms of duty or monetary gain. Bronn (Jerome Flynn), the hired swordsman who protects Tyrion Lannister (Peter Dinklage), clearly presents profit as his motive for killing. For example, in season three "The Bear and the Maiden Fair," he tells Tyrion, "You pay me to kill people who bother you." Bronn is an affable and sympathetic character with a love of wine, women, and song. The Hound, however, challenges Bronn about his true motives for killing. In season two "Blackwater" the Hound refuses to participate in the revelry of Bronn and the other men who are singing, drinking, and cavorting with prostitutes in the moments before the battle of Blackwater. The Hound claims that Bronn's love of women and wine does not make him any less of a cold-blooded killer. He tells Bronn, "Killing is the thing you love most. You're just like me." Similarly, The Hound rejects the claim made by Sansa Stark (Sophie Turner) that her father Ned only killed out of obligation when necessary. In season two "A Man Without Honor," Sansa attempts to thank The Hound for saving her from being raped but meets with a challenging response in the following exchange:

> Sansa: "I beg pardon sir. I should have come to you after to thank you for saving me. You were very brave."
> Hound: "Brave. A dog does not need courage to chase off rats."
> Sansa: "Does it give you joy to scare people?"
> Hound: "No it gives me joy to kill people. Spare me. You can't tell me that Lord Eddard Stark of Winterfell never killed a man."
> Sansa: "It was his duty. He never liked it."
> Hound: "Is that what he told you? He lied. Killing is the sweetest thing there is."

In the tradition of fantasy as escapism, *GoT* appeals to viewers with hopes of transcending or avoiding death. Whereas the White Walkers are frequently viewed as an allegory for the threat posed by climate change and a populace too distracted by political infighting to acknowledge the threat of possible global extinction and the need to work for collective solutions (Chau & Vanderwees, 2019), an interpretation supported by George R.R. Martin himself (Sims, 2018), they can also be viewed as a personification of death. This option is given voice by the characters, as when Gendry (Joe Dempsie) answers Arya's query about the enemy by saying,

Richard Brake portraying the Night King in season four of the HBO television series *Game of Thrones* (2014). In this scene, the Night King is raising those recently slain in battle to be wights in his Army of the Dead (photo credit: HBO).

"This is death. You want to know what they are like. That's what they are like. Death" ("A Knight of the Seven Kingdoms").

Not at the rational-discursive level but at the intuitive and unconscious level, the destruction of the Night King (Vladimir Furdik) and his army of the dead ("The Long Night") offers a powerful visual message of denial that death can be overcome by human technology and skill. Manifestly, the Night King is defeated by dragon's glass and by Arya Stark's training as an assassin that gives her the skill to wield it. Symbolically, these images confirm the viewer's subconscious hope that death can be defeated by the latest scientific advances in medical technology and by disciplined adherence to the fitness fad *du jour*.

The ways in which the visual and narrative elements of *GoT* potentially facilitate viewers' psychological efforts to deal with concerns related to death can be better illuminated by focusing on the cultural defenses articulated in TMT (Pyszczynski, Solomon, & Greenberg, 2015). The humanly created and consensually validated belief systems called cultural worldviews function to assuage death anxiety in two ways. First, culture allows people to conceptualize the world as an orderly, predictable, and safe place in which premature death can be avoided through adherence to culturally prescribed conduct. Second, culture makes the inevitability of death more palatable by describing means through which people can achieve literal immortality in a spiritual-religious sense, such that death will not mean the total extinction of the self, and symbolic immortality in a secular sense, in that they can imagine leaving some legacy that will be remembered after the destruction of the physical body.

While the gore and violence of *GoT* makes mortality salient to viewers in a way that potentially induces existential anxiety, the series also comforts viewers by presenting images and narratives confirming confidence in the possibilities of literal and symbolic immortality, thereby reinforcing psychological buffers against fear of death. Some characters express cynicism towards religious immortality. For example, Ser Davos Seaworth (Liam Cunningham) claims that "mothers and fathers made up the gods so their children could sleep through the night" (*Second Sons*). The show does, however, present viewers with images confirming the feasibility of literal immortality, in the resurrection of Lord Beric Dondarrion (Richard Dormer; "Kissed by Fire") and Jon Snow (Kit Harington; "Home"), both of whom are brought back to life, presumably through the divine power of The Lord of Light.

GoT offers viewers hope of death transcendence not only in a literal sense but also in a symbolic sense by promoting the narrative of the importance of legacy through power, lineage, and accomplishment. The symbolic quest to conquer death through the legacy of one's house is exemplified by Lord Tywin Lannister (Charles Dance) and his frequent lectures to his children Jaime, Cersei, and Tyrion about the importance of the Lannister name. The desire to achieve symbolic immortality by being remembered for great deeds is seen prominently in the character of Jaime Lannister. In the first episode of season four ("Two Swords"), we see Joffrey Baratheon flipping through the pages of *The Book of Brothers*, the historical tome that documents the life and accomplishments of all the knights of the Kingsguard. Joffrey pauses to read to Jaime a few of the more notable entries before stopping on Jaime's page. The audience sees recorded on the page a terse paragraph identifying Jaime as "The Kingslayer" for murdering King Aerys Targaryen. Joffrey taunts Jaime, saying, "Someone forgot to write down all your great deeds." When Jaime replies that there is still time, Joffrey mocks, "Is there? For a forty-year-old knight with one hand?" These comments obviously bother Jaime as he looks longingly at his page in the book before flipping it closed in disgust. In the end, Jaime gets the posthumous legacy he had hoped for with the assistance of Brienne of Tarth. Brienne was Jaime's unlikely friend, lover (briefly for one night), and life coach who temporarily put him back on the path towards humanity before he jilted her and went backsliding into his habitual pattern of casting off all other moral considerations and running to protect Cersei. In the series finale ("The Iron Throne"), Brienne revises Jaime's entry in *The Book of Brothers*. Omitting his incest, rape, and attempted child murder, she recasts Jaime's story in a favorable light, reflecting the audience's evolving attitudes towards the complex character over the series from contempt to sympathy. The new entry portrays Jaime as fighting heroically against the Army of the Dead and dying valiantly in the protection of his queen.

The fear of death in the absence of symbolic immortality is given expression in the conflict between humanity and the army of the dead. When asked what the Night King wants, Brandon "Bran" Stark (Isaac Hempstead Wright) replies, "An endless night. He wants to erase the world and I am its memory." In response, Samwell "Sam" Tarly (John Bradley) says, "That's what death is, isn't it? Forgetting—being forgotten. If we forget where we have been and what we have done, then we aren't men anymore we're animals" ("A Knight of the Seven Kingdoms"). Note the similarity here to the words of Ernest Becker (1975):

> What man fears most is not so much extinction, but extinction with insignificance. Man wants to know that his life has somehow counted, if not for himself, then at least in a larger scheme of things, that it has left a trace, a trace that has meaning. And in order for anything once alive to have meaning, its effects must remain alive in eternity in some way [p. 4].

For those involved in the creation and production of *GoT*, the success of the series provides them with a type of death-denying legacy—what psycho-historian Robert Jay Lifton (1976) would call the creative mode of symbolic immortality. Tyrion's speech during the series finale, in which he argues for Bran to be king, seems to be a thinly veiled argument from the series creators defending their work and hoping that it will stand the test of time. Tyrion exclaims to the council of nobles gathered to decide the fate of the seven kingdoms: "there is nothing in the world more powerful than a good story. Nothing can stop it. No enemy can defeat it" ("The Iron Throne"). Not everyone agrees that season eight of *GoT* provided a good story. As of July 17, 2019, a petition asking that HBO redo the final season of *GoT* with more competent writers had been signed by 1,689,550 people (change.org).

One of the most contentious questions regarding season eight was whether Daenerys' decision to charge the Red Keep on Drogon, scorch most of King's Landing, and kill thousands of innocent civilians in the process was in keeping with the psychology of her character (Pang Chieh Ho, 2019). Many viewers found the sudden shift in portrayal from selfless ruler and noble liberator to bloodthirsty tyrant too abrupt and viewed the writing as forced in order to provide a shocking ending inconsistent with a character who had demonstrated a history of compassion and a devotion to helping the weak and oppressed. So desperate were some viewers to dispel the cognitive dissonance between their view of Daenerys and her actions that theories began to emerge suggesting that Varys' attempts to poison her (strongly implied in the penultimate episode "The Bells"), while not fatal had been successful enough to induce madness.

The series does make efforts to establish the idea that Daenerys always possessed a dormant congenital predilection towards inflicting mass death by burning. Presumably, the same innate mental deficit led her father, the "Mad King" Aerys, to attempt to destroy King's Landing with wildfire. This tendency is foreshadowed in several places by Daenerys' impulse towards rash violence especially when she feels it is retaliation for injustice or that she has been slighted. Examples include burning Mirri Maz Duur (Mia Soteriou) at the stake in season one ("Fire and Blood"), crucifying 163 of the Slave Masters of Meereen in season four ("Oathkeeper"), and in season seven executing by dragon's fire two unarmed prisoners of war. Daenerys executes Sam's father Randyll Tarly (James Faulkner) and his brother Dickon Tarly (Tom Hopper) after they have surrendered in battle but refuse to bend the knee and acknowledge her as queen ("Eastwatch"). The case is also strengthened by references to longstanding conventional wisdom regarding madness as endemic to the Targaryen constitution.

In season two ("A Man Without Honor"), when Tyrion is trying to get Cersei to help him control Joffrey's cruelty, Cersei wonders if Joffrey's malicious temperament is a consequence of his incestuous lineage. When Tyrion tries to comfort her by pointing out the long history of Targaryen marriages between brothers and sisters, she reminds him that many in the Targaryen family went mad reciting the old saying "When a Targaryen is born the gods flip a coin." Varys repeats this saying to Jon Snow at the beginning of episode five in season eight ("The Bells"): "they say every time a Targaryen is born, the gods toss a coin and the world holds its breath."

Regardless of whether Daenerys' behavior is consistent with her character or explicable within the context of the story, it does have several unfortunate sexist ramifications. First, it legitimizes a longstanding sexist tactic in American politics of trying to discredit female candidates by arguing that women's hormones and physiology make them too unstable to be good leaders (Sinclair, 1984). Perhaps the most offensive of such fear mongering is the suggestion that a woman president would be likely to start nuclear war due to PMS. With dragons easily serving as a signifier for modern weapons of mass destruction, it is hard for viewers of *GoT* not to see in the series' conclusion parallels to these historic—sexist—arguments. Second, there is a sexist double standard in that male pursuit of power is normalized as rational self-interest, whereas the same female pursuit of power is villainized as irrational, deviant, madness, and evil (Dockterman, 2019). Third, by focusing on Jon Snow's romantic rejection

Daenerys Targaryen portrayed by Emilia Clarke in the HBO television series *Game of Thrones* (2011–2019) pictured here with her dragon, Drogon (photo credit: HBO).

of her as the precipitating event leading to Daenerys' destruction of King's Landing, *GoT* perpetuates the sexist trope of hell hath no fury like a spurned female lover and turns a complex and powerful female character into a lazy cliché of the crazy ex-girlfriend (Leon, 2019).

Daenerys' behavior is consistent with the *GoT* emphasis on resisting simplistic depictions of morality (Chau & Vanderwees, 2019) and with psychological theories of the underpinnings of evil. In his analysis of human violence and cruelty, Baumeister (1999) argued that the image of pure evil is a myth and that perpetrators of evil almost never identify with that moniker but instead view their actions as morally defensible and even heroic. He writes, "most people who do evil do not think of themselves as evil … most of them regard themselves as good people who are trying to defend themselves and their group against the forces of evil" (p. 62). Similarly, Becker (1975) took a bleak view of human nature viewing the human penchant for violence as difficult to change. However, he disagreed with Freud that this penchant for violence stemmed from an innate aggressive urge. Rather for Becker, what people need most is the hope for immortality achieved through heroism. Consequently, they must defend their fragile, socially-constructed immortality projects from the threat posed by different Others. Becker viewed evil as an ironic effect of the human drive for heroism in the quest for symbolic immortality as a means of dispelling the terror of death from consciousness. In order to be a hero, one must conquer an enemy. In order to purify the world, the group deemed responsible for the impurity must be expunged. This is the paradox that evil is always done in the name of the heroic quest to vanquish the evil *Other*. Becker put it this way: "man, of all animals, has caused the most devastation on earth—the most real evil. He struggles extra hard to be immune to death because he alone is conscious of it, but being able to identify and isolate evil arbitrarily, he is capable of lashing out in all directions against imagined dangers of this world" (p. 150).

Daenerys certainly serves as a cautionary tale against the dangers of too fervently pursuing the quest for symbolic immortality. She justifies her atrocities as necessary in order for the fulfillment of her heroic mission until the bitter end. This "destroying the world to save it" justification is all too commonly documented in the historical annals of real-world atrocities (Lifton, 2000). However, she is not alone in her failure to overcome the delusional blindness of self-righteousness. Fueled by delusions of grandeur that he is predestined by the Lord of Light to rule the seven kingdoms and to save the world from a night full of terrors, Stannis Baratheon (Stephen Dillane) murders his brother Renly Baratheon (Gethin Anthony) and his daughter Shireen. Had Stannis had the power of dragons at his disposal when he attacked King's Landing at the Battle of the Blackwater, would he have shown mercy or restraint? Is it fair to wonder then whether there is an element of benevolent sexism underlying the support of characters and viewers alike who assumed that because Daenerys was a woman, she must have a nobler disposition—a more compassionate nature—that would somehow inoculate her against the corrupting power of the quest for heroism so frequently predicted in psychological theory and so ubiquitously documented in history?

Although it is possible that some viewers might find in the Daenerys storyline existential wisdom about the folly of extreme heroic pursuits, there is also the insidious possibility that other viewers may simply respond with a sense of satisfaction from the validation of their pre-existing sexist worldviews. The problematic nature of this later response was articulated by Romano (2019) who expressed frustration and disappointment that *GoT* kills off most of the strong female characters and ends with a return to male dominated politics with Bran as ruler and Breanne the only female on the small council. She notes that while Sansa is queen in the North, the ending still sends a patriarchal message that male rule is superior, and the status quo is left unchanged and unchallenged.

The complexity of different audience reactions might be elucidated through the distinction Oliver and Bartsch (2011) make between two qualitatively different types of responses to media. Enjoyment is associated with positive affect and can be described as a pleasurable reaction in response to the pleasant feeling elicited by the media or in response to the gratification of wish fulfillment. In contrast, appreciation can be experienced in the absence of positive affect and even concomitant with negative affect. In Aristotelian terms, appreciation is not hedonic but eudemonic because it is associated with the gratification of higher order needs to find meaning and purpose in existence. So, while enjoyment of *GoT* might be a problematic sign of viewers' violent or misogynistic impulses, appreciation of the series might reflect the fact that it provides viewers the opportunity to grapple with complex and challenging social, political, moral, and existential issues. A similar type of distinction can be applied to the potential terror management function that watching *GoT* might provide to viewers. While *GoT* potentially provides some hedonic benefits to viewers in the form of satisfaction or catharsis through the symbolically gratification of wish fulfillment for immortality, it could also elicit a type of eudemonic appreciation that forces viewers to confront the existential reality of death and to process how life can be conceptualized as meaningful in the face of death's inevitability.

In applying a catharsis perspective that combines insights from dispositional alignment, excitation transfer, and TMT, the appeal of *GoT* can be located in the fact that its graphic depictions, or gore, and violence evoke the potential for negative affect in the form of death anxiety and concerns about creatureliness but then quells those anxieties by reinforcing cultural beliefs that offer a sense of immortality and transcendence. These cultural messages are all the more appealing because of the sense of catharsis provided by alleviating existential concerns raised by the extreme violence in the series.

It may seem odd to suggest that the violence in *GoT* increases viewers' confidence in the convictions of their worldview given that it is notorious for evoking outrage in response to the deaths of favorite characters. The series is often associated with the tendency to undermine viewers' sense of justice and fairness by killing off well-liked and morally admirable protagonists. Notable examples include the execution of Ned Stark in the penultimate episode of season one ("Baelor") and the treacherous betrayal of the Starks by Walder Frey (David Bradley) in the penultimate episode of season three ("The Rains of Castamere") that results in the murder of Robb Stark (Richard Madden), his mother Catelyn Stark (Michelle Fairley), his wife Talisa Stark (Oona Chaplin) and their unborn child at the Red Wedding. The seeming triumph of evil characters is upsetting to viewers, but this unsatisfactory state of affairs is temporary and only serves to enhance pleasure in response to the villains' eventual violent demise. As Zillmann (1998) noted, "Similarly distressing is witnessing the grand benefaction of an utterly evil and undeserving character. For good reason, such benefaction may exist transitionally, but it is exceedingly rare as the final resolution of drama" (p. 204). While the unjust deaths in *GoT* may have shocked and angered viewers at the time, the negative dispositions created in response to the characters responsible for the perceived injustices tremendously enhanced the gratification of seeing justice restored through retributive violence enacted against them. Petyr "Littlefinger" Baelish's (Aidan Gillen) deception and betrayal, which led to Ned's arrest ("You Win or You Die") and Joffrey Baratheon's order to have Ned beheaded ("Baelor") created intense aversion to these characters, which intensified audience's cheers when Joffrey is poisoned in season four ("The Lion and the Rose") and when Little Finger is killed by Ayra Stark in season seven ("The Dragon and the Wolf"). Similarly, the trauma viewers experienced in response to the calamity inflicted on the Stark family via the carnage of the Red Wedding ("The Rains of Castamere") exponentially intensifies viewers' pleasure when Arya Stark avenges her family by killing Walder Frey, donning his flayed face as a mask, impersonating him at a feast, and poisoning everyone in his household except for one girl witness to convey the message that "the North remembers" and "winter came for house Frey" ("Dragonstone").

While there may be some psychological benefit afforded to *GoT* viewers in the form of buffering defenses against death terror, there are also some potential adverse consequences to the extent that the cultural messages that ameliorate anxiety prevent more genuine confrontation with the inevitability of mortality as endemic to the human condition, promote acceptance of violence against others, and reinforce societal messages that perpetuate misogyny. The images of resurrection may augment distal defenses by offering conforming assurances about the possibility of literal immortality. Additionally, focus on violent rather than natural death may facilitate proximal terror management defenses by strengthening the belief that premature death can be avoided. The bolstering of TMT defenses protects viewers from existential anxiety, but it does not force them to struggle with or confront the reality of death, thereby denying them the possibilities for the prioritization of values and the opportunity for growth that come from such existential struggles.

Similarly, the destruction of the White Walkers may abate existential dread through the symbolic defeat of personified death, but any potential benefit of such catharsis must be weighed against the possibly deleterious effects of a narrative that normalizes and legitimizes violence as a solution to conflict and promotes and/or condones the elimination of the dehumanized *Other*. While not writing specifically about *GoT*, the potential for such negative effects was expressed by Desilet (2014), who voiced concern that the convenience of the dehumanized target of zombies and their malleability to signify any type of "enemy other" facilitated support for hostile attitudes and aggression against whichever outgroup impressionable viewers happened to be prejudiced against. He further argued that "the dramatic trope of the faceless enemy is a bit too convenient for good drama. But it is conveniently just right for the gratuitous conflict necessary for generating endless opportunities for gratuitous violence. And there is nothing like a defaced, dehumanized human to make a viewer feel good about shotgunning the head off an ugly body" (p. 173).

The most frequently criticized aspect of the cultural messages conveyed by *GoT* is the focus on its sexual objectification of women and promotion of misogyny and rape culture. In her analysis of the first 30 episodes of *GoT*, Needham (2017) notes that there are 44 scenes of female nudity compared to only 23 scenes of male nudity. She further reveals that there are only two scenes of male nudity without female nudity. Additionally, most of the female nudity is deemed gratuitous in that it functions only to titillate male viewers in the absence of advancing the plot. Needham concludes that "as a consequence of both sexposition and unnecessary nudity, men become the suppliers of story and plot while women decorate the scene, which they make visually appealing to those who enjoy the sight of exposed female nudes" (p. 6). Needham argues that the deleterious effects of *GoT* include not only the reduction of female identity to merely sexual objects for male pleasure through the frequent utilization of the filming technique of the "male gaze" but also the pervasive tendency to subjugate women's sexuality as inferior to male sexuality and to promote the acceptance and even vicarious participation in sexual violence against women through numerous rape scenes. She suggests that rape scenes, such as Khal Drogo's (Jason Momoa) rape of Daenerys on their wedding night ("Winter Is Coming"), "make female sexuality something to consume voyeuristically by paying men, both Khal Drogo who has purchased Daenerys' virginity with forty-thousand Dothraki soldiers, or viewing heterosexual men who are paying in HBO subscriptions" (p. 10). Needham further asserts that any potentially positive feminist message offered by the depiction of strong and empowered female characters such as Daenerys and Ygritte (Rose Leslie) is undermined and nullified by the fact of their continued sexual objectification.

Men's sexual objectification of women as well as their hostile attitudes, derogation, and violence against women undoubtedly have complex causes. They are likely rooted in political motives as men seek to maintain patriarchal power and perhaps also in reproductive strategies where men attempt to control female sexuality out of concerns about cuckoldry. In addition to these political and biological influences, there is also a potential existential motive underlying men's attitudes towards women. TMT can add an additional layer of explanation by showing how the threat of death anxiety may exacerbate both men's objectification of women and men's negative attitudes towards women.

While the issue of human corporeality and creatureliness threatens to undermine the psychological equanimity of people regardless of gender, the female body is particularly problematic given its greater ties to reproduction in the form of menstruation, pregnancy, and lactation. This tendency for the female body to elicit concerns about creatureliness, and therefore, to undermine terror management defenses and leave people prone to existential anxiety, can also be used to explain misogyny and the sexual objectification of women. Goldenberg, Morris, and Boyd (2019) asserted that heterosexual men are ambivalent about the female form in that they find it both alluring and attractive but also threatening to the extent that it reminds them of their own creatureliness and mortality. They suggest that one way men attempt to resolve this ambivalence is by trying to ignore and diminish women's personhood and reduce them to merely symbols of beauty and to narrow the focus of their attention to a constellation of sexualized body parts. Goldenberg et al. posited that "although men's attraction to women is problematic in the attempt to keep the awareness of mortality at bay, literal objectification of the female body may help to reconcile this dual threat/attraction motive" and that objectification of women "might strike the right balance for men by tapping into their attraction toward women ... but circumventing the potential threat associated with (real) women's bodies" (p. 236).

Goldenberg et al. (2019) further claim that male ambivalence about the female body might also underlie misogyny and hostility towards sexually seductive women. The physical aspects of sex are one of the most powerful reminders of our corporeality and similarity with other animals. When men find themselves having lustful thoughts or impulses, these feelings may undermine their attempts to deny their physicality and focus on the symbolic and transcendent aspects of their identity, thereby disrupting the terror management system and leaving them vulnerable to death anxiety. Rather than faulting themselves for their failure to deny their corporeality, men may blame the women who were the object of their sexual attraction and feel hostility towards them. Similarly, Goldenberg and Roberts (2004) suggested that

> men's sexual arousal itself can pose an existential threat. For, if as terror management theory posits, we defend against anxiety associated with the awareness of death by creating cultural systems of meaning that allows us to feel more significant than other animals, then ... animal desires have the ability to threaten the efficacy of this defense. Then it makes sense that women, the objects of sexual arousal, would be degraded by men [p. 81].

Goldenberg and Roberts (2004) agree with traditional feminists' notions that misogyny is a consequence of patriarchy but elaborate that they view misogyny as driven not merely by the desire to protect and maintain male social and political power but also as a consequence of the fact that womens' bodies elicit existential anxiety in men, and men have the power to shape societal conventions and mores to protect themselves from this threat. Goldenberg and Roberts assert that both the tendencies for men to objectify the female body sexually and the tendency for men to express negative attitudes about and feel hostility towards women who are the objects of their lust are "rooted in the power of *men's power* to protect themselves from the threat of women" (p. 82).

To test these TMT ideas about the role of existential anxiety in promoting misogyny, Landua et al. (2006) had heterosexual male college students read two police reports. The police reports were fictitious and created for the purpose of the study by the researchers but were designed with input from actual law enforcement to look real. One report described a case in which a male suspect physically beat and injured one of his male friends. The other report described a case in which a male suspect physically attacked and injured his live-in girlfriend. Participants in the study were asked to recommend a punishment, by selecting from a set of provided choices that varied in severity of jail time. Before reading the cases, half the men were assigned to write a brief essay about their own death, whereas the other half wrote about a different unpleasant topic (undergoing a painful dental procedure). Participants were also assigned to think about either a time when they got intensely excited when watching a sporting event or a time when they felt animalistic lust in the absence of any romantic feelings directed towards a sexually attractive woman they did not know. The experimental manipulations had no impact on men's recommended punishments for violence committed against other men. In contrast, however, men who had been reminded of their mortality and who had reflected on previous lustful feelings towards women recommended significantly more lenient punishments for male perpetrators of domestic violence against women.

TMT in general, but especially the work on how female corporeality elicits both objectification and misogyny, can offer useful insight into one of the more controversial and provocative scenes from *GoT*—the sex scene between Arya Stark and Gendry Baratheon in the second episode of the final season ("A Knight of the Seven Kingdoms"). Leah (2019) noted the visceral discomfort many viewers reportedly felt in response to this scene. In a series that frequently depicts coercion, exploitation of sex workers, incest, orgies, and rape, it seems odd that this scene, which was clearly consensual, should be one of the more controversial ones. One possibility is the ambiguity of the age of the actress and the character. Maisie Williams, who portrays Arya, was 11 years old when the series began, and although she was 22 when the scene was filmed, audiences may have been uncertain as to her age and may have gotten accustomed to thinking of her as a child. Similarly, Arya was clearly a child at the beginning of the series, and it is ambiguous as to how many years have passed in the diegetic world in which the events of the series have transpired.

Marcotte (2019) admits to her own discomfort in response to watching Ayra's sex scene with Gendry and to her initial attempts to explain her queasiness as due to concerns about the young age of the character. However, she quickly condemns her reaction and the similar reactions of other viewers and dismisses the possibility that it is age that underlies these reactions. She notes that the character of Ayra is considered old enough for adult decisions and responsibilities (after all, her younger brother Bran is deemed ready to be King of the Seven Kingdoms). Furthermore, no similar controversy was voiced over the scene in season three ("Walk of Punishment") when Podrick Payne (played by actor Daniel Portman, who would have been 21 at the time the episode aired), a teenaged character who if not younger certainly was more naïve than Arya, loses his virginity in a brothel orgy. Marcotte describes a societal double standard in which young men's initial sexual experiences are celebrated as a laudable foray into full adult masculinity, whereas young women's first sexual experiences are lamented as tragic losses of innocence. Marcotte places the source of the controversy surrounding Arya's sexuality as derived from the fact that the scene violates sexist cultural conventions that view sexuality as debasing the purity of women and that expect female characters to be coy rather than assertive in initiating sex.

Cultural taboos against assertive female sexuality are likely the source of audiences' aversion to this controversial scene. However, TMT offers further insight into the visceral power of this reaction. Existential threat is already highly salient in the episode ("A Knight of the Seven Kingdoms") as the threat of the impending confrontation with the army of the dead clearly puts death on the minds of characters and viewers alike. This threat is potentially subdued by viewer's hope that the human characters will be able to conquer the looming threat. Arya's gender-counter-normative ability as a warrior makes her a likely candidate for contributing to what the audience anticipates to be a strong visual confirmation of the triumph of good over evil and subsequently a symbolic victory over death itself. To make Ayra's nude body the object of the male sexual gaze provokes an awareness of corporeality that intensifies the already present existential threat posed by the death imagery in the form of the menace of the White Walkers. Consequently, the sexualizing of Arya exacerbates viewers' proneness to death anxiety while at the same time detracting from their ability to conceptualize Arya as the heroic source of comfort against that anxiety.

While TMT enhances an understanding of the discomfort many viewers felt in response to Arya's sexuality, it does not seem to explain as readily the actions of the character herself, because her motives seem more life-affirming than death-denying. It is clear that the possibility of death in the battle against the Night King and his Army of the Dead does motivate Arya to initiate a sexual interaction with Gendry, as she says, "We're probably going to die soon. I want to know what it's like before that happens." Although sex is a potential existential threat to the extent that it triggers awareness of corporeality and therefore mortality, it is also potentially a source of comfort against death anxiety. There is the obvious life-affirming symbolism of sex in that it can lead to the propagation of new life, so in this sense, sex offers a means of symbolic immortality. Sex is also potentially a means of feeling a close sense of personal intimacy and connection to another person and close relationships have been identified as a way to abate death anxiety by activating the feeling of a safe haven provided by proximity to an attachment figure (Mikulincer, Florian, & Hirschberger, 2004).

Ayra's action does not, however, seem to be defensively motivated. While she does have a longstanding friendship and connection with Gendry, she does not desire a long-term romantic relationship, a fact made evident by her rejection of his later marriage proposal. In episode four of season eight ("The Last of the Starks"), at the banquet hall celebration after the defeat of the army of the dead, Daenerys elevates Gendry's status from Robert Baratheon's bastard heir, making him lord and ruler of the Baratheon family castle—Storm's End. He leaves the celebration to find Arya practicing archery in an empty hallway where he informs her of his new, good fortunes and title. He impulsively proclaims her beauty, professes his love, and gets down on one knee to ask her to marry him. She kisses him but then refuses his proposal, claiming that she is not a lady and never has been. Her refusal ends with the simple phrase "That's not me." The line is a reference back to her earlier statement to her father in season one and reinforces her consistency in rejecting notions of domesticity and motherhood as suitable life goals. In episode four of season one ("Cripples, Bastards, and Broken Things"), while sharing with her father Ned Stark the progress in her sword lessons, which Ned does not approve of but has reluctantly allowed, she asks him if she can be lord of a holdfast someday. He pushes her to consider more gender-typical socialization towards marriage and family, telling her that she shall be wife of a high lord and that her sons will be knights. She responds by telling him, "no—that's not me."

These facts indicate that Arya's sexual advances toward Gendry, while certainly precipitated by the possibility of impending death, were not defensive attempts to abate anxiety by seeking symbolic immortality or clinging to traditionally defined standards of behavior. Leah (2019) emphasized this point, noting that she perceived Arya's sexual initiation as an empowering and life-affirming choice for the character.

So, for viewers who can tolerate the increased anxiety and avoid responding reflexively, there is a potential existential lesson to be gleaned from the way Arya faces her own mortality—namely that confrontations with the reality of death need not elicit defensive shrinking back from life but can at times for some people be an impetus for zestful and more authentic living.

5

Death-Denying (Super)heroism

Gender, Trauma, and Violence
in Marvel's The Punisher *on Netflix*

Ernest Becker (1962) described people as "Homo Heroica"—stressing the quest for a sense of heroism as the fundamental human need: "This is the uniquely human need, what man everywhere is really all about— each person's need to be an object of primary value, a heroic contributor to world-life—the heroic contributor to the destiny of man" (p. 76). Becker viewed the fundamental role of culture as providing a means for heroism and while the exact standards and definitions of what constitutes the heroic varies across culture, all hero projects share the same function of easing existential fears by elevating human existence beyond the realm of the biological and into the more enduring symbolic realm. Becker (1973) articulated the death-denying function of heroism thus:

> We admire most the courage to face death; we give such valor our highest and most constant adoration; it moves us deeply in our hearts because we have doubts about how brave we ourselves would be. When we see a man bravely facing his own extinction we rehearse the greatest victory we can imagine. And so the hero has been the center of human honor and acclaim since probably the beginning of specifically human evolution [pp. 11–12].

According to Becker (1973), the desire to overcome death anxiety gives rise not only to the quest for a personal sense of heroism but also to the admiration and veneration of others who offer hope of transcendence: "the hero was the man who could go into the spirit world, the world of the dead, and return alive" (p. 12).

Building on Becker's ideas about heroism, Koole, Fockenberg, Tops, and Schneider (2013) offered a TMT analysis of the popularity of superhero films in the 21st century. They asserted that the historical appeal of heroes from mythology, folklore, and religion was derived from their death-denying properties and that the modern superhero has now

96

replaced the religious-mythical heroes from which they were inspired and derived. Koole et al. suggest that identifying with superheroes offers one type of vicarious solution to the psychological quest for death transcendence and that superheroes symbolize death transcendence in several ways. First is their ability to avoid death. In violent confrontations with regular criminals and supervillains, they time and again prove exceedingly difficult to kill. Kool et al. write, "by identifying with invulnerable and eternally young superheroes, people may psychologically reduce their own sense of vulnerability to death and decay" (p. 140). Just as the direct or proximal defenses demonstrated in TMT research involve exaggerating one's invulnerability, superheroes might offer visual reassurance of the possibility that premature death due to violent or accidental causes can be avoided.

In addition, the fact that their superpowers seemingly break or at least bend empirical assumptions about the operations of the laws governing the physical universe could offer viewers hope that the inevitability of death can be overcome. If any of these laws such as gravity are not immutable, then perhaps the starkest reality imposed by the natural world (death) is not unavoidable. TMT research has shown that reminders of death increase the appeal of supernatural beliefs (Norenzayan & Hansen, 2006) and religious beliefs (Vail, Arndt, & Abdollahi, 2012) and increase the desire for the ability to fly, which is one of the most common powers for superheroes (Cohen, Sullivan, Solomon, Greenberg, & Ogilvie, 2011). Superheroes are often described as being imbued with religious imagery (Richardson, 2004). For example, Kozlovic (2006) noted that superheroes are "associated with the skies, metaphorically heaven (i.e., the iconic domain of angels, Jesus, God, heaven and the home of the Good), thus, subtly implying that these superheroes resonate with divinity." Consequently, the supernatural and religious aspects of superheroes can potentially help viewers assuage existential anxiety by augmenting confidence in beliefs about literal immortality. As Koole et al. observed, "by bending steel with their bare hands, superheroes may bend the natural laws that dictate that life must be finite" (p. 141).

Further, superheroes offer the same kind of model for symbolic immortality as regular heroes but on a grander scale. As Koole et al. noted, "Superheroes are undeniably American icons" (p. 136). They embody the American value of individualism and oftentimes come to symbolize American nationalism. For example, Superman fights for "truth, justice, and the American way" and Captain America embraces American nationalism in his name and his costume. Given that TMT research has shown increased nationalistic bias to be a defense initiated in response to reminders of mortality (Nelson, Moore, Olivetti, & Scott, 1997), it seems possible that part of the appeal of superheroes to American audiences is the ways in which they reinforce viewers' hopes of symbolic immortality in the form of nationalistic values and identity.

Superheroes also offer hopes of symbolic immortality in that they are champions of morality and protectors of all that is good and best in society. They vanquish evil forces; oftentimes, those bent on global destruction. What better way to feel that one's life has mattered in the cosmic scheme of things than to vanquish evil that otherwise threatens to extinguish the continuity of the human project? TMT research shows that mortality salience increases: appreciation for heroes as evidenced by larger rewards recommended for someone who provided a tip leading to the arrest of a dangerous criminal (Rosenblatt, Greenberg, Solomon, Pyszcynski, & Lyon, 1989), intentions to act pro-socially as evidenced by more giving to charitable causes (Jonas, Schimel, Greenberg, & Pyszczynski, 2002), efforts to punish wrongdoers such as higher bails for women accused of prostitution (Rosenblatt, Greenberg, Solomon, Pyszcynski, & Lyon, 1989) and harsher recommended penalties for moral transgressors (Florian & Mikulincer, 1997). Thus, to the extent that the heroic actions of the superhero have long lasting consequences for the aim and scope of history that far exceed the heroic aspirations possible for the typical person, identification with superheroes might serve as a vicarious means of symbolic immortality.

The argument that the appeal of superheroes lies in their ability to help audiences ameliorate death anxiety is complicated by a trend in the depiction of superheroes to pursue smaller rather than cosmic scale heroism and to be portrayed as increasingly flawed and morally ambiguous. Koole et al. (2013) acknowledged this trend and argued that increasing scientific rationalism has made it more difficult for many segments of the population to believe in supernatural mythologies including the superhero variant of these myths. Subsequently, recent efforts to make superheroes potentially credible have involved appeal to scientific causation, more realistic special effects, and more complicated and multifaceted character portrayals. These increasingly complicated character portrayals have been concomitant with another trend—namely the deconstruction of the superhero whose motives and impact are questioned in an increasingly morally relativistic and uncertain world: "the superhero film increasingly confronts its viewers with the absurdity of existence and the pointlessness of being a hero" (Koole et al., p. 147).

Similarly, Palumbo (1983) describes the morally compromised superhero of the postmodern age as representing an existential hero—a character who struggles with the absurdity of the human condition regarding issues of alienation, guilt, freedom, and death but who strives to construct some limited sense of meaning for life in the absence of any inauthentic belief in absolute significance or morality.

This chapter presents a TMT analysis of a prime example of a conflicted and angst-ridden protagonist whose motives and impact are questionable in an increasingly morally relativistic and uncertain world but for these very reasons may be more appealing because they align with viewer's increasingly postmodern sensibilities. An analysis of this type of hero is particularly interesting because it reveals a psychological ambivalence among fans stemming from a desire for images of supernatural feats that fuel hopes of transcending human limitations coupled with the simultaneous longing for identification with an all too human existential hero who grapples with issues of finding meaning and purpose in a turbulent and ephemeral world. Watching series depicting such existential superheroes can be simultaneously both palliative towards death anxiety but also potentially provocative of personal confrontation with existential issues.

This chapter offers an analysis of *The Punisher* (2017–2019), a recent, popular series on Netflix that brings a tormented and morally ambiguous (super)hero from the Marvel universe to the small screen. The eponymous protagonist Frank Castle survived extreme trauma, exhibits moral failings, and grapples with existential issues. While Frank responds to trauma in stereotypically gendered ways, externalizing his rage by knocking down brick walls with a sledgehammer when he is not exacting his lethal brand of justice, the show also interrogates cultural ambivalence about masculinity. The psychological complexity of the character stems in part from the fact that he operates on multiple levels of meaning.

The Punisher fits a long-standing pattern, in which superhero narratives serve as modern religious myths offering viewers hope of transcending the limits of the empirical world (Koole et al., 2013). It also fits a more recent trend of ambiguous heroes who offer audiences a means of grappling with epistemic and existential issues related to meaning and morality in a zeitgeist of moral relativism (Koole et al., 2013; Palumbo, 1983). *The Punisher* raises universal existential issues, such as the need to believe in a just world characterized by an unwavering, inerrant fairness, but also presents currently salient socio-historical challenges, such as concerns about gun violence and how to deal with veterans returning from war.

The Punisher character first appeared in *The Amazing Spider-Man* 129 (in February 1974). In describing the Ross Andru cover art for that comic, Worcester (2012) writes, "The white boots and white gloves he wore neatly symbolized the binary, black-and-white nature of his thinking, and added a somewhat implausible note of visual contrast. Seen peering through the scope of a high-caliber rifle, he was the personification of the grim reaper" (p. 331). Since his debut, The Punisher has had an enduring and prolific

Frank Castle, aka The Punisher, portrayed by Jon Bernthal in season one of the Netflix series *The Punisher* (2017), pictured here donning his trademark black body armor emblazoned with his iconic white skull (photo credit: Jessica Miglio/Netflix).

career, appearing in dozens of comic series and three feature length films. The most recent and perhaps most critically acclaimed instantiation of the character has been on the Netflix small screen. Actor Jon Bernthal portrayed Frank Castle (aka The Punisher) in season two of *Daredevil* in 2016 and then continued the role in two seasons of the character's own self-titled series (2017–2019). The appeal of the extreme violence, massive body count, and extensive death iconography that define *The Punisher* can be interpreted as an example of the defense mechanism of identification. By identifying with the instrument of death, perhaps viewers hope they can avoid being its victim.

Several incidents from season two illustrate this point nicely. The first occurs in episode three ("Trouble the Water"). Frank is in a small-town jail in rural Michigan after killing several assassins who came after him and the teenaged girl, Amy Bendix (Giorgia Whigham), he was protecting at a motel where they were hiding out. When an army of paramilitary hitmen attack the jail, the sheriff releases Frank so he can assist in the fight. The officers watch from inside the jail as Frank single-handedly eliminates dozens of attackers. One of the deputies inside says, "You ever seen that [W]estern where the guy comes to town and it turns out he's the devil or death or something." Another replies, "As long as he's on our side." This is a reference to Clint Eastwood in *High Plains Drifter* (1973) and not only a meta nod to the Western genre's influence as the precursor to the modern action hero but also a clear emphasis of the point that The Punisher is understood as death personified.

Homeland security agent Dinah Madani (Amber Rose Revah) rescues Frank and Amy from the battle in Michigan and brings them to New York because she wants Frank's help in dealing with the recently escaped Billy Russo (Ben Barnes), the villain from season one. In episode five ("One-eyed Jacks"), Frank and Amy are biding their time in Madani's New York apartment as they formulate a plan. While passing the time, Amy is teaching Frank a card trick hustle called Three-Card Monte. No matter how slowly she shuffles, he can't keep track of the Queen, and keeps picking the Jack. She tells him everyone knows the game is rigged, but they all have their reasons for playing. When he asks her what his reason is, she says, "You think you can beat anybody no matter how stacked the deck." Amy's analysis is spot on, but Frank's belief is well founded because he always survives, no matter what the odds. Later in the season, when Frank is going after Billy, Amy expresses concerns that Frank may be killed in the encounter because she has come to care for Frank as a surrogate father figure and because she knows his death will leave her vulnerable and at the mercy of the people chasing her. Frank dismisses her worries, saying, "I'm not the one who dies, kid; I'm the one who does the killing" ("Flustercluck"). This incident makes clear that Frank is immune to death because he is its instrument, and therefore, cannot be its victim. The appeal of Frank's violence is that it offers viewers the illusion of invulnerability to death by reinforcing the notion that death is something that happens only to others.

Worcester (2012) suggests that The Punisher character "represents the frustrations of millions of people who feel powerless and who fantasize about striking back at their enemies be they real or imagined" (p. 329). This powerlessness can be extended not just in reference to other people and social structures but to the existential human condition. The aversion to feeling powerless against personal mortality is explicitly mentioned in season one ("Crosshairs") in a conversation between Billy Russo and William Rawlins (Paul Schulze). Billy Russo was Frank Castle's best friend, and they served together in Afghanistan in a secret program called Operation Cerberus, led by CIA agent William Rawlins, that involved capture, torture, and execution of supposed terrorists. After a particularly ill-advised mission, in which Frank and Billy are among a few survivors, Frank confronts and attacks Rawlins, intent on beating him to death. Billy pulls Frank away but not before he has pulverized one side of Rawlins' face. Through the course of the show, viewers learn that Cerberus was a cover for a drug smuggling scheme in which Billy was a conspirator with Rawlins and that they killed Frank's family and tried to kill him in order to keep their secret. When Rawlins and Russo discover that Frank is still alive and coming after them, they discuss plans on how to deal with him. Russo is talking about how Rawlins used to enjoy torturing people during Cerberus and how Rawlins would relish the moment when his captives would realize that their deaths were inevitable. Russo goes on to say,

> I saw that same look on your face once, that fear, when Frank gave you that milky eye. He was gonna keep right on going to and you knew it. All of your grand ambitions choked out of you in a shitty tent. And who was it? Remind me, who was it who pulled him off you? Oh yeah, I did…. You know what I think. I think the only reason you wanted Frank dead was so you could pretend like he never made you feel like a man about to die.

It has been argued (Koole et al., 2013) that at least part of the appeal of superheroes is that they help fans symbolically assuage existential anxiety. Superheroes have an uncanny ability to avoid death. In their myriad violent confrontations with criminals, they time and again prove hard to kill. Although Frank Castle technically has no superpowers, his ability to always win violent confrontations regardless of how badly he is outnumbered or how much he is injured in the process certainly borders on the preternatural and exceeds the limits of realistic human performance. As Nelson (2019) noted, "Frank's endurance often stretches credulity." For example, he avoids detention by two police officers, incapacitates them, and steals their car armed only with a rock ("Front toward Enemy"). After saving his friend, reporter Karen Page (Deborah Ann Woll), from an attack on her life by right-wing domestic terrorist Lewis Walcott (Daniel Webber), Frank manages to escape a skyscraper swarming with federal agents and law enforcement officers even though he is severely injured after being shot repeatedly. In an interview with police, Karen quips, "You think a man like Frank Castle walks into a building he doesn't know how to get out of?" ("Virtue of the Vicious"). The series is palliative towards existential anxiety by presenting a world in which violence brings restorative justice and the innocent are protected by a hero who can overcome all threats and dangers no matter how seemingly implausible the odds.

In addition to universal existential themes, *The Punisher* also serves as a mechanism for presenting specific socio-historical challenges that are highly salient in contemporary cultural dialogues. The series highlights concerns about violent crime, the ethics of warfare, the limits and excesses of police force, the debate about gun rights, and the problems of how to deal with veterans returning from war.

Gilbert (2017) noted that the cultural zeitgeist when the character made his first comic cameo in 1974 was different from the release of the Netflix series in 2017. The salience of high-profile mass shootings that year—for example, the 58 people killed in Las Vegas and 26 in Sutherland Springs, Texas—potentially problematized the appeal of a show about a comic book series that fetishes guns and a character whose only power is an exceptional skill at killing people with guns. Gilbert goes on to admit that she finds the show entertaining but suggests that "it isn't an easy ride" and that it is uncomfortable to watch amid cultural concerns about gun violence. Similarly, Madison (2017) argued that the show is not pro-Second Amendment but rather makes salient the adverse emotional and physical consequence of gun violence. These claims might reflect a political bias in that they fail to acknowledge that for viewers who feel comfortable with guns and who conceptualize them as a source of safety, the anxiety engendered by the salience of real-world mass violence likely make guns and fictional characters who use guns to eliminate dangerous people more appealing.

The show's stance on guns is not all decidedly negative. Reporter Karen Page, who is a supporter of Frank and at times and within limits a champion of his vigilantism, is also a gun rights advocate who carries a pistol in her purse. Having a handgun allows Karen to escape when held hostage by disgruntled, veteran-turned-terrorist bomber Lewis Walcott. The liberal senator Stan Ori (Rick Holmes), who serves as the voice of gun control in debates and interviews with Karen, is depicted as wimpy and craven. When Ori fears for his life because he has publicly denounced Lewis, he hires Billy Russo's company Anvil to protect him. Billy is happy to take the senator's money but points out the hypocrisy of a vocal anti-gun activist being in a position to need people skilled with guns to make him feel safe. When an armed and maliciously intentioned Lewis breaks through Anvil security and interrupts an interview between Karen and Senator Ori, Ori whimpers and pleads for his life before using Karen as a shield and running out of the room leaving her in danger ("Virtue of the Vicious").

In an interview with *Esquire* (Rodrick, 2018), actor Jon Bernthal identifies as a gun owner and claims that the motive to protect his family is his rationale for keeping a gun in the house. He expressed dislike for extreme sides of the gun debate that advocate for no access to guns or unfettered access. When asked about the popularity of *The Punisher* symbol among members of law enforcement and the military, he claimed he was honored at being able to give expression to a character with whom these brave people identify. He did not express similar pride when asked about the alt-right protestors in Charlottesville, VA, who donned the symbol.

Some (for example, DiPaolo, 2011) have criticized *The Punisher* comics for endorsing a conservative ideology that emerged in the 1970s as a backlash against the progressive counter-cultural movements of the 60s that were blamed for the breakdown of traditional values and a subsequent rise in lawlessness. Such critics also take issue with the apparent racism underlying The Punisher's brand of vigilante justice, in that his victims are frequently non–White.

Worcester (2012) rejects these criticisms, arguing that "the Punisher is indifferent to ordinary political discourse" and "an equal-opportunity avenger" (p. 339).

The Netflix series does not contribute to these concerns about racism and in some ways works to distance itself from endorsing a "make America great again" political ideology.

In the character of O'Connor (Delaney Williams), we find a caricature of negative stereotypes about the typical Trump supporter. He is a bitter and frustrated, old, White man, who feels marginalized and threatened. He uses racial slurs and views the government as tyrannical in its infringement of Second Amendment rights. These sentiments are epitomized in one of his outbursts during the veterans' support group he attends, when he says, "The real persecuted minority in this country today is the Christian American patriot" ("3 a.m."). O'Connor is presented in a very negative light rather than a sympathetic one. He pretends to be a decorated Vietnam vet, but it is later revealed that he served after the war was over and never saw combat. He is presented as a frustrated loser who uses lies and fear mongering to try and manipulate actual combat vets like Lewis Walcott into supporting his dubious political agenda. He has no conviction or courage. When Lewis and O'Connor are confronted by police while protesting in support of Second Amendment rights outside a courthouse, O'Connor sneaks away, leaving Lewis to be arrested, and does not even bail him out of jail. When Lewis learns of O'Connor's lies about his combat service, he confronts him and ends up killing him in the ensuing altercation ("The Judas Goat"). The series continues to villainize the political right in season two with a set of bad guys and plot lines clearly inspired by Trump-era politics. One reviewer suggested season two was trying to "rip from as many headlines as possible" with plot lines featuring cult-like religious conservatives manipulating digital media and Russian mobsters bent on gaining influence over American politics (Schedeen, 2019). Similarly, Tassi (2019) noted that "you can see the overall Trump-era parallels pretty clearly" as the villains in season two include neo–Nazis, Russian blackmailers, and alt-right conspiracy mongers.

The Punisher character is extremely popular among many in the military and in law enforcement and some even co-opt the character's iconography to decorate their equipment (Reisman, 2017). Chris Kyle (the inspiration for the 2014 movie *American Sniper*) was one of the most famous Punisher fans to describe publicly how his unit took on the moniker of "The Punishers" and displayed the character's iconic skull. Some people find *The Punisher* fandom among military and law enforcement unseemly because they worry that such fandom may promote emulation and a disregard for rules of engagement and due process in real life. Character co-creator Gerry Conway, commenting on Chris Kyle's fandom, said, "I don't think they understood the fundamental truth the Punisher is not a man to admire or emulate" (Reisman, 2017). Despite these objections, there are more legitimate reasons for the character's appeal to fans in the military and law enforcement. First, they admire the character's intensity and perseverance as he doggedly accomplishes his missions against daunting odds and through extreme injury and duress. Second, the ideal of infallible justice depicted in *The Punisher* helps alleviate frustrations over the fact that justice is never so precise or absolute in the real world.

Beauchamp (2016) argues that The Punisher is a mythical folk hero in military culture and is best understood as a cultural response to societal ambivalence towards veterans. We need warriors to protect national security, but what do we do with them when they are not fighting? Can those who have been socialized and trained to be the most effective killers in the name of nationalistic goals be re-socialized to be productive and peaceable members of a society not at war? Beauchamp (2016) noted how Netflix's *The Punisher* gives voice to "an unspoken collective guilt" that rests pervasively but uneasily in the cultural recognition that "what was once useful on the battlefield becomes a liability in the civilized world."

Frank Castle's seemingly inherently violent nature, methodical proficiency in utilizing his lethal skills, and lack of self-doubt make him seem more like a weapon than a person. This view is expressed explicitly by Rawlins. When he admits to CIA deputy director Marion James (Mary Elizabeth Mastrantonio) that he used drugs to fund torture and assassination in operation Cerberus and now needs to kill Castle in order to keep it quiet, Rawlins tries to ease James' conscience by telling her, "Think of it as decommissioning unwanted ordinance. That's all Castle is—a weapon we no longer have any use for" ("Danger Close").

The series promotes sympathy for the damage done to veterans in the demands of their service and expresses a collective guilt about society's utilization of them for unsavory jobs to protect national interests and safety. For example, agent Madoni goes to see Curtis Hoyle (Jason R. Moore), a friend and brother in arms to Frank and Billy, who now runs a support group for veterans. Madani wants to see what Curtis knows that might help her track down Billy. He tells her he can't talk now because the group is about to start: "if I make these guys wait for you then it makes them feel like they don't matter and that is pretty much how they feel 24/7 so I'm not going to do that" ("One-eyed Jacks"). The series also comments on how the training and experiences with violence necessary for success in combat complicates veterans' return to peaceful civilian life. Frustration at the lack of meaning in civilian life is expressed by Billy who tells his therapist Dr. Krista Dumont (Floriana Lima), "I was the best version of myself out there in the service—swift, silent, deadly, we all were all of those things. We were a family. We were fighting for something" ("Scar Tissue").

One of the most interesting themes explored in both seasons of the series is the cultural ambivalence about traditional notions of masculinity. *The Punisher* interrogates popular notions about the concept of toxic masculinity by offering an apologetic for the need for violent men to do the dirty work of keeping family and country safe from the evils of the world that supposedly can only be bested through brute aggression. Frank Castle is not a trope for toxic masculinity. His love, devotion, and faithfulness to his late wife and mourning for the loss of his children are frequently depicted in flashbacks and conversations to show that Frank is a romantic and a family man. But the same capacity for violence that makes him a national protector makes him a domestic danger. He is shown having a violent outburst towards his son in a flashback ("Two Dead Men") and admits that after returning from combat to be physically present with his family, he was often emotionally absent and longing for return to his unit.

The series adopts a common dualistic solution to ambivalence about masculinity seen in other Marvel comic characters such as the Incredible Hulk in which the sensitive and caring family man needed for day-to-day domesticity, and the brutish male rage and power needed in times of emergency, have to be dissociated (Genter, 2007). The sensitive, intellectual side of modern masculinity desirable for white-collar jobs and domesticity is personified in the character of David Lieberman (Ebon Moss-Bachrach). Lieberman was an NSA analyst who discovered the misconduct involved in Operation Cerberus and tried to report it, an action that resulted in his attempted assassination. Assumed dead, Lieberman must remain in hiding to keep his family safe. Or, said another way, riffing on the opening sequence of an earlier comic-based TV show (*The Incredible Hulk* 1977–1982): David Lieberman is believed to be dead, and he must let the world think that he is dead until he can find a way to recruit a raging spirit to avenge him.

Without a hulking alter ego dwelling within him, Lieberman must look externally, so he convinces The Punisher to help him bring the people behind Cerberus to justice. Frank wants vengeance for his family, but Lieberman just wants to be able to safely return to his.

The Bruce Banner vs. Hulk dichotomy is a salient feature of the duo's strained partnership, illustrated with devices such as Lieberman's fondness for chamomile tea in contrast to Frank's black coffee. Frank has dreams about attending a dinner with the united Lieberman family (illustrating his longing for the domestic life he romanticizes after the loss of his family), but the dream takes a nightmarish turn when masked assailants burst in and kill all the Liebermans (symbolizing not only Frank's guilt over his culpability for the deaths of his own family but also his awareness that he will always put those around him in danger). Once Rawlins has been killed and Russo neutralized, the threat to the Liebermans is removed, and it is safe for David to return home. Symbolizing cultural ambivalence about both masculinity and veterans, Frank drives David to the doorstep but refuses to join him in the lavish family celebration awaiting inside; the man needed for national and domestic security is too volatile to enjoy its benefits.

The theme of ambivalence about male violence and its incompatibility with domesticity is further explored in season two. Season two begins with Frank aimlessly driving across the country ("Roadhouse Blues"). He stops at a bar in rural Michigan where he develops a brief romantic relationship with bartender Beth Quinn (Alexa Davalos). After an

David Lieberman (Ebon Moss-Bachrach, standing) and Frank Castle (Jon Bernthal, seated) having a tense conversation in season one of the Netflix series *The Punisher* (2017, photo credit: Netflix).

old-fashioned display of chivalry in defending Beth from an aggressively harassing customer, the two have a one-night stand that turns into a genuine emotional encounter. Frank takes Beth and her son Rex (Jagger Nelson) out for pancakes where they laugh and discuss benign topics like hockey, leaving viewers to wonder if there is a possibility for Frank to have a happy domestic life again. After initially driving away to continue his migrant wanderings, Frank has a change of heart and returns to the bar to see Beth again. However, any hopes of domestic tranquility are quickly dashed when Frank intervenes to save the troubled teenage girl Amy Bendix from a team of highly trained mercenaries. In the chaos that ensues with sprays of gunfire from multiple combatants, Frank kills or disables all of the attackers and saves Amy, but Beth is injured in the process. It is now clear that Frank will always be a danger to those around him, and he is, therefore, too unstable for traditional family life, but his hyper-violent masculinity can be of use to those in need. Again, the point here is that violent masculinity is a necessity in an emergency but a liability at other times.

Frank's initial appearance as a wandering drifter, which Miller (2019) described as "Frank's just bopping around America, enjoying the sights in a vagabond way," is another frequently employed device to deal with the ambivalence towards male violence. A common trope in action-adventure television series of the 1970s and 1980s involved a male protagonist or protagonists—a solitary figure (*Kung Fu* 1972–1975, *Knight Rider* 1982–1986), a duo (*The Master* 1984), or a group (*The A-Team* 1983–1987) forced into a transient life of drifting from place to place (Bassett, 2016). This "man/men on the run" theme gives expression to a culturally emerging ambivalence about the changing nature of masculinity. Male physicality and male sensitivity are presented as incompatible, conflicting forces. The hero enters the right situations to be helpful when needed but then moves on before such hyper-masculinity can have its prolonged destructive consequences. This apologetic offers viewers a guilt-free, cathartic expression of the appeal of hyper-violent masculinity and a justification for the lack of long-term emotional availability, while still facilitating a sense of heroic participation in the world.

After the initial episode of season two, however, *The Punisher* shifts from the man-on-the-run motif to a different narrative device prevalent in Marvel comics and their on-screen adaptations, in which an older and seasoned character tries to find some level of redemption in mentoring a younger character. Abad-Santos (2019) pointed out that the storyline in season two utilizes an old, familiar device of having a powerful but jaded and emotionally-withholding, older character take a "vulnerable youngster under his wing and vows to protect them at all costs." Recent cinematic examples include Wolverine's (Hugh Jackman) protection of the young mutant Laura (Dafne Keen) in *Logan* (2017) and Tony Stark's (Robert Downey, Jr.) mentorship of Peter Parker (Tom Holland) in *Spider-Man Homecoming (2017)*. The relationships between Frank and Amy certainly fits this pattern, but it also offers a further exploration of tensions between the desire for a dominant male protector in a dangerous world and the concerns about the dangers such a man poses given his questionable stability and fitness as a domestic caregiver. In fact, most of season two is a meditation on both the potential powers and perils of the extreme measures people take in the name of protecting those they love. This idea is given voice by Russian crime boss Nikolai Poloznev (Dikran Tulaine) who tells Frank, "Isn't that what we all want, Mr. Castle—to give our children a better life than we had" ("One-eyed Jacks"). As Miller (2019) observed, "Nearly everyone on this show seems to agree on one fact: protecting your family is worth killing for."

The fervent desire to protect family name and legacy is what creates the circumstances that drive one of the main plots of season two. Eliza (Annette O'Toole) and Anderson Schultz (Corbin Bernsen) are billionaires who use their wealth and the propaganda of their alt-right media outlets to promote their conservative Christian political agenda as well as their own financial and family interests. They are grooming their son, Senator David Schultz (Todd Alan Crain), to become president. The only problem is that David is gay, and his parents insist on keeping this a secret for reasons they claim are based on electability but probably have to do more with their own prejudices and potential embarrassment. Amy Bendix is among a group of teenaged grifters hired to take compromising pictures of David kissing another man. Russian oligarch Nikolai Poloznev planned to buy the pictures not to sabotage David's campaign but to wield influence over him once he did become president. When the Schultzs discovered the plot, they sent John Pilgrim (Josh Stewart) to retrieve the photos. Pilgrim kills all of the other teenagers, but Amy escapes with the photos. Schultz's mercenaries would have killed Amy as well had it not been for Frank's intervention. Frank kidnaps David Schultz to interrogate him as to what he knows and use him as leverage against his parents but discovers that David knew nothing about the photos or his parent's murderous efforts to keep them suppressed. In the series finale, realizing that Amy will never be safe as long as the Schultzes are alive, Frank goes to their home, shoots Eliza Schultz, and then gives Anderson Schultz a choice ("The Whirlwind"). He offers to keep secret the murder and mayhem the Schultzes have caused in order to allow David's political career to go forward if Anderson kills himself. If not, he will expose everything. We hear the gunshot indicating Anderson's choice. The Schultzes' misguided devotion to the urgency of their desire for symbolic immortality through their legacy and name is portrayed as folly. Their plight serves as a warning against privileging the success of one's own family over the suffering of others and over any sense of moral scruples.

While complicity in violence and murder to protect the reputation and career of their son is deemed folly in the villainized characters of the Schultz, violent father figures who destroy any and all who pose physical threats to their children are venerated as heroic in the characters of Frank Castle and John Pilgrim. Amy objects to Frank's methods and often encourages him to use less lethal tactics but also admits on several occasions that she is grateful to Frank and knows she would be dead if it weren't for Frank's killing a bunch of people. Although Frank cares for Amy and would do anything to protect her, his violent nature and dangerous lifestyle make him ill-suited for a long-term caregiver. In the series' conclusion, Frank and Amy are waiting at a bus station. Amy invites Frank to go with her, saying, "This is your last chance. We're good together." Frank tells her that she is a kid and should go act like one because he can't have her on his conscience. He makes her promise not to get involved in any more shady activity, gives her some money, and puts her on a bus to Florida. Frank's violence is redeemed as heroic because it saved Amy and allowed her to live a normal life.

The character of John Pilgrim is more complicated because, unlike the people killed by Frank who are presented as unambiguously evil, Pilgrim has a more complex past and his victims are less clearly unredeemable. Pilgrim was part of a neo–Nazi gang in New York before finding true love with his wife Rebecca (Allie McCulloch) and becoming a true believer in a Christian congregation led by the Schultzes. Pilgrim is depicted as a somewhat sympathetic character because of his love and devotion to his wife and children. He is presented as a pawn who was manipulated by the Schultzes, who were providing treatment and care for Rebecca, who was suffering from a terminal illness. Once Rebecca died, the Schultzes used Pilgrim's sons as leverage to get him to continue in his mission. In the final confrontation, Pilgrim explains to Frank that the Schultzs have his boys and that he will do whatever he has to in order to save them. He asks Frank what he would have done to save his own family. A mutual understanding and perhaps even respect is created between the two men who both see in the other the same unrelenting persistence to both suffer and dole out any amount of punishment in the perceived protection of family. Frank wins a grueling junkyard brawl and is about to kill Pilgrim only to change his mind and grant clemency when Pilgrim asks him to please not hurt his boys when he goes after the Schultzes. After Frank has eliminated the Schultzes, we see Pilgrim reunited with his sons. While Frank rejects the role of permanent caregiver to Amy in favor of devoting his full-time efforts to vigilantism, Pilgrim seems to embrace the role of father with the implicit assumption that he will henceforth be a Christian man of peace and abandon his violent ways. Although he has shown potential for change in abandoning the hateful ideology of his past, the ruthlessness with which he killed so many leaves one to wonder about what type of stable home environment he will provide for two young sons.

The Punisher does potentially challenge viewers to contemplate important social issues such as the mental health of veterans and interrogates cultural ambivalence about masculinity and the tension between violence and domesticity. It also briefly raises existential issues about how the trauma of loss can produce a tendency to withdraw from caring about others in order to protect against the threat of further loss. For example, Curtis tells Amy that Frank is so gruff with her because he cares about her and is worried about getting hurt again the way the death of his family hurt him. Curtis says that Frank would "rather stay mad at the world than risk being a part of it" ("My Brother's Keeper"). Despite these occasional moments that stimulate thoughtful reflection on social and existential issues, the show is mostly palliative rather than provocative. The series offers a balm against death anxiety by encouraging identification with a seemingly indestructible titular character, and thereby, facilitates the illusion that death can be avoided by dispensing it out to others. The show also adheres to the melodramatic tendency to reinforce a belief in a just world where violence can be utilized by the hero in a precise way to eliminate evil with no messy collateral damage. Foutch (2019) suggested the show lost some of the provocative elements of the first season in exchange for a more sensationalized approach is season two, writing, "*The Punisher* has swapped bullets for brains."

While some characters such as Curtis, Madoni, and Amy express reservations about Frank's lethal methods and show remorse over their own uses of violence, these objections appear to be merely a strawman argument offering viewers plausible deniability of their own motives for watching. Frank's lack of remorse and refusal to contemplate the potential consequences of his violence serves as a device to allow viewers a guilt free enjoyment of his violence and to share his certainty that justice will always be neat and inerrant. In one episode, as Frank goes to confront Russian gangsters, Amy says, "It's almost like you are looking forward to it." Her comment applies to viewers as well, who are eager to see Frank in unrestrained, full-punishing mode with maximum violence directed at dehumanized targets ("One-eyed Jacks"). Similarly, in a later episode, Amy has been forced to shoot and kill an armed assailant who was attempting to abduct her. She is visibly shaken and distraught, but Frank tells her the assailant's blood is not worth a single one of her tears ("Flustercluck"). Here again, the show's dialogue is giving viewers permission to enjoy the violence without reservation.

The violence in *The Punisher* is seductively appealing because of the force with which it reinforces a comforting belief in a just world and the power with which it buttresses illusions of invulnerability; however, a thoughtful viewer might do well to interrogate their enjoyment of this type of violence and to recognize the terror management defenses underlying its appeal. We now turn to another Marvel comic-inspired show on Netflix for an example of how television violence can offer less comforting and more nuanced contemplation of existential and social issues.

6

Death-Confronting (Super)heroism

Facing Existential and Social Problems in Marvel's Jessica Jones on Netflix

Jessica Jones shares many commonalities with *The Punisher*. They both portray titular characters who are survivors of extreme trauma, exhibit ethical flaws, and interact in a gritty and morally ambiguous world. In contrast to Frank Castle's externalized rage, Jessica Jones primarily internalizes her rage in the form self-recriminating guilt and self-destructive alcoholism. Both series confront viewers with existential and social problems. *Jessica Jones* engages viewers on a universal level by highlighting issues of identity, free will, and vulnerability to overwhelming external forces, while also giving expression to currently salient socio-historical challenges such as growing outrage over the longstanding traditions of sexist mistreatment of women. Unlike *The Punisher*, *Jessica Jones* is less palliative and more evocative by refusing to offer simple solutions to existential and social problems and encouraging the idea that while it is necessary to confront these struggles, the process is arduous.

The character Jessica Jones first appeared in 2001 in the comic *Alias* that was created by Brian Michael Bendis and Michael Gaydos as part of the Marvel Max series that was marketed to older audiences by allowing more explicit depictions of sex and violence. The series *Jessica Jones* (2015–2019) aired for three seasons on Netflix as part of a small-screen Marvel multiverse including other heroes like Luke Cage and Daredevil.

Jessica Jones appeals to viewers on a universal level by exploring existential issues. One of the most salient of which is related to free will versus determinism. The plot of season one revolves around supervillain Kilgrave (David Tennant), who used his mind control powers not only to keep Jessica Jones (Krysten Ritter) as his sexual slave and consort but also to conscript her superhuman strength for his nefarious purposes, including the murder of Reva Connors (Parisa Fitz-Henley), who he ordered Jessica to kill in order to protect the secrets of his identity. Kilgrave exerts his power over myriad others in his quest to regain control over Jessica, leaving a wake of destruction and forcing characters and viewers to grapple with issues of control.

Taylor and Brown (1988) noted that the self-deluding tendency to overestimate personal control over life circumstances was a vital lie—a necessary illusion to ward off depression and anxiety and facilitate psychological equanimity. This need for the illusion of control is illustrated by nurse Claire Temple (Rosario Dawson) who, while helping Jessica get the incapacitated Luke Cage (Mike Colter) to safety, says, "I want everything to be my fault good or bad. It means I have some control ... keeps me dreaming that I can change things for people" ("AKA Smile"). However, such control is a double-edged sword. As theorists like Erich Fromm (1941) have pointed out, people are all too willing to give up their freedom to toxic, authoritarian leaders in order to avoid the anxiety over future wrong choices and the guilt over past mistakes. Relinquishing autonomy frees people from guilt or responsibility for their actions. Kilgrave's victim Malcolm Ducasse (Eka Darville) expresses these sentiments when he acknowledges that "there was a kind of freedom being under Kilgrave's control. You're not a slave to guilt, fear, or even logic. You just do what you're told" ("AKA You're a Winner").

Another important universal theme resonant throughout the series is exploring the ways in which defensive shrinking back can lead to self-destructive behavior. Firestone and Firestone (1998) view self-destructive behavior as a defense mechanism against anxiety rooted in the psychodynamics of childhood but enacted in adulthood, to ward off the painful awareness of the inevitability of death. From their perspective, self-critical thoughts promoting self-punishment and self-loathing are present to some degree in everyone but increase in intensity concomitant with the amount of trauma experienced. These negative thoughts and feelings give rise to self-destructive behaviors varying on a continuum from self-denial, in the form of avoiding challenging professional and interpersonal activities in favor of manageable and predictable forms of routine, to actual self-harm, in the form of micro-suicidal behaviors such as substance abuse or recklessness, all the way to actual attempts at self-annihilation.

Jessica is the epitome of self-destructive behavior. At one point, she admits her previous suicidal ideation to best friend and adopted sister Trish Walker (Rachael Taylor). In season two ("AKA Sole Survivor"), Jessica and Trish are at a remote beach location where Jessica used to come with her family. Jessica tells Trish that she thought about suicide in the early days after surviving the crash that killed her family: "After they died, I thought about coming back because I knew no one would ever find a body out here. I could just disappear." Although Jessica is no longer overtly suicidal, she continues to engage in micro-suicidal behaviors in the form of reckless sexual behavior and extreme alcohol abuse. Jessica criticizes Malcolm for his sexual addiction, telling him that "sticking your dick in anything that moves is the same as sticking a needle in your arm" ("AKA Three lives and Counting"). But this attack is hypocritical given Jessica's own penchant for using sex as a distraction to temporarily numb the pain of her past traumas. She routinely has casual sex with strangers such as in a bathroom stall at a bar with a stranger who objectified her by telling her she had a nice ass ("AKA Freak Accident") and sometimes wakes up after a night of drinking uncertain as to whether she is alone or with a one-night stand.

As noted by Rautiainen (2017), "Jessica mostly seems to deal with her trauma and guilt by consuming copious amounts of alcohol. She is seen drinking whiskey or other alcoholic drinks in 10 of the 13 episodes (in season one)" (p. 54). As fellow super-strong hero Luke Cage tells her in season one, "Jessica Jones, you are a hard-drinking, short-fused, mess of a woman" ("AKA You're a Winner!"). Jessica drinks to the point of passing out most nights, and Malcolm routinely has to drag her out of bed and bring her an energy drink to help her become functional to start most every workday at Alias Investigations. After a knife wound results in the loss of her spleen, the doctor explains to Jessica that she will need to make a swift change in any reckless lifestyle behavior, to which Jessica asks where a liter of bourbon a day would fall on the reckless scale ("AKA I Have No Spleen"). Jessica's own mother (Janet McTeer) convicts her on the way her alcoholism is constraining her from full engagement with life, saying, "You're drunk 24/7. You're numbing yourself. Is that a life?" ("AKA Playland").

Similar to the issue of self-destructive defenses, another recurring theme of the show is that caring about and trying to help others makes one vulnerable to physical dangers as well as emotional suffering but that callous indifference promotes isolation and meaninglessness. Psychodynamic scholar Norman Brown (1959) labeled this the tension between fear of death and fear of life. Through the course of season one, we learn that Jessica's drug-addled neighbor Malcolm, a character towards whom she has frequently shown compassion, has all along been a pawn of Kilgrave. Kilgrave got Malcolm addicted and uses both mind control and the promise of drugs to manipulate Malcolm into spying on and taking photos of Jessica. Further, we learn in a flashback ("AKA The Sandwich Saved Me") that it was Jessica's heroic intervention in fighting off assailants who were

Jessica Jones (Krysten Ritter) engaged in her common practice of binge drinking bourbon in the Netflix series _Jessica Jones_ (2015–2019, photo credit: Netflix).

beating Malcolm in the street that revealed her powers to Kilgrave in the first place, sparking his fascination with and victimization of her.

Jessica's wisecracking, tough-edged, no tolerance for sentimentality or bullshit demeanor is an intentional means of keeping others at a distance. In their final confrontation, Kilgrave tells Jessica that his mistake was trying to make her love him when she is incapable of love ("AKA Smile"). In the same episode, Malcolm tells Claire Temple that he doesn't want powers because he likes people too much, and people with powers such as Luke and Jessica are by necessity separate from people—even from each other. Her powers do partially account for her isolation, as they attracted Kilgrave's attention. Jessica does not want close relationships because she does not want Kilgrave to be able to hurt those close to her as a means of manipulating her. However, more than this, her aversion to closeness is also a defensive reaction to extreme trauma. Prior to being victimized by Kilgrave, Jessica lost her parents and brother in a car crash (a crash she feels guilty for causing and for surviving), and she found the murdered body of her boyfriend Stirling Adams (Mat Vairo). Trish recognizes Jessica's attempts to keep others at a safe emotional distance as a defense mechanism and calls her on it. When Jessica tries to explain that the timing is wrong for any relationship with Luke Cage and that things would be different if not for the crisis of trying to neutralize Kilgrave, Trish says, "You'd push him away like everybody else" ("AKA Take a Bloody Number"). Jessica admits her desire to avoid pain as the motive for trying to not care about others. After shooting Luke in self-defense from his Kilgrave-induced attack, she is dragging him into the hospital against a voiceover of her inner dialogue: "Pain is always a surprise. I try to avoid landmines, avoid caring, but until it hits, you have no idea what pain is" ("AKA Smile").

As the series goes on, Jessica begins to recognize this pattern of defensive behavior in herself. In season two, Jessica learns that her mother, Alisa Jones (Janet McTeer), is still alive but spends most of the season trying to thwart her mother's murderous rage. Jessica decides to take a chance that her mother is redeemable and to help her mother escape to Canada where they will live together, perhaps as some type of crime fighting duo. However, this unlikely dream is thwarted when Trish kills Alisa, in what she viewed as the only way to save Jessica. The experience does serve as an awakening for Jessica as to her need for connection to others and how isolated she had been. In the season two finale ("AKA Playland"), she says, "I've gone through life untethered, unconnected. I wasn't even aware that I had chosen that. It took someone coming back from the dead to show me that I've been dead too. The problem is—I never really figured out how to live."

Despite this realization, Jessica continues to have difficulty overcoming her habitual pattern of self-protection through isolation. Her romantic involvement with building superintendent Oscar Arocho (J.R. Ramirez) that began in season two comes to a quick end in season three ("AKA You're Welcome"). Oscar comes to Jessica's apartment to return an article of clothing she left at his place, but this is just a pretense to talk about their relationship, which they both admit has changed from romantic to platonic with a shared affection for Oscar's son Vido (Kevin Chacon). When Jessica points out to Oscar that he could have sent Vido to return the clothing, he asks if she always thinks like a detective. Jessica replies, "That's why I never liked magic. I always figured out the trick." Oscar wants to confirm with Jessica that they are both in the same place of just wanting to be friends because he has found a new potential romantic partner and wants closure in their relationship before he moves on. In reference to his new relationship, Oscar tells Jessica, "It's nice having someone you can let in who lets you in too." Jessica replies, "Yeah, that is the one trick I never quite figured out."

Other characters continue to point out Jessica's defensive aversion to closeness in season three. Trish states, "I've envied your powers but never the PI stuff—stalking out suspects for weeks on end, like watching paint dry. Probably why you like it, being alone, keeping people at a distance, focusing on someone else's shit so you don't have to look at your own" ("AKA You're Welcome"). Even her nemesis, serial killer Gregory

Sallinger (Jeremy Bobb), notes, "Your intentionally indifferent rebel rock garb, they are your cape, your mask, and your armor—your longing for distinction. How about your chosen profession—private eye? It's a lazy cliché. The individualist hero" ("AKA A Lotta Worms"). The show is being somewhat meta here by recognizing that Jessica's cynicism about humanity and her tortured isolation are tropes of film noir and the private detective genre. Further, this trope helps the series subvert the tendency in the superhero genre to relegate female characters to serve mainly as romantic interests for male characters. Rautiainen (2017) noted that female crime fighters in comics were "generally portrayed as less powerful and competent than their male counterparts, who were often forced to rescue their well-meaning but ineffectual partners from various villains" (p. 16). And depictions of women in superhero films and television are similarly problematic in that "female characters are often quite insignificant for the advancement of the plot, and they usually have to be rescued by male characters at some point" (p. 28).

It is perhaps a feminist victory that the series resists any temptation to force Jessica into a happily ever after romantic ending in which a successful resolution to her story requires the love and validation of a man. In the series finale, Jessica ends her romantic involvement with her lover—the somewhat super-powered Erik Gelden (Benjamin Walker). Erik has the ability to feel the badness in people (although not to the level of knowing the specifics of their misdeeds). The catch is that the presence of evil in others makes him physically sick and causes him great pain. Erik is compatible with Jessica in many ways including his cynicism, moral ambiguity, reluctance to be a hero, predilection for black leather clothing, self-destructive behavior, and the fact that his powers cause him suffering. While Erik is at times of some use to Jessica in his ability to read people's goodness or badness, he is always in a subservient position to her, and although she does seem to have genuine feelings for him, their relationship never becomes a central or defining feature of Jessica's identity. In fact, at points in the season there is an intentional inversion of the gender dynamics historically prevalent in the superhero genre, with Erik being the one who needs rescuing from Sallinger by Jessica ("AKA Sorry Face") and Erik relegated to having value only to the extent that he pleases Jessica. In episode five ("AKA I Wish"), after a night of lovemaking, Erik wakes up in bed to find Jessica already at work. He tries to talk her out of going after Sallinger and when he is unable to do so, offers to help her. Jessica refuses, saying she won't be able to protect him. He says it is a good thing he proved his masculinity all night, to which Jessica replies, "You think you did," and then with a smile says, "Feel free to leave me one of those burgers." In the series finale, it is clear that Erik wants to continue in a romantic and crime fighting relationship with Jessica, but she rejects both. Jessica tells Erik that she thinks he is a good guy but does not trust him. The series ends with Jessica on her own. She arranges a meeting between Erik and Detective Eddy Costa (John Ventimiglia) so that they can team up to continue to catch bad guys. She leaves the keys and responsibility of running Alias Investigations with Malcolm. It is unclear what exactly Jessica will do, but she will do it self-sufficiently.

Despite having several romantic interactions with Luke Cage (season one), Oscar Arocho (season two), and Erik Gelden (season three), the fact that Jessica is ultimately deprived of any "normal" relationship is consistent with a common theme in Marvel comics that Palumbo (1983) labels existential heroism. Spider-Man is the prototypical example of the existential hero in Palumbo's analysis. The trauma he experienced in the loss of his parents, the guilt he feels over his culpability in the death of Uncle Ben, and his dual identity with the sacrificial demands required of being a superhero and the dangerous attention this role brings to those he loves all work together as powerful forces that alienate Spider-Man from potential friends, love interests, and from society. All of these characteristics apply equally well to Jessica Jones. The series gives a knowing wink to the similarity of its titular character to Spider-Man but in typical sardonic Jessica fashion. In season two, Jessica's mother is trying to convince her that they can team up and use their powers for good. She is arguing that their special abilities should not be hidden or suppressed but utilized to their full potential. Jessica stops her, saying, "If you say with great power comes great responsibility, I swear I'll throw up on you" ("AKA Playland"). Despite Jessica's aversion to the mantle, she is an existential hero, nonetheless.

The existential dilemmas posed in the super-powered fictional realm of *Jessica Jones* are really the same questions all people must address in their own mundane lives. Psychotherapist Robert Firestone (1993) argued that most people prefer the illusion of intimacy rather than true feeling and genuine love, and consequently, withhold their real passion to avoid the painful yet poignant sadness that love, like all things, is ephemeral. The problems facing Jessica Jones and similar existential superheroes are not unique to those with powers. As MacDonald (2019) states, "Watching larger than life characters removed from our own contexts allegorically shoulder our pressing political and existential questions opens a space for us to make sense of as well as negotiate and resist our everyday worlds" (p. 19). In reality, all people must answer these questions. Is it OK to be vulnerable to loss? Perhaps it is safer not to feel too deeply in order to avoid the pain of loss. Is it acceptable to love someone fully and completely at the risk of losing them to rejection or ultimately, death?

In addition to addressing existential issues such as free will and the self-limiting defenses people employ to avoid anxiety, the show also at times directly confronts the issue of mortality. For example, early in season two, Jessica is continuing to search for clues about the cause of the accident and what happened to her that resulted in her acquiring her powers. In her inner dialogue we hear her thoughts: "There are worse things than death. Once you're worm food it's over—painless, quiet, while the rest of us are stuck digging holes, picking up the pieces and remembering, or I don't know trying to" ("AKA Sole Survivor"). This claim that it is living that is hard and that there is nothing about death to be feared can be traced back to the first-century Roman stoic philosopher Seneca, who argued that it was illogical to fear death because it represented the total annihilation of the self. Since one would no longer be conscious post death, they could not experience pain or distress by the fact of their death, and as long as they were conscious, they had not yet died. Seneca viewed the span of individual existence as a mere blip between periods of not being. If one did not worry about where they were or what they experienced before birth, they should not worry about where they would be or what they would experience post death, because to Seneca, the answer was the same insensate oblivion. Although this argument is meant to be palliative, its logical coherence does not necessarily quell the terror of the awareness of the inevitable demise of the self. The prospect of annihilation, the possibility that one will cease to exist, and even worse that their existence will not have mattered, is not comforting but the very thing that elicits dread in self-aware being while still alive. From a TMT perspective, it is the avoidance of the dread of annihilation that motivates people to seek out heroism and to sustain the illusion of permanence and immortality through the perceived enduring impact of their heroic projects. The pursuit of immortality can oftentimes have tragic consequences, causing harm to self and others. These tragic consequences are seen in the characters of Jeri Hogarth (Carrie-Anne Moss), who is consciously facing her own death in the form of a terminal ALS diagnosis and Trish Walker, who remains unaware of how her need for symbolic immortality dominates her behavior.

Jeri Hogarth is a partner at a high-powered legal firm known for defending wealthy clients via any means necessary. Jeri is as unabashedly ambitious as she is ruthlessly unscrupulous. Jeri is at the height of her legal career, receiving a distinguished legal award at the beginning of season two but still unrepentant in her selfish pursuits. After receiving the award, she dismisses advice from her legal partners that she should settle a lawsuit filed by her former assistant with whom she was sexually involved. Jeri evokes the classic victim-blaming excuse of justifying her behavior by commenting on the provocative way in which her assistant dressed ("AKA Start at the Beginning"). It is in this same episode that she gets her terminal diagnosis. Initially, Jeri attempts to distract herself with illicit drugs and group sex with prostitutes ("AKA Freak Accident"). Then, she turns her hopes to finding a cure. When conventional medicine proves ineffective, she seeks a supernatural alternative. She comes to believe that a convict named Shane (Eden Marryshow) acquired super-healing powers as a result of the same type of secret experimentation that created Jessica's powers. Jeri pulls strings to get Shane released from prison on the condition that he heals her. Initially, Jeri thinks the healing was successful, but later discovers the whole thing was a scam orchestrated to rob her. Deprived of any hope for long-term physical survival, she turns her attention to the quest for symbolic immortality.

Jeri's legal partners are using her diagnosis to force her out of the practice. She wants Jessica to find dirt on her legal partners that she can use against them. She confides in Jessica that she has ALS and that it will kill her in the span of a few years. She says,

> It's ironic, isn't it? I've spent my whole life amassing this power and control thinking somehow it would protect me. If I believed in God I would say her sense of humor is for shit. I thought about taking the buyout, living on an island, drinking rum, making love to beautiful women. Nothing but time to contemplate my future. My future is nothing but a goddamn horror show. I'm alone, I'm estranged from my family. All I have is my clients, my firm, and the respect of my colleagues. The only thing I will leave behind is my name on that door.

In the absence of any belief in religious immortality, Jeri turns to the symbolic realm by looking to careerism, accomplishments, and the legacy of her name on a law firm as something that she can leave behind. Rather than reprioritize how best to live her remaining years, Jeri doubles down on her pursuit of conventional notions of success by working with even greater immoral zealotry for legal wins at any costs. She takes on horrible clients whom she knows are guilty and dangerous such as serial killer Gregory Sallinger in hopes that the notoriety will bring in more money and clients to her firm. Jessica sees the flaws in Jeri's behavior and tries to convince her that her death-denying project is misguided. After learning that Trish's mother, Dorothy Walker (Rebecca De Mornay), an unabashedly superficial and selfish character, left part of her estate to a charity to help girls in the arts, she tells Jeri, "Dorothy had no clue that she was about to die and even she wanted to do something good before she checked out. You know you're dying, what are you doing?"

Jessica's insight into Jeri's misguided efforts to deal with her pending mortality are consistent with the wisdom of existential psychology.

Summarizing his years of experience as a psychotherapist studying how people attempt to come to terms with their mortality, Yalom argues for the futility of trying to achieve symbolic immortality by "leaving behind your image or your name" (2009, p. 83). He draws on insights from Shelley's poem "Ozymandias" to make the point that individual identity inevitably fades, regardless of the extent of one's wealth or power—even a Pharaoh will eventually be forgotten and scattered "boundless and bare" across "the lone and level sands" of obscurity. A better balm against death anxiety, suggested by Yalom, is to cultivate a sense of rippling. Rippling is the idea that each of our lives has some small effect on the lives of others around us and that those other people have impact on the lives of others, and therefore, we can conceptualize our existence as meaningful to the extent that we positively impact other people and imagine that impact spreading and perpetuating over generations. Similarly, TMT researchers have documented a Scrooge Effect (Jonas, Schimel, Greenberg, & Pyszczynski, 2002) named after the character in Dickens' *A Christmas Carol*, who after being shown in a confrontation with the Ghost of Christmases Yet to Come the fact that his death left no impact, changes from an inwardly directed life of solitude and material accumulation to an outwardly directed life of compassion and caring for others. Several TMT experiments have shown that reminders of death can increase prosocial behavior such as giving to charity (Vail et al., 2012).

Jeri never learns these existential lessons and continues to struggle in vain to quell the threat of her imminent death through the ruthless pursuit of symbolic immortality. In addition to her quest to promote her identity through her name and legal firm, Jeri also adopts another strategy by seeking to rekindle a romance with her first love Kith Lyonne (Sarita Choudhury). Even though Kith is now married, Jeri initiates a romantic and sexual relationship; however, she soon realizes that Kith and husband Peter (John Benjamin Hickey) have an open marriage and that Kith will not leave him. Jeri directs Malcolm to dig up dirt on Peter that she can use to break up their marriage. Malcolm discovers that Peter has been embezzling money from the charity set up to honor his daughter who died from cancer. The release of this information leads Peter to kill himself and causes heartache as well as legal and financial struggles for Kith and her son. Jeri's actions are motivated not by a genuine love for Kith, but by a desperate and selfish need to avoid being alone, and the misguided hope that obtaining the love of Kith will somehow provide a sense of meaning and purpose to her existence.

Becker (1973) recognized this *romantic solution* to the problem of death anxiety as one sometimes attempted as an alternative to pursuing symbolic immortality through accomplishment. He observed that for some people "the love partner becomes the divine ideal within which to fulfill one's life. All spiritual and moral needs now become focused on one individual. Spirituality, which once referred to another dimension of things, is now brought down to earth and given form in another individual human being" (p. 160). Similarly, Firestone (1993) labeled addictive couple bonds as a commonly deployed defense against death anxiety. However, he noted that this defense is ultimately self-defeating because the desire for the relationship is motivated by an emotional hunger and a desperate need rather than any genuine concern, respect, or admiration for the other person.

Jeri is able to protect Kith against the lawsuits being brought against her. Further, Jeri even shows a willingness to sacrifice herself for Kith by trading places with her when she is held hostage. However, these efforts are not enough to give her the happy ending she desires. Kith is thankful for Jeri's help and willingness to sacrifice herself but is not interested in a continued romantic relationship with Jeri. She sees too clearly all the dangers still posed by Jeri's years of involvement in shady activities. Kith tells Jeri, "I know you don't want to die alone, but you're going to." Jeri's personal growth comes too late, and her dogged pursuit of salvation through careerism and emotional hunger for merger with another are revealed as tragic folly.

The character arc of Trish Walker offers a parallel but distinctive cautionary tale of terror management defenses gone wrong. In contrast to Jeri, Trish does not have a terminal illness, but her quest for fame and her need for heroism are clearly driven by terror management defenses. Trish was a child celebrity on the now transnationally syndicated television show *It's Patsy.* After a series of well-publicized struggles with drug addiction and several failed musical and acting efforts, Trish now finds herself as the host of a radio talk show program called *Trish Talk*.

Trish is increasingly frustrated with the banality of her vapid talk show and longs to make a more heroic contribution to the world. As her attempts to help uncover the secrets of Jessica's past by investigating IGA (the clandestine entity they view as responsible for the experiments on Jessica after her accident that led to her powers) are increasingly thwarted, Trish's frustration boils over into an on-air tirade ("AKA Shark in the Bathtub, Monster in the Bed"). Trish grows disgusted by her guests' misplaced outrage over the dangers of gluten. Trish uses the opportunity to express her anger over what she views as her own complicity in misdirecting society's attention towards pseudo problems in order to avoid confronting more threatening social ills and the frightening realities of our shared existential predicament. She launches into the following impromptu rant:

Trish Walker (Rachael Taylor) on the set of her call-in radio program *Trish Talk* in the Netflix series *Jessica Jones* (2015–2019, photo credit: David Gies-brecht/ Netflix).

> You clearly care about gluten very deeply but here's the thing—it doesn't mat-ter. Diet, hair volume, space-saving packing tips—none of it matters, when there's war, sex trafficking, elusive companies conducting illegal human research, on kids no less. I could go on. No, no, I will go on—racism, global warming, child pornography, murder, poverty, true human suffering that too many people refuse to look at. Denial is the warm bed that no one wants to get out of and *Trish Talk* is the comforter on that bed. I keep you complacent. I keep your eyes down, but you know what? This show is bullshit. I've been spouting bullshit. Wake up, people; face the truth. Bad shit happens every day and every single goddamn person has the power to do something about it. So, do something, I'm going to start with throwing off the covers and getting the hell off this show. I quit.

Trish's reaction illustrates what Heidegger (1927/2008) labeled as a conflict between guilt and anxiety. While one could avoid existential anx-iety by inauthentic living, as if personal existence was not finite, the safety of the everyday mode of existence brings with it a sense of guilt for not living authentically and fully, with a passion and urgency derived from the truthful recognition of the limited scope of one's days. Likewise, Rank (1941) described this as the tension between the fear of life, which caused people to shrink back from a full engagement with their existence, and the fear of death, which was a consequence of embracing the reality of finitude and zestfully pursuing one's autonomous goals. Similarly, Firestone (1993) articulated preoccupation with pseudo problems as a specific pattern of defense people use to avoid death anxiety. By focusing on daily hassles and elevating them to the level of all consuming emergencies, people avoid confronting difficult existential issues by filling their thoughts with more manageable trivialities. Firestone suggests, people "prefer to occupy their minds with melodrama and pseudo problems while shutting off feelings for real issues in their lives. When preoccupied with these concerns they are tortured by real life situations, yet seem immune to death anxiety" (p. 508). Getting worked up over a perceived slight by a coworker, the sloppiness of a neighbor's yard, the lack of sufficient acknowledgment by friends of one's social media posts, the unforeseen frustrations of a home renovation project gone awry, or the dangers of gluten are all means of distraction from the existential predicament of finding one's self thrown into a perilous and transient existence.

Trish attempts to find a more meaningful way to use her media talents but fails a screen test for the serious and hard-hitting journalistic cable outlet ZCN. Subsequently, the only job she can land is on a cable shopping network. Trish is disgusted by the vapid consumerist worldview that she is forced to promote in her job hawking cardigans on *Trish Style*. Trish sees as flawed the stereotypical notion that women can find meaning in their appearance and consumerism by shopping. However, by setting out to become a super-powered vigilante, she embraces an equally flawed quest for meaning in the stereotypically male system promoting physical dominance as a means to restore simplistic notions of justice.

In season two, Trish finds Dr. Karl Malus (Callum Keith Rennie), the scientist whose experimental treatments saved Jessica and her mother, Alisa Jones, from the injuries caused by their car accident but also gave them super-strength, and convinces him to continue his experiments on her. The procedure initially seems to have failed and almost kills Trish, but in season three, we learn that while Trish does not have strength like Jessica, she does have powers. She can see in the dark, has cat-like reflexes and agility, enhanced speed and fighting skills, and can jump from extreme heights and always land on her feet.

In her analysis of the show, Bastien (2018) suggests that Trish's desire for powers stems from her history of abuse. As a child, Trish was physically and emotionally abused by her mother and sexually abused by movie producer Max Tatum (James McCaffrey). She has felt powerless and now wants to feel safe in a world where she has been frequently victimized. Trish envies Jessica's power perhaps because she believes that having powers of her own would make her less vulnerable to future abuses and empower her to prevent the abuse of others. This is clearly at least one of the factors motivating Trish. When Dr. Malus describes the severe risks to Trish and asks if she is having second thoughts, she replies, "Have you ever felt powerless." When he responds that "everyone has," she retorts, "Not everyone had an abusive mother and a super-powered sister" ("AKA Three Lives and Counting"). In season three, Trish tells Jeri, "It doesn't matter how powerful I am, I'll never forget what it's like to feel helpless" ("AKA Everything"). Similarly, when Trish tells Sallinger that killing him will not be murder but justice, he accuses her of lying to herself and suggests that she does what she does because it makes her feel powerful ("AKA Hellcat"). Trish's desire for power is partially a response to her past victimization, but it also stems from a more universal existential motive to overcome the banality of life and feel like one is having a meaningful impact on the world.

In addition to the desire to overcome these feelings of helplessness, Trish is also driven by the need for recognition and the desire to feel that she is making a special contribution to the world. Trish's fear of being ordinary is revealed in season two when she confronts the producer Max Tatum, who years ago sexually abused her when she was auditioning for a part in one of his movies ("AKA Freak Accident"). Max is a major contributor to the hospital system, and Trish is trying to get him to use his influence with the hospital to help her obtain medical records she hopes will shed light on her investigation into the secret experimentation on Jessica that led to her powers. She threatens to go public with his abuse unless he helps her obtain the records. After hearing her demands, Max responds, "You know what you are, you're a B list radio personality who has to resort to dirty threats to stay relevant." He dismisses her ultimatum, saying, "It won't make any difference. You'll still be exactly what you always feared you'd be—utterly goddamn ordinary." In season three, after obtaining her powers and teaming up with Jessica for furtive crime-fighting-adventures at night, while keeping her *Trish Style* day job as a cover, Trish is not satisfied because no one knows about her heroics. She asks Jessica, "Are you still a hero if nobody thinks you are?" Jessica replies, "Like I give a shit what other people think." Trish apparently does care what other people think. Unable to be happy with helping anonymously and perhaps still craving the attention she had as a star, Trish sends a tip to the media and allows herself to be photographed in her vigilante costume doing super-powered acrobatics. She wants people to know that her super-powered alter-ego is out there.

After Sallinger tortures and murders Dorothy Walker, Trish becomes set on vengeance and as the brutality of her vigilantism increases to lethal levels, she increasingly comes into conflict with Jessica. In flashbacks, we see Trish's audition for the show that made her a child star. She tells her mom that she got the part of the best friend, not the lead. Her mom replies, "You weren't born to be a best friend. A best friend is a sidekick. It's nothing." The relevance here is to show Trish's desire for super-heroism and that she now feels the need to go on her own rather than be constrained as Jessica's sidekick ("AKA Hellcat").

Ouellette (2019) compares Trish Walker to Daenerys Targaryen from *Game of Thrones* in that both characters have some admirable traits and start out with good intentions but become increasingly blind to their moral failings with delusions of grandeur and visions of themselves as uniquely capable of carrying out the extreme measures required to purge evil from the world. Trish's solo vigilante efforts start out well-meaning, but the body count rises concomitant with her self-righteous convictions. The death of her first victim, corrupt police officer Carl Nussbaumer (Larry Mitchell), was accidental. To protect Erik from the charging Nussbaumer, Trish kicks him from behind, and he hits his head on a metal beam and dies ("AKA Hellcat"). Her second victim, arsonist Jace Montero (Chaske Spencer), is a crime of passion. In trying to coerce a confession out of Montero, Trish gets carried away in her anger and ends up beating him to death ("AKA Hellcat"). Her third murder is premeditated. Even though Jessica has gotten a confession out of Gregory Sallinger for Dorothy's murder, and he is now in prison awaiting trial with more than enough evidence to convict him, this does not satisfy Trish's sense of vengeance. Trish attacks the chained Sallinger while he is being taken to court and pummels him to death in an elevator ("AKA A Lotta Worms").

Jessica realizes that Trish has crossed a line and must be stopped. When Trish refuses to turn herself in and attempts to flee the country, the stage is set for a showdown in the series finale ("AKA Everything"). Trish is hiding in a coffin waiting to be transported to Thailand by a group of paramilitary smugglers when Jessica thwarts her escape. When she realizes she is about to be discovered, Trish breaks out of the coffin and initiates a physical confrontation with Jessica. The intended symbolism here is the death of the relationship between Trish and Jessica and the death of the person Jessica loved who has now been lost to the new vigilante persona. However, from a TMT perspective, the visual imagery of death fits nicely with the narrative arc of Trish's behavior as driven by her death-denying quest for heroism. It is not much of a fight as Trish is clearly no match for Jessica, but the sequence does serve the purpose of showing that Trish is so desperate to continue her mission that she is willing to use lethal force— even against Jessica. Trish leaps in the air with a knife and makes a thrust that would have been fatal, but Jessica absorbs the blow with her hand and effortlessly slams Trish to the ground with one arm with the knife still impaled through her other hand. In the next scene, Trish is in a police interviewing room listening incredulously as Detective Costa reads the list of charges against her: murder, aggravated assault, and the attempted murder of Jessica. As the list of charges is read, a pained expression goes over Trish's face and she says out loud with a sense of dawning awareness, "I'm the bad guy." Only in that moment does she finally realize the extent of her descent into evil.

In addition to the universal existential issues raised so provocatively in the series, *Jessica Jones* also addresses social issues related to gender that are at the forefront of cultural conversations. As a counterpoint to *The Punisher's* apologetics for male violence, *Jessica Jones* presents a narrative of female empowerment and gives expression to concerns over issues of sexual abuse, discomfort over ways in which consent is blurred through coercion, and a growing cultural outrage over the longstanding traditions of sexist mistreatment of women as seen in the #MeToo and #TimesUp movements as well as the pink hat women's marches.

Nussbaum (2015a) suggests that the show taps into audience discomfort over challenging notions of sexual consent and abuse and "seethes with modern ironies, as if culled from a freshmen handbook aimed at preventing sexual assault." Because Kilgrave used mind control rather than physical force, there is an ambiguity about consent and the possible responsibility of victims. Kilgrave's mind control is symbolically like a date rape drug. Nussbaum goes on to note that Kilgrave's power to make Jessica sexually submissive to his will is eerily similar to other popular, but potentially problematic, cultural narratives about heterosexual relationships, such as ancient vampires seducing adolescent human girls in supernatural romances like *Twilight* or of the supposed female fantasy to be dominated by a powerful man presented in *Fifty Shades of Grey.*

Sims (2015) claimed that a lead female character like Jessica Jones was desperately needed in the male-dominated Marvel universe and that she was both "its most flawed" and "most fascinating" hero. Similarly, Deggans (2018) asserted that Jessica Jones is "one of the most complicated and challenging female heroes on television." Head of original series at Netflix Allie Gross stated that *Jessica Jones* was not reactionary but prescient in addressing gender issues (Wattercutter, 2018). However, executive producer Melissa Rosenberg acknowledged that season two's focus on Jessica's rage was a way for the writers to vent their own anger over Donald Trump's defeat of Hillary Clinton in the 2016 presidential election (Deggans, 2018).

Jessica Jones represents a double feminist victory in that it not only challenges patriarchal social standards limiting the expression of anger exclusively to men but also avoids the benevolently sexist tendency to depict female anger as infallibly righteous and morally justified. Gilbert

(2018) noted that the women in *Jessica Jones* are portrayed as morally complicated and "just as likely as men to be distorted by greed, ambition, pride, and power." In spite of these advances, there are critics who see room for improvement. Bastein (2018) faults the series for reducing womanhood merely to rage in response to victimization and for a lack of attention to intersectionality. She suggests that the show depicts an array of white women who have the privilege to acquire and wield power for themselves but do not use that power to address systemic change in systems of oppression.

MacDonald (2019) situates *Jessica Jones'* merger of the superhero and film noir motifs in historical and contemporary context. MacDonald suggests that just as the film noir of the 1940s and 1950s resisted the optimism prevalent in media at the time by giving expression to post–World War II cultural concerns, so too does *Jessica Jones* not only give expression to anger at patriarchy and misogyny but also resists expectations that contemporary feminism focuses on optimistic messages of female success within the existing system rather than expressions of anger and calls to reshape that system. MacDonald views Kilgrave as an allegorical embodiment of the current social ills of toxic masculinity, rape culture, male privilege, and entitlement. She further sees Jessica's decision to try to stop Kilgrave from hurting others instead of simply fleeing to keep herself safe as symbolic of the difficulty women face in deciding whether to speak out against patriarchy and misogyny because of the tendency to be blamed for somehow creating the problem they are merely pointing out. The emotional struggles Jessica faces, not only from her original victimization by Kilgrave but also from her repeated failed attempts to stop him that yield further aversive consequences to herself and those around her, symbolize the difficulty that women face when they criticize, challenge, or resist the status quo. Jessica eschews traditional stereotypical notions of femininity in her dress and her personality. While a slave to Kilgrave's mind-control powers, he forced her to conform to his notions of female beauty, making her wear pastel-colored dresses and extensive make-up—a look she would never adopt of her own free will, choosing for most of the series her uniform of ripped blue jeans and a black leather jacket. She also rejects gendered expectations that women be polite and deferential in interactions with men. MacDonald notes that one of the most telling ways in which Jessica evidences resistance against patriarchal expectations is in her ongoing resistance to Kilgrave's instance that she constantly smile. Kilgrave coerces Jessica into sending him a picture of her every day, a concession she makes in order to get Kilgrave to leave Malcolm alone. While agreeing to send the pictures, she refuses to concede to his demand that she smile in the pictures. The tendency for men to encourage women to smile is a frequent tactic used to attempt to enforce male dominance and relegate women to presenting themselves in ways that are pleasing to men. Jessica also clearly and forcefully holds Kilgrave accountable for his rape of her. She makes clear to him in forceful and unambiguous terms that he raped her and does not vacillate in response to his attempts to blame her or mitigate his culpability. In these ways, *Jessica Jones* offers viewers a needed role model who has the courage to fight back against rape culture, misogyny, and patriarchy, but also offers an honest depiction of the challenges and difficulties inherent in such fights.

This theme of pointing out not only the dangers of male privilege but also of the difficulties faced by women who expose and resist it, is continued in Jessica's fight against season three's villain Gregory Sallinger. Mancuso (2019) makes this point nicely by accurately describing Sallinger as "basically an internet troll, a man with an inflated sense of ego and rage built from the fact that he's painfully ordinary." Similarly, Virtue (2019) points out that Salinger's only powers are "seething white male privilege and a determination to tear down powerful women." The clearest illustration of this occurs in episode seven ("AKA The Double Half-Wappinger"). Sallinger casts himself as the victim of Jessica's misplaced super-powered vigilantism. He tells the press, "Perhaps I'm an easy target, single white male and she's this feminist vindicator … they're taking back the night or something. I've worked hard for every advantage I've gotten. Powered people, they feel entitled, they feel superior. They refer to themselves as heroes." Here Sallinger becomes a trope for White male privilege and the tendency towards hostile sexism and blaming women who refuse to conform to traditional and submissive gender roles as the source of societal ills.

As a series, *Jessica Jones* is commendable for its efforts to raise challenging existential and social issues. This is especially difficult to do given the insight from TMT, that existential anxiety often promotes preferences for epistemic certainty in the form of tradition and stereotypes. For example, Hoyt, Simon, and Reid (2009) demonstrated that reminders of death strengthened traditional gender biases leading men to show a greater preference for a male over a female political candidate. Similarly, Schimel et al. (1999) found that mortality primes intensified gender stereotypes, leading men and women to generate more explanation for behaviors that violated than those that conformed to gender expectations and increasing liking for job candidates that conformed to gender stereotypes (e.g., a male candidate interested in a reporting job covering sports and a female candidate interested in a reporting job covering fashion). Despite the desire for cognitive rigidity potentially raised by the stimulation of existential anxiety, *Jessica Jones* challenges stereotypes and subverts traditional gender biases in the superhero genre.

Jessica Jones was ahead of its time having a lead female character in 2015 and preceded the trend of female lead superheroes in films such as *Wonder Women* (2017) and *Captain Marvel* (2019). Rautiainen (2017) highlights that, "as a protagonist, Jessica is quite exceptional among female Marvel heroes" (p. 71) in that she is the main protagonist who drives the story and around whom all the other characters revolve. Rautiainen does note that contrary to the physique that would be expected to give credibility to her super strength, Jessica's appearance conforms to traditional male preferences for female beauty in the "slim but curvy" body type. Perhaps this reflects the assumption that an overtly muscular female character would be seen as too threatening or intimidating to male viewers. Importantly, despite her attractiveness, Jessica is not portrayed in excessive or gratuitously sexualized ways, and there are no close-ups or body pans that facilitate the sexual objectification of the male gaze. Gilbert (2018) claims the show uses "its superhero not for spectacle, but to convey something deeper about the world." Similarly, MacDonald (2019) argues that Jessica Jones offers viewers not only a needed role model who has the courage to fight back against rape culture, misogyny, and patriarchy, but with honest depictions of the challenges and difficulties inherent in such fights, but also one who gives viewers a chance to "think symbolically and in imaginative ways about what we desire to see differently in the world" (p. 19).

Jessica Jones raises challenging questions about existence and society but refuses to offer easy or comforting answers, thereby placing it more in line with the film noir genre than the superhero genre. Several commentators have suggested that this may be a reason why the Marvel experiment on Netflix lacked the sustained success of its film counterparts. The Marvel Universe on Netflix contains 13 seasons of TV across six series in just over four years—three seasons of *Daredevil* (2015–2018), three seasons of *Jessica Jones* (2015–2019), two seasons of *Luke Cage* (2016–2018), two seasons of *Iron Fist (2017–2018),* a one-season miniseries mashup of the four heroes *The Defenders* (2017), and then two seasons of a spin-off from *Daredevil, The Punisher (2017–2019).* The Marvel inspired content on Netflix came to an end with the third season of *Jessica Jones.* Virtue (2019) noted that while the cinematic Marvel heroes were succeeding in both their cosmic battles for the fate of the universe and with continuing box office success, their television counterparts could overcome smaller scale villains but "ultimately could not prevail over corporate synergy." Li (2019) pointed out that while the decision to cancel all the Marvel shows on Netflix is complicated, one factor was likely the launch of the Disney+ streaming service; because Disney owns the rights to the Marvel universe, Netflix may have decided not to compete with Disney in that arena. Mancuso (2019) suggested that the third season offers an appropriate ending to *Jessica Jones* and to the entire Marvel universe on Netflix because of its lack of grandiosity. She claimed that the focus of these series is on the unseemly side of humanity and not on saving the universe from cosmic destruction, which is the focus of the large screen entries in the Marvel universe (e.g., *Avengers: End Game* in 2019) and consequently "as an ending, not only to a series but an entire universe, *Jessica Jones* season three feels right in its low-keyness." In contrast to the cosmic heroism of movie superheroes who likely quell existential anxiety through hopes of transcendence and buttressing viewers' cultural defense systems by affirming the fairness of the world, *Jessica Jones* offers a more troubling but realistic picture, in which there are social and existential struggles worth engaging despite the pain and difficulty inherent in confronting them.

7

Moral and Existential Dilemmas and the Quest for Death Transcendence in the FX Television Series *Sons of Anarchy*

The television series *Sons of Anarchy* (*SOA*), which aired for seven seasons on the FX network (2008–2014), depicts a frenetic, gritty, and brutal world inhabited by rival motorcycle clubs, drug cartels, gangsters, and myriad law enforcement agencies, in which viewers encounter ambiguous and morally complex characters that they love to hate and hate to love. The show was very popular, with the penultimate season averaging approximately five million viewers, making it the third most watched drama on basic cable at that time (Bibel, 2013). The final season had even higher total viewership and became the most watched season of any series on the FX network (Patten, 2014).

SOA presents the gunrunning and other illegal exploits of the Sons of Anarchy Motorcycle Club Redwood Original (SAMCRO) based in the fictional California town of Charming. The main protagonist Jax Teller (Charlie Hunnam) struggles to reconcile his devotion to the club with his moral qualms about its increasing violence and instability. This struggle grows over the course of the series as Jax learns about the horrible secrets of the club's past and as his new roles as father and husband place increasingly conflicting demands on his loyalties.

Jax's deceased father John Teller (Nicholas Guest) was a founding member and the original president of the club. Jax's mother Gemma (Katey Sagal) is now married to current club president Clay Morrow (Ron Perlman). Clay and Gemma were culpable in the death of John Teller to ensure the club's continued involvement in the gunrunning trade, a fact unknown to Jax. Clay is committed to keeping his past secrets in order to maintain his position as club president, which he uses to pursue his own greedy objectives.

Jax has discovered a manuscript written by his father and is start-ing to share his father's disillusionment with the club. Jax wants to find a new, less violent and more sustainable direction for the club. Gemma is an overly involved and manipulative mother, who works to keep the secrets of the past from Jax but also to ensure his continued involvement in the club and his future position as club president.

This show has sometimes been dubbed "Hamlet in black leather" (Sheffield, 2012), and the similarities to and influences of Shakespeare's tragedy on *SOA* have been well documented (Corn, 2013; Withers, 2010) and acknowledged by the show's creator Kurt Sutter (Sepinwall, 2008). However, Sloboda (2012) noted that *SOA* is not committed to being merely a modern re-envisioning of *Hamlet* and therefore is not constrained by the original text. She writes, "*Hamlet* flavors *Sons of Anarchy* without defining it," because "the show is a self-aware composite, partially but not entirely dependent upon earlier material that it simultaneously builds upon and interrogates" (p. 88). Although the influence of *Hamlet* yields many oedi-pal themes in *SOA* that are ripe for Freudian analysis, such an analysis has already been offered (Zanin, 2013). Further, there are additional elements of the show that can be examined through theoretical perspectives other than psychoanalysis and without reference to *Hamlet*.

Two of the show's central elements that will be the focus of this chap-ter are (1) vivid reminders of mortality through graphic portrayals of vio-lent death and frequent depiction of death iconography in the symbols of SAMCRO and (2) complex and ambiguous portrayals of morality in terms of difficult ethical decisions as well as fluctuating displays of vice and vir-tue. This chapter offers an analysis of the central elements of mortality and morality present in *SOA* through the lenses of TMT and Moral Founda-tions Theory (MFT; Haidt, 2012), which conceptualizes moral dilemmas as the result of the conflicting responses produced by a set of distinct moral senses.

Mortality in SOA

Viewers of *SOA* are constantly reminded of human mortality, given the extremely violent nature of the show. Of the shows on basic cable between 2012 and 2013, *SOA* was ranked the fourth most violent with 176 acts of violence depicted on screen (Parents Television Council, 2013). Mortality is made salient not just by the show's violence but also by the pervasive death imagery that decorates the club's buildings and the mem-bers' clothing and bodies. As Elsby (2013) notes, "The reaper is the defin-ing symbol of the Sons of Anarchy Motorcycle Club. Whether in tattoo

From left, Bobby Munson (Mark Boone Junior), Jax Teller (Charlie Hunnam), and Chibs Telford (Tommy Flanagan) at the table bearing the grim reaper insignia of SAMCRO, conducting club business in sessions they call "church" in the FX television series *Sons of Anarchy* (2008–2014, photo credit: FX).

form or emblazoned on a cut or hoodie, it identifies its bearer as someone closely allied with death, as someone who both shows courage in the face of death and, in warranted circumstances, is prepared to mete it out" (Section 4, para. 1). The prominence of death in the show can be illuminated through the application of a theory that gives awareness of mortality prominence as a motivating force in human psychology.

The death-denying dynamics laid out in TMT can be seen in the motives of SAMCRO. Although the central protagonists of the show sometimes refer to themselves as the "reaper crew" and don a grim reaper insignia, their violent behavior is motivated by a symbolic flight from, rather than identification with, death. The original vision of SAMCRO founders was to break free of the stifling entanglements of traditional society to live off the social grid free to embrace the open road. Corn (2013) noted the importance of this desire for freedom, stating, "The Sons of Anarchy pursue an ideal of not being commanded or controlled" (Section 2, para. 6). He goes on to suggest that this desire for freedom resonates with viewers, claiming that "part of their attraction to us as viewers is that they embody a freedom that middle-class Americans have traded away for the comforts of physical security and social responsibility" (Section 2, para. 6).

From the TMT perspective, the urge for freedom is a response to our embodied nature and to the biological limits that impose the inevitability of death. Ironically, a common response to this existential anxiety is to give up some of our autonomy for the reduced anxiety that comes from immersion in larger social structures that are stronger and more enduring than the individual. Although SAMCRO has rejected the mainstream American cultural worldview and its traditional political and religious institutions, they have replaced it with an alternative cultural system replete with its own religious (the inner sanctum of the club house where official business is conducted is called church) and political (club officers wear patches to signify their status) structures and symbols. SAMCRO's pursuit of freedom is elusive because the need to protect the club from external and internal threats becomes an all-consuming task that constrains personal goals and conflicts with personal morals. As John Teller observed, "On the fringe, blood and bullets are the rule of law and, if you're a man of convictions, violence is inevitable" ("Seeds"). The members of SAMCRO are engaged in the death-denying defenses described in TMT. They have created a countercultural organization, but they are still seeking to merge their identity into a larger entity and are willing to kill and die to protect this symbolic identity.

TMT explains that because avoiding existential terror motivates people to construct symbolic extensions of their identity that will transcend their corporeal limitations, threats to these symbols are met with the same type of violent reactions as threats to physical life and limb. TMT research has shown that reminders of death increase aggression against those who express different political attitudes (McGregor et al., 1998), evidenced by increased support among American university students for extreme military action including civilian casualties and the use of chemical and nuclear weapons in the war on terror, and increased support among Iranian university students for martyrdom attacks (Pyszczynski et al., 2006).

These same violent defenses of the symbols of cultural identity are observed in the fictional world of *SOA*. For example, in the episode "Patch Over" from season one, upon exiting a convenience store, Jax finds a MC wannabe sitting on his bike posing for pictures. For Jax, his bike is not just a mode of transportation but a symbol of his identity. Consequently, the poser gets his face smashed in with a helmet for his disrespect. An even more violent punishment is enacted on an excommunicated member who is desecrating the integrity of SAMCRO's insignia and reputation by continuing to display the club tattoo. In the episode "Giving Back" from season one, we meet a former member of SAMCRO named Kyle Hobart (Brian Van Holt) who was kicked out of the club because his cowardice resulted in the imprisonment of another member. We learn in the backstory that Kyle was driving the getaway car on an arson mission with

Opie Winston (Ryan Hurst), when he got scared and drove off, prematurely leaving Opie to get arrested. The episode takes place years after this event, with Opie out of prison. Kyle has been given permission to attend a community function sponsored by the club so that he can hear his son's band play. However, Kyle foolishly uses the opportunity to try to ingratiate himself back in with the club and to pitch them a money-making scheme. When SAMCRO discovers Kyle still has his club tattoo, they chain him to a garage lift, douse him in alcohol, and use a blowtorch to burn off the tattoo along with most of the flesh on his back.

Not only will people use violence against others to protect the symbols and institutions in which their social identity is vested, but they are also willing to die for them. For example, one TMT study found that reminders of death increased British participants' expressed willingness to die for their country (Routledge & Arndt, 2008). It may seem ironic that people are willing to sacrifice their physical existence to defend their symbolic identities, because the motive for the construction of these symbolic identities was to help attenuate anxiety about the vulnerability of the corporeal self to decay and death. However, if the goal is immortality, it makes sense that the symbolic aspects of identity would be privileged over the corporeal aspects to the extent that they are perceived as more enduring.

A prominent example of such self-sacrifice in *SOA* occurs in the episode "Na Triobloidi" from season two when SAMCRO prospect Kip "Half-Sack" Epps (Johnny Lewis) is stabbed to death attempting to protect Jax's infant son Abel from Cameron Hayes (Jamie McShane), a member of the real IRA who blames the MC for the death of his son Edmond (Callard Harris). Half-Sack is posthumously inducted into the club as symbolized by the placement of a full member cut on his coffin. Similarly, in season five ("Laying Pipe"), Opie volunteers to be the payment of a blood debt the club owes to drug kingpin Damon Pope (Harold Perrineau). In vengeance for the death of his daughter, Pope has used his connections to get some members of SAMCRO arrested. Pope informs Jax that one person from the club will be killed in prison and Jax must decide who it will be. The corrupt guards have staged a fight in solitary confinement in order to implement Pope's wishes. With knowledge of the dilemma his best friend Jax faces, Opie takes action by attacking one of the guards to ensure that he will be selected as the sacrifice. Opie is thrust into a locked room where he faces four other combatants who beat him to death with a lead pipe.

Members of SAMCRO are not only willing to sacrifice themselves to save the lives of their fellow members but also to preserve the future of the more abstract concept of the club. For example, in season five, Otto Delaney (Kurt Sutter) bites off his own tongue so he will be unable to testify against the MC ("J'ai Obtenu Cette"). At an even more abstract level, Jax has been known to risk his life over his cut (the symbol of his club membership). When Jax, Opie, and Bobby Munson (Mark Boone Junior) are captured by a rival motorcycle club (the Mayans), Mayan president Marcus Alvarez (Emilio Rivera) tells them to send Clay a message that the truce between their two clubs is over. In an attempt to make his point, Marcus orders his men to take the Sons' cuts. When Jax tells him "that ain't gonna happen," Marcus points a pistol at Jax's head and says, "You will lay it at my feet." Jax calmly responds, "Pull the trigger, man. That's the only way this leather is coming off my back." Being a member of SAMCRO is so important to Jax's sense of identity, and his cut is such an important symbol of that identity, that Jax is willing to die to protect it ("Potlatch").

Of course, the most obvious example of self-sacrifice for symbolic immortality occurs in the series finale ("Papa's Goods") with Jax's suicide—a sacrifice, loaded with Christian religious symbolism, he makes in order to preserve the legacy of his MC. In large part due to the actions and decisions of Jax, SAMCRO is in dire straits facing existential threats on several fronts. Knowing his own survival and the survival of the MC are mutually exclusive, Jax executes some of the club's most dangerous enemies in order to ensure the continued existence of SAMCRO but knows he must also offer himself as a sacrifice. Jax's death will reestablish a sense of peace among the various MCs and end the cycle of retributive violence begun by Jax in his search for revenge over the death of his wife Tara (Maggie Siff). Jax chooses to take his own life because the club had already voted that he must meet Mr. Mayhem (be executed) and Jax wants to save his brothers the pain of having to kill him. He hops on his motorcycle and without a helmet leads dozens of police cars on an extended chase. Finally, he sees his opportunity in an oncoming truck. He steers directly into the path of the truck and raises both arms in semblance of crucifixion. The truck driver, realizing impact is imminent, lets out a surprised expletive, "Jesus," making sure viewers don't miss the intended symbolism. Jax's blood flows to the side of the road where a crow is eating bread, symbolizing the Eucharist in that the body and blood given for SAMCOR by their *savior* will afford them new life. Gravett (2017) comments on the Christian imagery of sacrifice in *SOA*, noting,

> Sutter makes his case for Jax as the "Adam" transformed, or the Christ figure. Much as the political execution of Jesus via crucifixion paradoxically becomes for early Christians the new standard for freedom from a life of sin and defeating the inevitability of death (Rom 7:21–8:11, for example), Jax's sacrificial death will remove the virtual certainty of SAMCRO's demise and create the possibility of new life for his MC family [p. 200].

Jax Teller (Charlie Hunnam) with arms raised in semblance of crucifixion moments before he sacrifices himself for the club in the series finale of the FX television series *Sons of Anarchy* **(2008–2014, photo credit: FX).**

While Jax is presented as a Christ-figure, it is symbolic not literal immortality that he offers. Sensing that his death is imminent, Jax attempts to find some sense of heroism that will give meaning to his existence so that his death will not be in vain but will contribute to the continued well-being of the entity into which he has invested his identity. The events of the finale epitomize the theme of the entire series in that members of the MC must be willing to kill and die for the club.

The extreme violence SAMCRO requires of members in the protection of their physical lives, their club, their reputation, and their symbolic identity creates a sense of moral turmoil, especially for Jax. He is frequently depicted sulking alone on rooftops or in cemeteries reading about his father's discontent or journaling about his own feelings of disillusionment, confusion, and self-loathing brought on by the violence and mayhem he feels compelled to enact or condone. We share Jax's moral confusion because the complexities of the characters and the overwhelming power of the situations in which they find themselves yield an intense ambivalence, in which viewers simultaneously feel revulsion and admiration.

Morality in SOA

Eberl (2013) asserted that "part of the show's appeal stems from recognizing the members of SAMCRO as kindred spirits who exemplify—albeit to dramatic extremes—the mixture of virtue and vice found in every human being's moral character" (Section 2, para. 1). Eberl offered an analysis of *SOA* through an Aristotelian perspective on ethics, in which people are neither inherently good nor evil but have the capacity for both. Morality is explained from this perspective as a matter of degree, as virtue represents feeling or acting in the appropriate way for a situation, whereas vice represents too little or too much of a feeling or action in a given situation. Although this perspective has utility, the moral complexities encountered in *SOA* might be further informed by the application of a modern theory of morality that conceptualizes right and wrong not as the mere excess or absence of a single moral dimension but as a complex interaction among competing moral dimensions.

Moral Foundations Theory (MFT; Haidt, 2012; Graham et al., 2013) asserts that moral reactions are the product of six distinct moral foundations. These moral foundations are labeled using a dimensional approach with the favorable pole listed before an unfavorable pole. These dimensions are care/harm, fairness/cheating, authority/subversion, liberty/oppression, sanctity/degradation, and loyalty/betrayal.

The care/harm foundation focuses on whether we inflict pain and suffering on others or attempt to relieve their distress and discomfort. Dr. Tara Knowles exemplifies the care end of this dimension as she tends to the sick and injured in her occupation as a physician. However, Tara is also capable of harming others, as when she punches hospital administrator Margaret Murphy (McNally Sagal) in the face and threatens to kill her if an ethics complaint is not dropped ("The Culling"). Moral violations of the care/harm foundation are perceived when we encounter the suffering of others. For example, this foundation drives our moral reaction when Lyla Winston (Winter Ave Zoli) shows up at *Diosa* burned, beaten, and scared due to an Iranian torture porn operation ("Straw"). A strong violation of the care dimension occurs when Clay and Bobby check in on their ammunition suppliers at the Wahewa Indian reservation and discover Chief Charlie Horse (Randolph Mantooth) enacting an ancient form of tribal punishment on a man who is buried up to his chest and dying slowly from the hundreds of flesh-eating ants covering his head ("Dorylus"). Moral reactions to the care/harm foundation are particularly strong when injury is inflicted upon the weak and defenseless, such as when a drug dealer sells crank to Jax's pregnant ex-wife Wendy Case (Drea de Matteo), resulting in their son Abel being born prematurely with uncertain chances of survival ("Pilot").

The fairness/cheating foundation focuses on the rule of reciprocity in social exchange. This foundation informs decisions about who is trustworthy and a good partner for cooperative efforts. People who have demonstrated a history of fairness are good candidates for future dealings, whereas those who have demonstrated a history of cheating are not. While the fairness/cheating foundation might typically inform decisions about cooperation, people in Charming typically have to deal with SAMCRO out of necessity or fear rather than out of trust. As club president, Clay has a history of cheating. For example, he has an agreement to provide protection for Sheriff Wayne Unser's (Dayton Callie) trucking business. Clay takes money from Unser with the understanding that the club will protect a shipment of electronics from potential hijackers. Instead, SAMCRO hijacks the shipments as a way of extorting Unser to stay on in his capacity as Sheriff, so he can continue to turn a blind eye toward the MC's illegal activities ("Seeds").

Jax initially tries to operate more fairly in his time as MC President. Although he must frequently be dishonest and manipulative in his dealings with others, he tries to be true to the intent if not the letter of his agreements. Take for instance the quandary in which Jax finds himself in season six. Jax wants to get SAMCRO out of the gun business, but the IRA will not allow this unless a suitable substitute is found for their gun distribution needs. Jax makes a deal with the IRA to break Clay out of prison so that he can organize a new network for the gun running. Jax has also made a deal with District Attorney Tyne Patterson (CCH Pounder). Patterson has been under a lot of pressure to find the source of a KG-9 gun used in a highly publicized school shooting, and SAMCRO is her prime target. To protect the club, Jax tells Patterson he will lead her to the guns and to Galen O'Shay (Timothy V. Murphy) of the IRA as the source of the guns. To complicate matters even further, Jax has promised the IRA gun business to organized crime boss August Marks (Billy Brown) as appeasement of Marks' vendetta against club member Tig Trager (Kim Coates). Jax cannot possibly honor all three of these agreements and has been dishonest by entering into three competing agreements simultaneously. He does, however, deliver a solution that protects the interests of all three parties. Jax kills Clay and Galen to gratify his own personal need for vengeance. He convinces IRA representative Connor Malone (Scott Anderson) to make the IRA believe that Clay and Galen double crossed them and had to be killed in self-defense. Consequently, the IRA will use August Marks to run their guns. This satisfies Jax's agreement with both the IRA and Marks. As for Patterson, Jax leaves a shipment of KG-9s at the scene where Clay and Galen were killed, giving her the perfect scapegoat for the school shooting case. The fact that Jax has dealt fairly if not completely honestly is attested to by Sheriff Eli Roosevelt (Rockmond Dunbar) who exclaims to Patterson, "Teller kept his promise. He gave you Galen and the guns" ("Aon Rud Persanta").

The authority/subversion foundation deals with showing the proper respect, deference, and obedience to authority figures as well as social institutions and traditions. Despite the word anarchy in the club's name, there is a clear power hierarchy, and deference to authority is expected. The traditions of SAMCRO are patriarchal and misogynistic, and women are expected to know their place. On the way to Nevada to patch over an allied club called the Devil's Tribe, Jax rescues a naïve young woman named Susie (Mircea Monroe) from her abusive boyfriend and invites her to ride with him. Later at the Devil's Tribe's club house, Susie tries to get Jax's attention while he is talking business. The Tribe's president Jury White (Michael Shamus Wiles) attempts to subtly correct her by saying, "Girls, these beers are warm." She fails to pick up on the hint and responds that they just pulled the beers from the keg. At this point a more experienced woman named Cherry (Taryn Manning) intervenes and shepherds Susie away. Cherry tries to explain to Susie the importance of female submission to male authority. She says, "Never throw these guys any lip." Susie defends herself, saying, "I didn't. I just asked them a question." "That's even worse," Cherry replies ("Patch Over"). The authority foundation is seen not just in cross-gender relations but also in expectations for male deference to higher status club members. For example, when club prospect Half-Sack makes the off-color comment that Gemma gives him a "MILF chubby," Clay takes this statement about his wife as a lack of proper respect for his authority as club president ("Patch Over").

The liberty/oppression foundation deals with concerns over excessive limitations or infringements on personal freedoms and with abusive or tyrannical behavior from leaders. The Sons of Anarchy view the government and its representatives as oppressive in their restrictions of individual freedoms. Clay calls ATF agent June Stahl (Ally Walker) a "fascist pig" and claims that her desire to bring down the club is fueled by a resentment of their liberty. He tells Stahl, "You hate the fact that we get the same rights and freedoms as you do" ("Sleep of Babies"). Whereas government agencies are viewed as oppressive by their very nature, SAMCRO does recognize the necessity of deferring individual interests to legitimate authority within its own internal power structure. Authority figures can, however, lose their legitimacy if they misuse their power. In the early seasons, Jax's subversion of Clay's authority creates tension in the club. However, in the latter seasons, Clay's true tyrannical nature is gradually exposed to the club. It becomes clear that Clay has put his own interests ahead of the club and has abused his power as president. Once Clay is revealed as an oppressive bully, the club has no moral problem with removing him as president, kicking him out of the club, and eventually killing him.

The sanctity/degradation foundation deals with protecting the purity of the physical or political body from perceived physical or spiritual contamination and defilement. This foundation can be triggered by any perceived defilement such as lack of hygiene or violation of food taboos but is especially salient in perceptions of sexual immorality. At first glance SAMCRO's lax sexual mores might suggest they are immune to feeling disturbed by violations of the sanctity foundation. They have wild orgies at patch over parties and when club members get out of prison. They are involved in pornography through their partnership with Luann Delaney (Dendrie Taylor) and her *Cara Cara* studio and are involved in prostitution through their partnership with Nero Padilla (Jimmy Smits) and his *Diosa* escort service. They show acceptance, and in Tig's case attraction, to the transsexual Venus Van Dam (Walton Goggins). However, they have little patience for Chucky Marstein's (Michael Ornstein) compulsory public masturbation and are disgusted and outraged when they learn about the history of Venus' mother Alice (Adrienne Barbeau) and her involvement in child abuse, incest, and child pornography ("Sweet and Vaded").

The loyalty/betrayal foundation deals with devotion to our social identity and the preferential treatment of in-group members. Mahon (2013) argued that loyalty involving self-sacrifice for the good of the group and a willingness to support fellow club members even at extreme costs is the most highly valued trait among members of SAMCRO. Betrayal of the club, particularly if it involves cooperation with law enforcement, is the most egregious violation of the Sons' moral code. There are several instances over the course of the show where the loyalty of club members, such as Filip "Chibs" Telford (Tommy Flanagan), Otto, Opie, and even Jax, are called into question because they are erroneously suspected of being rats, are pretending to be disloyal to the club, or are flirting with the idea of making a deal with law enforcement only to change their minds in the end. One of the most dramatic examples of betrayal occurs when Juan Carlos "Juice" Ortiz (Theo Rossi) makes a deal with Sheriff Eli Roosevelt and Assistant U.S. Attorney Lincoln Potter (Ray McKinnon) to help them acquire evidence of SAMCRO's involvement with running drugs for the Mexican Cartel. Juice steals a brick of cocaine from a cartel shipment to give to Roosevelt and Potter as evidence. However, when he is caught by fellow club member Eric Miles (Frank Potter), Juice kills Miles and frames him as the thief ("With an X").

According to MFT, any particular moral reaction can be the product of a single foundation or of any of the possible interactions among the various foundations. In addition, different moral reactions between individuals or within the same individual across time or situation can be conceptualized as a difference in the relative weighting of the six foundations. Further, moral ambiguity may arise when different foundations yield competing moral responses to the same situation. Tamborini (2011) suggested that differences in viewers' reactions to television programs could be explained by individual differences in the relative importance ascribed to each of the six moral foundations. He predicted that people would prefer to watch programming that validated their own moral sensibilities. By extension, it seems possible that viewers will feel moral ambiguity in response to fictional situations in which moral foundations that they value are put into conflict.

We might condemn a character like Tig when he describes his enjoyment of necrophilia ("Old Bones"), because we perceive it as a violation of the sanctity/degradation foundation. Yet, we might applaud Tig's generosity when he gives $12,000 to his daughter Dawn (Rachel Miner) in the episode "With an X" and his compassion when he rescues an injured pit-bull from a dog-fighting ring ("J'ai Obtenu Cette"), because we perceive these behaviors as upholding the care/harm foundation.

Even if a particular situation seemingly involves only one moral dimension, such as loyalty, it is not always easy to do the right thing because loyalty to different entities may call for contradictory actions. For example, Jax feels competing loyalties to his family and the club. As he tells Piney Winston (William Lucking), "I'm trying to find some kind of balance, Piney. The right thing for my family, the club. Every time I think maybe I'm heading in the right direction, I end up in a place I never even knew could feel this bad" ("So").

The problem is made more complicated by the fact that different moral foundations may yield conflicting perceptions of right action. In *SOA*, loyalty frequently comes into conflict with other important virtues. For example, Tara Knowles wants to stay loyal to Jax and to the Club (the loyalty/betrayal virtue), but she also has to make sure her children, Thomas and Abel, are safe (the care/harm virtue). When Gemma drives stoned and has a wreck with the boys in the car, when Wayne Unser (a frequent babysitter) is attacked by neo–Nazis at the garage, but most pointedly when the IRA blow up the clubhouse and all inside barely escape with their lives, it becomes clear to Tara that her boys are not safe as long as they have ties to the MC. Another example of conflicting moral foundations occurs in season four, when Jax faces a moral conflict between his need for justice and his loyalty to the club. In Jax's mind, killing Clay Morrow is required to reestablish justice since Clay killed his father John Teller and his best friend's father Piney Winston, and tried to have his wife Tara killed. However, Jax needs Clay alive to help get the club out of dealing guns, which he views as an essential step for SAMCRO's long-term survival. In this case loyalty trumps justice, as Jax delays his personal vengeance against Clay in the best interest of the club ("To Be Act 2").

The Reciprocal Relationship Between Mortality and Morality

Thus far, mortality and morality have been discussed as separate elements in *SOA*, however, there is a reciprocal influence of these central elements that warrants analysis. Morality influences mortality and mortality influences morality. Morality influences mortality because moral transgressions are used to justify violence and make it more palatable to the audience. Presenting the victim of violence as morally flawed or deserving of his/her fate makes it easier for viewers to override their natural aversion to the suffering of others. Violence is acceptable and perhaps even admirable when it serves as a mechanism for satisfying justice. For example, Clay's murder of a carnival clown by castration and exsanguination is difficult to watch particularly because of the victim's pleading and groveling ("Fun Town"). The fact that earlier in the episode the clown had raped and beaten a girl makes his gruesome fate less disturbing. In season six, when defending the club's decision to kill Clay, Tara offers Nero an account of all of Clay's many transgressions and concludes with the verdict that "he should have been dead a long time ago" ("Aon Rud Persanta"). In the same episode, when trying to explain to IRA representative Connor Malone why he had to murder both Clay and Connor's former boss Galen O'Shay, Jax says, "They earned that blood." The characters' moral justifications for their violent behavior mirror the audiences' need to justify morally their consumption of fictional violence, as viewers try to convince themselves that the blood they witnessed was earned.

Inversely, mortality influences morality because the existential anxiety experienced by the audience in response to violent and graphic reminders of death creates a yearning for the increased meaning and safety established by perceived moral certainty. According to TMT (Pyszczynski et al., 1997), when we feel vulnerable to existential anxiety, we deploy a set of psychological defenses aimed at bolstering our perception that we are making a valuable contribution to a heroic project defined as meaningful and enduring through our immersion in a specific cultural worldview. Pyszczynski (2016) suggested that morality was an important aspect of cultural worldview that helped assuage existential anxiety by offering hope for literal and symbolic immortality. Morality is linked to notions of literal immortality because most religions describe fate in the afterlife as predicated upon living up to the demanding ethical standards and rules of proper conduct articulated in religious texts and teachings. Similarly, morality is linked to symbolic immortality because living up to culturally defined standards of conduct is an essential criterion for being considered worthy of posthumous honor, and these standards often involve morality.

Many of the heroic figures deemed worthy of post-death veneration are presented as paragons of one or more culturally valued moral virtues.

Evidence for the terror management function of morality comes from previous research showing that reminders of death increase people's concerns about adhering to moral standards as shown by harsher punishments for those who act immorally by breaking the law or transgressing the rules of proper conduct (Florian & Mikulincer, 1997). In addition to influencing reactions towards other people's moral behavior, contemplating mortality has also been documented to increase people's personal intentions to act morally, in the form of increased generosity towards charities (Jonas, Schimel, Greenberg, & Pyszczynski, 2002), more interest in helping others when prosocial norms were salient (Jonas et al., 2008), and reduced likelihood of cheating when the moral virtue of honesty was salient (Schindler et al., 2019).

To the extent that morality is a component of death-denying cultural worldviews, reminders of death may enhance aversive reactions to moral transgression, but, as seen in MFT, notions of morality are multidimensional rather than monolithic. Kesiber and Pyszczynski (2011) asserted that many of the virtues enumerated by MFT serve defensive functions in helping to ameliorate death anxiety. For example, concerns about fairness are essential in maintaining psychological defenses against death anxiety because, if the righteous are not rewarded, how can people hope to attain literal or symbolic immortality by adhering to culturally prescribed standards of conduct? Similarly, issues of in-group loyalty are often motivated by desire for symbolic immortality by advancing or protecting the social/political entity that will serve as a death-transcending legacy. In the same way, moral questions of sanctity are also motivated by existential defense as they involve protecting notions of transcendence by denying or disguising human activity (e.g., sex and eating) that might otherwise serve as a reminder of human corporeality and creatureliness. Violations of the care/harm foundation evoke personal vulnerability to premature death and highlight the fragility of the human condition. Given the role that all the moral virtues described in MFT play in symbolic defenses against existential anxiety, it seems reasonable to assume that reminders of death would intensify distress in response to the violation of any single virtue and would also exacerbate moral confusion resulting from the tensions between competing virtues.

Consequently, imagery of violence and death leaves people craving the security of a worldview in which the universe conforms to the principles of human justice and morality. However, this craving may be particularly intense when the violence is unexpected and unjustified. For example, following Opie's death, Jax seems to have lost his already tenuous grasp on morality. He is disoriented without Opie to serve as his moral compass. In a journal entry to his sons Abel and Thomas, Jax writes, "Since my best friend was killed, I've lost my center. 'Op' was always my pull back to true north" ("A Mother's Work").

Although confrontations with mortality can be disorienting because they challenge the assumptions of cultural worldview, these confrontations can also be opportunities for personal growth and the reassessment of values and goals. Fosl (2013) noted how this personal growth in response to mortality is illustrated in *SOA*. Using the terminology of German philosopher Martin Heidegger, Fosl pointed out how the tragedy of Opie's death led Jax to a greater authenticity, in which he strived to find his own path as club president. Adopting the conventional values of others may help one deny the reality of mortality, but it does so at the cost of living inauthentically. Jax's moral struggles stem in part from his excessive reliance on other people and the many conflicting sources of information he receives (e.g., his father's manuscript, Clay, Piney, Opie, Tara, Gemma) about the nature of his future and the future of SAMCRO. When Opie's death deprives him of his habitual moral crutch and reminds him of his own mortality, Jax must become the author of his own sense of meaning for his life and the club.

Jax appears to be cognizant of the relationship between morality and mortality. He seemingly endorses an existential worldview, in which each person must be the author of his/her own sense of morality and shows an awareness of how the transience of life in a violent world intensifies this necessity. In season five, he writes to his sons, "Every day is a new box, boys. You open it and take a look at what's inside. You're the one who determines if it's a gift or a coffin" ("Orca Shrugged").

The same dynamics between mortality and morality that illuminate the behavior of characters in the series may also operate in the minds of its viewers. The violence inherent in the show's content might increase death-related thoughts that in turn might increase concerns about justice. For viewers of *SOA*, the struggle with moral ambivalence may be intensified by the salience of mortality induced by the show's violence. The violent acts committed by characters on the show can elicit feelings of both revulsion and admiration in viewers. The same quest for death transcendence that drives the characters to extreme behaviors drives viewers to seek moral justifications for those behaviors, but the moral ambiguity presented in *SOA* often frustrates the easy satisfaction of this drive. While critics might condemn the graphic violence in *SOA* as low-brow pandering to a base need for sensation seeking, it is possible that the awareness of mortality engendered by the use of violence is an important contributor to the show's moral complexity. Rather than viewing the violence in *SOA* as gratuitous, it might be possible to view it as a means of vicarious confrontation with mortality that could potentially influence some viewers to examine their own moral assumptions. The lives of SAMCRO members have an urgency given the precarious nature of existence in their dangerous world. Their actions have a gravity given the life and death consequences of their decisions. So too is the meaning of our lives and actions enhanced by an awareness of finitude. If Jax Teller can come to see life as a box, the meaning of which must be determined by each individual, then maybe we can as well.

Certainly, there are many motives for watching television, and people likely watch *SOA* for different reasons. Some viewers may simply enjoy the spectacle, as the titillation of violence and taboo violation offers vicarious arousal of the fight or flight system. Other regular viewers might not technically speaking enjoy the show at all but rather their reaction might be labeled appreciation. In an attempt to explain why people would intentionally subject themselves to sad or tragic media, Oliver and Bartsch (2011) made a distinction between the reactions of enjoyment and appreciation. They defined enjoyment of media as an immediate, positive, hedonic or affective reaction that occurs automatically without reflection or rational thought. Enjoyment differs from appreciation, which is a positive response to media that emerges from the slow and effortful contemplation of meaning. The experience of appreciation is rewarding to viewers in that it offers them an enhanced sense of meaning through some new moral insight.

Tamborini (2011) applied MFT to the distinction between enjoyment and appreciation of media. He argued that when media content upholds a moral foundation valued by a viewer, that viewer experiences an immediate, intuitive feeling of enjoyment. In contrast, when media content pits competing valued moral foundations against each other, such as when the same behavior that violates one or more foundation upholds other foundations, then the viewer feels a sense of dissonance that motivates him/her to think about and attempt to resolve his/her discordant reactions to the content. This effortful contemplation may lead the viewer to meaningful insight about his/her moral values, and this meaning would yield the feeling of appreciation.

The addition of insights from TMT can enhance this analysis. If, as posited in TMT, reminders of death increase the need for moral confidence, then the experience of both enjoyment and appreciation might be more intense in response to violent media content that makes death thoughts salient. *SOA* offers viewers opportunities for both enjoyment and appreciation, the experience of which may be exacerbated by the violence in the show. In the final episode of Season three, when Jax's successfully executes a plan that allows SAMCRO to eliminate two of their most ruthless adversaries, ATF agent June Stahl and IRA representative Jimmy O'Phelan (Titus Welliver), the club's reaction is one of elation ("NS"). The audience's reaction to this event is likely one of enjoyment because there is an intuitive sense that justice has been served by the death of these two villains, who in their own separate selfish pursuits have directly and indirectly been responsible for numerous deaths. In contrast, when Gemma kills Tara at the end of season six ("A Mother's Work"), the audience's reaction is likely shock, horror, or outrage but definitely not enjoyment. So, after such trauma why did millions of viewers eagerly tune back in for the final season? Perhaps, because the emotional turmoil generated in response to the series' most tragic events spurred rumination about the characters' decisions and motives and challenged viewers to contemplate how their own moral values would hold up under similar circumstances. Alternatively, perhaps viewers kept watching in anticipation of the opportunity for a visceral reward at viewing Jax's assumed forthcoming revenge. A reward they eventually get with Jax's killing of Gemma in the series' penultimate episode ("Red Rose").

Although the violent deaths in *SOA* serve as an intense mortality salience prime that could potentially stimulate viewers to grapple with existential and moral issues in autonomous and deliberative ways, it could also have a more deleterious effect. For many viewers of the series, the violence may reinforce reflexive acceptance of established and conventional cultural worldviews that while offering the comfort of epistemic certainty perpetuate messages of misogyny and toxic masculinity as well as offering apologetics for extreme measures to protect one's in-group and heroic projects. For example, Cox and DeCarvalho (2016) criticize *SOA* for presenting "a contemporary form of white, hegemonic masculinity that is dependent on dominance, violence, and the oppression of Others" (p. 822) and for a misogynistic tone, in which "women are treated as disposable, undeserving of respect—and they exist for the pleasure and gratification of men" (pp. 831–832). *SOA* transmits a clear and consistent message that violence is the *sine qua non* of masculinity and that in order to be a real man one must be willing to use violence as a means of protecting self, family, and reputation. However, the tragic consequences of this violence are also often portrayed. As Cox and DeCarvalho suggest, "The violence on-screen often creates more problems, and sometimes, members are not successful in their mission at all. These latter outcomes call into question the club's view of violence as the answer and question the very foundation of violent masculinity" (p. 826).

Thus, it is hard to condemn unequivocally *SOA* for its glorification and promotion of violence or to praise it for its depictions of the limitations and tragic consequences of violence. The series resists easy categorization in that it has elements of both insidious and instructive types of screen violence. In many ways the depictions of violence in *SOA* fit the pattern Desilet (2014) labels as antagonal in that they encourage viewers to experience joyous emotional reactions when violent death is presented as righteously deserved and as reestablishing a sense of justice. Simultaneously however, *SOA* also meets the criteria for what Pizzato (2005) labels as complex, tragic violence in that characters are presented in morally ambiguous ways and are shown grappling with the moral turmoil generated by decisions about when and how to use violence. The untimely deaths of Jax as well as his father, mother, stepfather, and wife can all be presented as evidence of a warning against the tragic consequences of immersion in a culture of violence. Such an interpretation is complicated by the glorification of Jax as a martyr whose violence is necessary for the salvation of the collective good. Whether engagement with *SOA* serves as a catalyst for existential growth or merely buttresses automatic defenses is likely variable across different viewers and even over time within the same viewers. Viewers might do well then to stay mindful of varying reactions to the series and to interrogate the motives potentially underlying those reactions.

8

Giving Voice
to the Unmentionable

The Appeal of Transcending Mortality
and Corporeality in the NBC
Television Series Hannibal

Dr. Hannibal Lecter, AKA Hannibal the Cannibal, is one of the most intriguing characters of the modern horror/psychological thriller genre and has maintained a persistent ability to terrify and mesmerize fans across decades in multiple mediums. The character appears in four novels by Thomas Harris: *Red Dragon* (1981), *The Silence of The Lambs* (1988), *Hannibal* (1999), *Hannibal Rising* (2006) and in five feature films: *Manhunter* (1986), *The Silence of the Lambs* (1991), *Hannibal* (2001), *Red Dragon* (2002), and *Hannibal Rising* (2007). Shaw (2015) asserted, "Hannibal Lecter is one of the most fascinating evil geniuses in the history of the moving image" (p. 199). Similarly, Oleson (2005) claimed, "We love Lecter. He is the paragon of serial killers. There is something about this character that resonates in the popular imagination" (p. 189). Further, Wong (2015) suggests that Hannibal is "everything we fear and everything we want to be" (p. 7). In a survey that asked people to name their favorite movie monster, Hannibal was one of the most commonly mentioned, with reasons given for his appeal being that he is morally unconstrained, pure evil, and shows us the dark side of human nature (Fischoff, Dimopoulos, Nguyen, & Gordon, 2005). Perhaps, as Westfall (2015) observed, one of the reasons for our continued fascination with Hannibal is his ability to raise challenging questions about human nature and to serve as "the mirror in which we see our darkest desires reflected" (p. xix).

The most recent instantiation of the character is in the television series *Hannibal* created by Bryan Fuller, which aired on NBC for three seasons (2013–2015). In an interview, Bryan Fuller describes himself as a Fannibal (a self-generated moniker for the active online community of avid Hannibal fans) and describes the show as a work of fan fiction (Prudom, 2015). *Hannibal* might be labeled as a preboot in that it presents the initial interactions of characters from Red Dragon that precede the events depicted in the novel but is set in a contemporary time period, and while it preserves some of the iconic features of the characters, it takes liberties in the presentation of those characters and storylines that deviate from the book and movie material, while still paying homage and alluding to aspects of that material. *Hannibal* can be considered quality television based on its characteristics of "high production values, a reliance on complex ongoing storylines, an overwhelmingly positive reception by television critics" (Brinker, 2015, p. 303). The series received critical acclaim despite low ratings and controversy. For example, Nussbaum (2015) wrote that Hannibal feels like "a macabre masterpiece" and asserted that the show has an uncanny ability to fascinate and unnerve by artfully depicting carnality in a way that make "us crave something we thought we'd find disgusting." Further, Cain (2015) suggested that *Hannibal* "must go into the hallowed halls of great TV before its time." Likewise, Uhlich (2015) noted that despite the low ratings, regular viewers praised Hannibal as "one of the most inventive and distinctive series ever made."

The series lends itself readily to a TMT analysis because it raises the problems of mortality and corporeality but also offers palliative defenses against these concerns. People have limbs amputated, are impaled onto animal antlers, are disemboweled, have their organs surgically removed while still conscious, and of course are eaten. Sometimes, victims are even forced to eat parts of their own bodies. Such macabre displays not only serve as graphic reminders of human frailty and vulnerability to premature demise but also serve to illustrate our corporeality and the reality that we are biological organisms—assemblages of blood and guts. In the words of science fiction writer Terry Bisson (1991), all humans are "made out of meat."

Although potentially disturbing in the graphic nature of the gore displayed, death in *Hannibal* is often mitigated through a defensive lens; either the surreal artistic display of the killers' ritualistic presentations, or the sterilized scientific space of the FBI's forensic crime lab, or the aesthetic work of the titular gourmet showcasing his culinary skills over refined classical music accompaniment. There is an aesthetic anesthetization against terror by presenting death in ways that are unrealistic, dreamlike, captivating, beautiful, and imbued with cultural significance through the human enterprises of art and science. So, while the show does raise the existential threats of mortality and corporeality, it also offers viewers some relief by bolstering psychological defense against these threats. The most powerful form of death denial comes perhaps surprisingly in the character

Hannibal Lecter (Mads Mikkelsen) preparing to enjoy one of his signature gourmet dishes on the NBC series *Hannibal* (2013–2015, photo credit: Brooke Palmer/ NBC).

of Hannibal himself. His ability to outthink the machinations of others, avoid numerous attempts on his own life, and inflict death on others reinforces proximal TMT defenses by strengthening the belief that death can be avoided. Further, his intellectual, artistic, musical, and culinary prowess reinforce distal TMT defenses by elevating human cultural activity above the plane of animal existence and offering hopes for transcendence through symbolic immortality.

These terror management properties of the Hannibal character, while present in all versions, are most salient in Mads Mikkelsen's depiction on the television series. Hannibal's power, poise, and self-control are highlighted in the series in such a way as to make the character seem superhuman and ethereal. In addition, the series gives extensive attention to Hannibal's artistic and aesthete nature. I agree with Cain's (2015) assessment that Mads Mikkelsen's portrayal of Lecter is superior to Anthony Hopkins' film portrayals and that Mikkelsen's version is both more unsettling and captivating because Hannibal's "proclivity for cannibalism starts becoming the least disturbing thing about him" yet at the same time he is "persuasive, charismatic and *likeable*." The enhanced focus on the power and aestheticism of Hannibal in the television series are essential factors that increase the ability of the character to assuage viewer's death anxiety, thereby magnifying his allure and appeal.

The first way in which Hannibal bolsters terror management defenses is in his resilience. Hannibal is exceedingly difficult to kill, as time and time again he demonstrates an uncanny and almost preternatural ability to survive. He survives attacks from fellow serial killers Tobias Budge (Demore Barnes) in season one ("Fromage") and from Francis Dolarhyde the Great Red Dragon (Richard Armitage), who in season three tries to kill him in order to absorb his powers ("The Wrath of the Lamb"). He survives an assassination attempt by hospital orderly Matthew Brown (Jonathan Tucker) in season two ("Mukozuke") and twice escapes the lethal plans of Mason Verger (Gary Oldman), who tries to feed him to flesh-eating pigs in season two ("Tome-Wan") and who tries to personally eat him in season three ("Digestivo"). He survives being beaten and thrown out a window by Jack Crawford (Laurence Fishburne) in season three ("Contorno"). Hannibal even seems to have potentially survived the surprise series ending, in which Will Graham (Hugh Dancy) tackles him off a precipice, and they plunge in each other's embrace to the waters of the Atlantic hundreds of feet below ("The Wrath of the Lamb"). This initially seems like the last scene of the series but then after the credits we get a shot of Dr. Du Maurier (Gillian Anderson) dressed in a stunning evening gown and seated alone at a lavish dinner table with three place settings where she is about to eat her own exquisitely prepared leg. When asked in an interview about how he interprets the ambiguous ending of the series, Hugh Dancy thinks Hannibal survived the fall since "it's hard to believe that Hannibal would really die. Because he's not exactly mortal" (Bacle, 2015). This air of immortality facilitates viewers' proximal defenses against death anxiety by bolstering the comforting delusion that death can be avoided via intelligence, cunning, wit, and vigilance.

Hannibal Lecter offers viewers a sense of mastery over death, not only in his ability to survive attempts on his own life, but also in his ability to take the lives of others. Shaw (2003) advanced a general theory of the appeal of horror, in which the audience experiences both their utter helplessness against the forces of the world through their identification with the victims of horror violence and a sense of power and mastery over these forces through their identification with the perpetrator of horror violence. Shaw describes the pleasure derived from consuming horror as stemming from "the vicarious feeling of power that horror films provide their audiences" (p. 11). From this perspective, fictional depictions of killing both trigger our usually suppressed anxieties about personal vulnerability to death and offer a defense against this anxiety by allowing us to identify with the killer rather than the victim.

Hannibal frequently suggests that the appeal of killing is derived from how powerful it makes the killer feel. His argument for power often makes reference to God, whom Hannibal views as the ultimate killer and describes as "beyond measure in wanton malice" ("Ko No Mono"). Hannibal collects stories about church collapses and describes one in Sicily in which 65 grandmothers were killed during a special mass. He suggests to Will that if God is up there that he is certainly a killer ("Shiizakana"). For Hannibal, the supreme form of human activity is the striving to emulate God's power in the form of killing. Perhaps the most compelling example of this argument is found in a conversation between Hannibal and Will that occurs in season one ("Amuse-Bouche") and focuses on Will's reaction to killing the serial murderer Garret Jacob Hobbs (Vladimir Jon Cubrt).

> HANNIBAL: Killing must feel good to God, too. He does it all the time, and are we not made in his image?
> WILL: Depends on who you ask.
> HANNIBAL: God's terrific. He dropped a church roof on 34 of his worshipers last Wednesday night in Texas as they sang a hymn.
> WILL: Did God feel good about that?
> HANNIBAL: He felt powerful.

Power is commonly posited as the main aspect of Hannibal's nature that drives his appeal. For example, Shaw (2015) argued that what motivates audiences to identify and empathize with Hannibal is his god-like power and his embodiment of the Nietzschean Overman in his ability to exert his will to power and be the autonomous creator of the meaning of his existence. Shaw suggests that Hannibal is always "in complete control of himself, his environment, and all of the inferior individuals around him" (p. 199). No matter how tenuous his position seems, no matter how precarious the circumstances, no matter how astronomically the odds seem stacked against him, Hannibal Lecter is always one step ahead and always in control. As Will Graham explains to Jack Crawford, Hannibal does not ever worry and knowing he is in danger will not rattle him any more than killing does ("Dolce"). Similarly, Dr. Du Maurier tells Jack, "If you think you are about to catch Hannibal it's because he wants you to think that" ("Tome-Wan").

Perhaps the appeal of this power lies in the desire for autonomy and the imagined pleasure at the relief freedom from conventional moral and social constraints might produce. Consistent with this line of thought is the fact that Hannibal is often presented as a satanic figure, and this is especially true in the NBC series. Hannibal's identity as the devil is symbolized in the numerous scenes depicting Will's dreams or subconscious imagination where Hannibal is represented as both a stag and as the Wendigo, an evil figure from Algonquin mythology with a discolored human form and animal horns. Further, Piñeiro-Otero (2016) describes how the series' classical scores are at times intentionally selected to facilitate the presentation of Hannibal as Satan. He notes,

> pieces like The Golden Calf from Gounod's Faust ("Sorbet," #1x07) associate Lecter with the devil. This association will be taken up again later when Hannibal plays Suite No 4: La D'Au-bonne. The performance and adaptation to the harpsichord of this piece by Forqueray, whose contemporaries believed he played like the devil, links Hannibal to Satan himself [p. 183].

Mads Mikkelsen may have won the part of Hannibal on the television series because of his interpretation of Lecter as a Satan-like character (Westfall, 2015). Series creator Bryan Fuller acknowledges Mikkelsen's interpretation of the character of Hannibal "as a fallen angel ... as the devil, who is enamored with man" (Stephenson, 2013). Hannibal is devil-like in his ability to show others their hidden desires and manipulate them into doing his will. Hannibal's supernatural status is implied by Dr. Du Maurier who describes him as "wearing a very well-tailored person suit ... a human veil" ("Sorbet") and hinted at by Hannibal himself when he discusses with Dr. Frederick Chilton (Raúl Esparza) selfishness as the original sin of man according to Judeo-Christian morality ("Mukozuke"). There are several instances in the series where other characters refer to Hannibal as the devil, such as when Abel Gideon (Eddie Izzard) tells Will that the Chesapeake Ripper is the devil and when Gideon jokingly says to Hannibal, "I bet you're a devil at the bridge table" ("Mukozuke").

The fact that audiences find the cannibalistic serial killer Hannibal Lecter so fascinating and captivating could be explained in part as due to the draw of his Satan-like freedom from the constraints of social and moral restrictions and by his God-like power over life and death. What is left unanswered by this perspective is why audiences find Hannibal Lecter more captivating than the myriad other killers on the show. Why do audiences find themselves wanting those other killers to get caught but rooting for Hannibal to get away?

Oleson (2005) pointed out how public reaction to actual cases of cannibalism, such as Armin Meiwes, elicit outrage and disgust, in sharp contrast to audience reactions to Hannibal's fictional cannibalistic acts. The *Hannibal* series cleverly makes reference to Meiwes in season three ("Digestivo"). When Mason Verger has captured Will and Hannibal, he taunts them by saying, "You boys remind me of that German cannibal who advertised for a friend and then ate him—and his penis—before he died. Tragedy being the penis was overcooked. Go to all that trouble to eat a friend and you overcook his penis! They ate it anyway. They had to. They committed. But they didn't enjoy it."

The series is offering a keen insight that the reason people respond more favorably to Hannibal than to Meiwes is not just because one is fictional, but it is a matter of aesthetics rather than ethics. Oleson (2005) highlighted the importance of Hannibal's cultural refinement in generating audiences' admiration, suggesting that "perhaps they forgive him because Lecter is a figure of finely developed tastes who prefers fine books and music, expensive cars, and gourmet cuisine, who abhors discourtesy, and who exhibits impeccable manners" (p. 200). Similarly, McAteer (2015) notes that whereas real life serial killers tend to have low IQs and are motivated by psychological urges that push and compel them to kill, Hannibal is extremely intelligent and kills not out of a sense of need or deprivation but out of the pursuit of artistic and aesthetic aspirations. Likewise, Holt (2015) describes Hannibal as "an aesthete, one who prizes the rewards, the pleasures, afforded by art and beauty" and posits that "such aestheticism is in fact the very key to unlocking the mystery of his character" (p. 162).

The key to understanding the reason why Hannibal's cultural refinement is essential to his allure is recognizing the psychological concerns raised by cannibalism and how culinary skills and aesthetic appreciation potentially attenuate these concerns. One of the reasons cannibalism is so offensive is because it places human beings on the same plane of materialistic biological existence as other animals. As Wong (2015) notes, "The human being served with fava beans has no greater value than the fava beans" (p. 9). The horror of Hannibal Lecter is twofold: the threat he poses as a killer elicits the awareness of death, but his cannibalism elicits disgust about human corporeality. Corporeality is ideologically offensive to human psychology because it suggests our creaturely nature and thereby threatens beliefs in nonmaterial aspects of identity and undermines hopes of transcendence by raising the unpalatable possibility that all conscious experience no matter how seemingly sublime or noble is just a byproduct of the random flow of chemicals through meaty organisms. As Hannibal himself put it, "We are orchestrations of carbon" ("Mizumono").

TMT offers insight into the importance of Hannibal's cultural refinement as an essential factor in fostering audiences' identification with him. If the allure of Hannibal is his death-transcending power, then this allure would be nullified by any perception of his creatureliness and vulnerability to death and decay that plague all biological organisms. Terror Management theorist Jamie Goldenberg (2012) argues compellingly that the denial of human similarity to other animals is essential for psychological comfort. She suggests that all of our symbolic attempts to deny our mortality are undermined by our corporeality and by physiological constraints that remind us how our animal bodies fix us firmly to the physical plane of existence that our symbol-creating minds seek to transcend. Eating, sex, and excretory functions are all necessities of our existence as biological organisms, but they can be uncomfortable challenges to our desire for immortality. The recognition that we must eat, copulate, and excrete just as any other animal gives rise to the unsettling realization that if we are just like other animals then we share their same fate to die and to rot, and this realization calls into question the enduring value and meaning of our existence. These animalistic acts are rendered less psychologically threatening by imbuing them with cultural significance. Ritual, etiquette, manners, and artfully prepared and presented food are all means of elevating eating above the mere bestial act of energy intake necessary to keep biological machinery operating.

If part of the appeal of fictional killers lies in their ability to assuage consumers' own fears of death, then it might be difficult to identify with fictional killers whose violence seems carnal or animalistic in nature. Although we may be drawn to identify with the perpetrators rather than the victims of violence as a psychological defense to avoid feelings of our own powerlessness against death, this defense is rendered less than fully effective if the perpetrators of the violence are exposed as vulnerable to death through their creatureliness. Hannibal astutely claims that "we inherited our emotions from our animal ancestors. Cruelty is a gift humanity gave itself" ("Coquilles"). Contrary to this insight, it is quite common to present fictional killing as motivated by an inability to curtail baser animalistic urges. However, it is hard to admire killers who are merely driven by a deviant, sadistic type of sexual drive or a bestial hunger. To the extent that they are portrayed as powerless to resist the urges that drive them to kill, such characters might garner our sympathy but not our admiration.

It has long been known that dehumanizing outgroups by describing them in animalistic terms as less than human makes it easier to aggress against them. Hannibal gives voice to this position, stating that the tendency to see Others as less human than ourselves is universal ("Shiizakana"). Hannibal is frequently presented as viewing the people he kills and eats in animalistic terms. For example, Will tells his class at the FBI that the Chesapeake Ripper kills in sounders of three and that he uses the term *sounder* intentionally because that is how the killer thinks of his victims—as pigs ("Sorbet"). Likewise, when Dr. Chilton expresses frustration with psychiatry, telling Hannibal that he wishes he had more interest in the common mind, Hannibal replies, "I have no interest in understanding sheep—only eating them" ("Rôti").

An interesting variant on the relationship between dehumanization and violence has emerged from TMT research suggesting that presenting aggression as an animalistic act may actually reduce the appeal of violence. In one study, Motyl et al. (2013) showed that when reminded of the similarity between people and other animals, acting aggressively (hitting a punching bag) increased the salience of death-related thoughts, making people vulnerable to death anxiety. In another study, they demonstrated that participants exposed to essays arguing for human-animal similarities acted less aggressively (hitting a punching bag with less effort and for less time) than those not exposed to such arguments. In still another study, they found that when American university students were presented with arguments that violence was animalistic, they showed a decrease in support for war. These findings suggest that because reminders of death increase people's desire to distance themselves from other animals, presenting violence as an animalistic behavior could actually be a means of reducing aggression. So, while viewing victims of violence in animalistic terms makes it easier to aggress against them, presenting the act of aggression itself in animalistic terms makes violence less appealing. Applying this line of thought to reactions to fictional killers suggests that people should be more drawn to killers whose motives and methods are framed as uniquely human compared to those who seem more bestial.

The character of Hannibal Lecter offers death transcendence on two fronts; he exerts power over death by being its instrument rather than its victim, but he also imbues his violent acts with symbolic meaning so that they are more transcendent than mere animalistic acts. Hannibal may be driven by violent impulses that he acts on with brutality, but they are not bestial because he satisfies them in controlled and artful ways. Hannibal uses his culinary and artistic skills to transform his violent urges into symbolic and death-denying statements of his power. Hannibal's artistic, musical, and culinary abilities as well as his refined taste and appreciation of art, music, and cuisine reinforce and validate the human need to perceive ourselves as superior to other animals and to elevate human activity to a transcendent and sublime plane.

An interesting inversion here is the prominence that is devoted to highlighting Hannibal's sense of smell. While keenly perceptive in all sensory modalities, smell is Hannibal's most developed and refined sense. He is able to find another serial killer by smelling the scent of corn on the corpse of one of his victims ("Sakizuke"). He smells the scent of Freddie Lounds (Lara Jean Chorostecki) on Will Graham and knows that Will has lied to him about killing Lounds and is therefore likely setting a trap for him ("Mizumono"). The irony here is that smell is typically something that is stronger and more important in non-human animals, as people tend to privilege visual information over the olfactory influences of their mammalian ancestors. Holt (2015) recognized this irony, stating that "smell of course is a primitive sense, an evolutionarily old, beastly sense, and this is retained, regardless of how sophisticated, how intellectualized it is, in Lecter's aesthetic sensibility" (p. 167). Even though the prominence of smell is a trait he shares with other non-human animals, Hannibal uses his smell to enhance his enjoyment of fine food and wine and in these gourmand activities, as with his cultural refinement in dress and art, he distinguishes himself from other animals to overcome his creatureliness.

Hannibal transcends creatureliness through his expression of artistic creativity in multiple domains. He is not only a patron of the symphony, but also musically gifted—playing and composing for the harpsichord and theremin. He is a talented artist who does intricate drawings of people and places. Through the ritual display of his victims, Hannibal elevates killing to an art form as well. For example, one of Hannibal's early murders involved posing the bodies of a couple to resemble figures from Botticelli's painting *Primavera* ("Primavera"). Another artistic display occurs when after killing a city councilman who approved an environmentally detrimental development deal that allowed for building over a nesting area for endangered songbirds, Hannibal grafted the body into a lone tree in the middle of a parking lot. He cut open the mid-section, removed all the organs, and replaced them with beautiful bouquets of colorful but poisonous flowers ("Futamono"). This work of art is meant to symbolize not only the toxicity of the victim but also the continuity of the natural world and the vitalism of life to reclaim urbanized spaces.

Food is perhaps Hannibal's greatest art form. Food features prominently in the series with footage of Hannibal cooking in almost every episode. There are websites and even cookbooks devoted to recreating the meals depicted in the show (with some ethical and legal substitutions of ingredients). The names of each episode are taken from culinary terms for gourmet courses in French, Japanese, and Italian cuisine. World-renowned chef José Andrés served as a culinary consultant to ensure the authenticity of Hannibal's status as a gourmand. The attention to the details regarding food is illustrated in the claim by Rivera (2015) that "*Hannibal* is lavish in its attentions to all things culinary" and that the preparation of food depicted in the series is better than anything you can find on actual cooking shows.

If food is his greatest art form, then cannibalism is perhaps Hannibal's most death-denying act. Hannibal's gustatory preference for human organs offers symbolic power over death in several ways, the most obvious of which relies on the patterns of sympathetic magic and the law of contagion. By ingesting the life-giving organs, the cannibal symbolically absorbs their life force. This is the symbolism of the Christian Eucharist and the ideology behind fictional vampirism—"the blood is the life." Several scholars have noted Hannibal's similarity to vampires. For example, Westfall (2015) observed that Hannibal "has a clear resonance with

One of Hannibal's artfully displayed victims from season two of the NBC series *Hannibal* (2014) in the episode "Futamono." Baltimore city councilman Sheldon Isley (uncredited actor) has had his organs removed and replaced with poisonous flowers in punishment for his history of environmentally harmful legislation (photo credit: NBC).

that cannibalistic arch-villain of old, Dracula. Like the vampire, Lecter bides his time hiding among human beings as one of the most cultured and best educated of their number, awaiting his opportunity to strike" (p. xvii). The television series makes reference to these ideas about the power of incorporation, as when Matthew Brown, during his assassination attempt on Hannibal, describes how the Iroquois used to eat their enemies to take their strength ("Mukozuke"). Hannibal explicitly voices the death-denying appeal of cannibalism, avowing that "the feast is the life. You put the life in your belly, and you live" ("Sorbet").

Another way in which Hannibal's cannibalism has death-denying properties is the fact that he tends to dine on the rude and discourteous. Hannibal tells Will that Mason Verger is discourteous, and discourtesy is unspeakably ugly. He goes on to say that whenever feasible one should always try to eat the rude ("Tome-Wan"). Breikss (2015) asserts that "Hannibal does not eat the rude only for the sake of his cannibalistic urges. He prepares these meals in his ritualistic fashion for himself and his colleagues as a way to display their superior virtue, literally consuming rudeness as the means of its physical and symbolic disposal" (p. 140). By serving the organs of the rude people he has killed as exquisite fare for lavish dinner parties, Hannibal views himself as transforming something ugly into something beautiful. Much like euphemistic language, etiquette and courtesy, especially around eating and table manners, are designed to disguise unpleasant truths about our creatureliness and our corporeality and the assurances of mortality they imply. Think for example of how we might accuse those who display an appalling lack of table graces as *being raised in a barn* or *acting like an animal*. So, by eating the rude, Hannibal is not only trying to expunge the world of rudeness but also symbolically to assert his power over corporeality. In order to justify eating non-human animals, people must imagine that they are superior beings. Similarly, by eating other people, Hannibal is asserting himself as a superior being. When Hannibal is eating Abel Gideon's leg (a dish he also persuades Gideon to consume), he rejects Gideon's label of the action as cannibalism insisting that it is only cannibalism if they are equals, and they most certainly are not equals ("Antipasto").

Zanin (2015) argued that Hannibal's sense of artistry was derived from a "detestation of the frailty of the human condition" and interpreted his murders as a symbolic attempt to repudiate and transcend that condition through a passion for creative expression; as "In death, Lecter's victims are freed—reinterpreted on the canvas of a dinner plate" (p. 189). Hannibal tells Dr. Du Maurier that he used to keep snails as food for firefly larva and that the snails were fuel for the transformation of the larva into creatures of beauty. That is how he envisions the people he kills, as simply fuel for the acts of beauty that he creates ("Contorno").

Hannibal shows great skill as a gourmet chef but also great appreciation for food with his discriminating palate. In the same way, he shows great technical and artistic skill in his murders but also high standards in his critique of the murders committed by others. Holt (2015) thinks Hannibal "would object to the trophies produced by less sophisticated killers not on moral grounds but aesthetic ones" (p. 165). There are several instances in the series where Hannibal shows appreciation for the work of other artful killers. For example, Hannibal praises the work of his former patient turned serial killer Randall Tier (Mark O'Brien), telling Randall that he "bore screams like a sculptor bears dust from the beaten stone." When Randal describes how "ragged pieces of scalp cling to his teeth trailing the tails of hair like comets," Hannibal replies with a single word—"beautiful" ("Shiizakana"). Similarly, Hannibal responds with something like reverent awe to discovering James Gray's (Patrick Garrow) human mural. Gray has been selecting victims based on their skin hue to provide the right color palette he needs for his gruesome art. He gives victims an overdose of opioids and then glues them into the mural he is creating inside a corn silo. Looking down on the silo, the bodies are arranged to create the image of a human eye. Hannibal tells James Gray, "I love your work" and speaks about it with an appreciation for the transcendence to which it aspires, saying, "The eye looks beyond this world and into the next and sees the reflection of man himself. It's a killer looking at god" ("Sakizuke"). It is not just the will to power that Hannibal appreciates in these fellow killers but the artistry of their lethal craft. One imagines that Hannibal would be thoroughly unimpressed if he were to have met real life serial killer Ed Gein, not because he would find Gein's human furniture morally repugnant but more likely he would find it brutish, boorish, and in bad taste (aesthetically not ethically). In his creation and appreciation of art in both its more mundane and macabre forms, Hannibal is making a statement of his freedom from the creaturely plane of existence, from the constraints of traditional cultural morality, and from death itself.

In addition to artistic, culinary, and cultural refinement, Hannibal's dignity and self-control even in extreme circumstances is another important ingredient in his appeal as an antidote to concerns about creatureliness. The series finale makes an intentional allusion to Sherlock Holmes, as Hannibal and Will's final plunge was inspired by the short story "The Adventure of the Final Problem," in which Sherlock Holmes and Dr. Moriarty fall over Reichenbach Falls (Doyle, 1894). However, Hannibal shares much in common not only with Moriarty but also with Holmes in his analytic ability and mental control. Hannibal does not scream in pain even when branded like a hog with the Verger brand ("Digestivo"). Even with a noose around his neck and standing on a wobbly can, he still maintains his composure and talks rationally in a calm and even voice ("Mukozuke"). David Wolpe (2003) speculated that the appeal of characters like Mr. Spock and Sherlock Holmes to adolescent fans is because of the concerns puberty raises about the unruliness and uncontrollability of the body. Spock and Holmes are almost machine-like in the ability of their disciplined minds to exert control over the distractions of the body and to subjugate or ignore corporeal impulses in the service of their logical pursuits. Extending this line of thought to the present analysis, such self-controlled characters as Holmes and Lecter ought to have appeal to fans of all ages because of their ability to assuage concerns about creatureliness.

In season three, while Hannibal is in a cell at the Baltimore Hospital for the Criminally Insane, psychiatrist and hospital administrator Dr. Alana Bloom (Caroline Dhavernas) warns him not to try anything that would hurt Will. Hannibal tells Alana that she has Will in moral dignity pants because she refuses to hold him accountable for any of his actions. She threatens Hannibal that if he attempts to manipulate Will in any harmful way, she will take away his book and his drawing; (perhaps in response to his earlier moral dignity pants joke) she also threatens to even take away his toilet ("And the Woman Clothed with the Sun"). Alan knows that what Hannibal finds most aversive is not pain or isolation but indignity. She seems to have a keen insight that transcending his animal nature is what motivates Hannibal's artistic and intellectual strivings and that the best way to punish him would be to deprive him of those outlets. Later in the season, after Hannibal has orchestrated an encounter between Will and Francis Dolarhyde and sends Dolarhyde after Will's family, Alana follows through on her threat removing not only Hannibal's books and drawings but also his toilet ("and the Beast from the Sea"). This action suggests that without a toilet Hannibal will be forced to wear not moral but literal dignity pants (possibly the pinnacle of indignity). This punishment would likely annoy Hannibal more than any other because while he does not experience guilt over questions of good or evil, he does always strive to maintain dignity. Here the series presents a keen philosophical insight as expressed by novelist Milan Kundera in *The Unbearable Lightness of Being* (1984): "Shit is a more onerous theological problem than is evil. Since God gave man freedom, we can, if need be, accept the idea that He is not responsible for man's crimes. The responsibility for shit, however, rests entirely with Him, the creator of man" (p. 266).

It is difficult to imagine Dr. Hannibal Lecter wearing adult diapers because such an indignity robs him of his awe-inspiring sense of power and control. In fact, it may be difficult or at least unpleasant for fans to imagine Hannibal having to answer the call of nature in any way, because a large part of the appeal of the character is the way he seems to have complete mastery over his body and to transcend the baser aspects of existence, either by reigning them in with remarkable self-control or by transmogrifying corporeal acts into meaningful moments of artistic expression.

Oleson (2005) states that the appeal of the character of Hannibal Lecter stems from his contradictory nature. We are cognitively drawn to the puzzle of Lecter's contradictions. He fits some of the traditional social science models of serial killers but not others. He is capable of being charming, well mannered, and culturally refined on the one hand and savage, brutal, and sadistic on the other. Oleson writes that "the fact that the character of Hannibal Lecter is something of a paradox, a riddle, may help to explain his tremendous appeal" (201). From a TMT perspective, Hannibal's paramount contradiction is the ability to simultaneously threaten psychological equanimity by raising the specters of mortality and corporeality while also offering a balm against these threats. Hannibal thus both horrifies and captivates the imagination. Like Rudolf Otto's (1923) description of the Holy, an encounter with Hannibal Lecter is a *mysterium tremendum et fascinans*.

The appeal of Hannibal's power and refinement are enhanced by the activation of concerns about mortality and corporeality. Thus, *Hannibal* is not purely palliative, but the series also presents some stark and potentially unsettling perspectives about existence. Wong (2015) claims that honesty is Hannibal's most dangerous weapon because, like philosophical critique, Hannibal can disabuse people of their psychologically comforting illusions by laying bare the inaccuracy of their assumptions about themselves and the world. Wong argues that one such truth Hannibal holds is "humans' contribution to our world is no more valuable than that of invasive weeds" and "the ability to recognize this fact is central to Dr. Lecter's outlook. It's what enables him to eat people with the same lack of concern with which the rest of us sink our teeth into cows and artichokes" (p. 9). Hannibal clearly views human existence including his own as finite and has no hopes for any type of literal immortality. He tells Will, "Every life is just a piece of music. Like music we are finite events" ("Fromage"). Similarly, Hannibal tells Dr. Du Maurier that he thinks of his earliest memory and then imagines the future moment of his death and never imagines living past that span of time except by reputation ("Savoureux"). Hannibal unnerves viewers by breaking down their comforting death-denying illusions both cognitively through the narrative of his intellectual arguments about human mortality and more viscerally through the images of his murders and cannibalism. It is when we are thus unnerved and most vulnerable to existential worries that his death-denying properties of power and cultural refinement become all the more alluring and invite us to identify with him and his symbolic mastery over death.

Our identification with Hannibal is not free from ambivalence. Oleson (2005) noted that many critics express concern about what the appeal of fictional killers like Hannibal implies about human nature. He writes, "Indeed the vernation of a cannibal killer may imply that something has gone horribly awry within our culture" (p. 189). Although we may be drawn to the power of these characters, their appeal raises some concerns about our own morality. Jones (2015) posited that Hannibal depicts the dangers of empathy because empathy requires the suspension of moral judgment, thereby opening the empathizer to losing their own moral stance by becoming lost or engrossed in the perspectives of the other. Jones goes on to suggest that "what Hannibal is doing to Will, the show is doing to us" (p. 152), implying that like Will, viewers are threatened by exposure to Hannibal's sinister worldview. Stadler (2017) does not think such fears that empathy or identification with television characters could lead to dangerous mimetic contagion are well founded, but he does suggest that the depictions of cannibalism in Hannibal is a metaphor for viewers' concerns about the potential threat of empathic merger. Hannibal interrogates the potential harm of consuming fictional violence and uses the relationship between Hannibal and Will as a means of raising troubling questions about the moral and ontological implications of what our enjoyment of the show and empathy towards its titular character mean about us and our capacity for violence.

The discomfort Will feels in response to his enjoyment of killing is parallel to the discomfort audiences might at times feel at the recognition of their enjoyment in watching fictional violence and identification with fictional killers. Perhaps the allure of fictional killing stems in parts from its ability to "give voice to the unmentionable" by allowing us to recognize our own capacity for and attraction to violence. For example, when Jack and Will find one of Tobias Budge's victims on stage at the symphony with his vocal cords exposed and turned into cello strings to be played by the killer, Jack asks Will, "Is it me or is it getting easier for you to look?" Will replies, "I tell myself it's just an intellectual exercise" ("Fromage"). Jack's question to Will is really directed at the audience as well. The show is interrogating viewers about their own complicity by being consumers of such graphic violence. With repeated exposure, is it getting easier for us to watch more extreme images. Do we attempt to allay any concerns raised by this awareness by telling ourselves that it isn't real but just an intellectual exercise we are engaging in for entertainment? A similar interrogation occurs in season three. As Hannibal and Anthony Dimmond (Tom Wisdom) walk by various implements of torture on display at the Palazzo, Dimmond says, "An exposition of atrocious torture instrument appeals to connoisseurs of the very worst in mankind." Hannibal replies, "Now that ceaseless exposure has calloused us into the lewd and vulgar, it is instructive to see what still seems wicked to us." Dimmond joins in: "what still slaps the clammy flab of our submissive consciousness hard enough to get our attention" ("Antipasto"). This is a self-referential wink to the controversy surrounding the series for pushing the boundaries of violence on network television as well as a commentary on cultural debates about the contributions of television to the culture of violence.

Later in the same episode, Hannibal clubs Dimmond over the head in front of Dr. Du Maurier. He asks her, "Are you, in this moment, observing or participating?" She chooses to be an observer but is still complicit in the murder ("Antipasto"). Again, this question is also directed at viewers and interrogates us about our own motivations and moral culpability in the violence we are consuming. The potential dangers of desensitization to violence are again alluded to when Hannibal tells Jack that when Will is at a crime scene, he doesn't just reflect, but he absorbs ("Buffet Froid"). The implication is that viewers of the series are absorbing something as well, but what exactly is it that we are absorbing? Mason Verger tells Dr. Chilton that he wants to understand Hannibal Lecter to better understand himself ("Aperitivo"). This is not just true of Mason but may also apply to many viewers of the series who are captivated by Hannibal. Likewise, in giving Margot Verger (Katharine Isabelle) advice about how to survive her brother, Will says, "Hannibal has a certain personality style that we can all learn from, in moderation of course" ("Tome-Wan"). So what can viewers potentially learn from Hannibal?

There is certainly a *memento mori* lesson of the necessity of acknowledging and embracing the awareness of our mortality as a prerequisite to appreciating existence and living with a sense of urgency, meaning, and purpose. This message is conveyed humorously when Abel Gideon initially refuses the meal Hannibal has prepared for him (Gideon's own leg), and Hannibal tells him that the real tragedy is not to die but to be wasted ("Futamono"). The same wisdom is conveyed more seriously when Hannibal tells Will that "without death we would be at a loss. It's the prospect of death that drives us to greatness" and "most of what we do, most of what we believe, is motivated by death" ("Naka-Choko"). Similarly, Hannibal tells Jack's wife Bella Crawford (Gina Torres), who is dying from lung cancer, that the fact that his life could end at any moment frees him to appreciate fully the beauty in art ("Takiawase").

While a periodic acknowledgment of the finitude of existence does help people prioritize what is important to them and what they want to accomplish in their limited time on Earth, an unabated chronic contemplation of the precariousness of existence and its inevitable end in the annihilation of the self would likely be overwhelming to the point of nihilism. As philosopher La Rochefoucauld observed, "One cannot look directly at the sun or death." How can people maintain purpose in the face of finitude and ward off the nihilism illustrated by Tolstoy's question "Is there any meaning in my life that the inevitable death awaiting me does not destroy?" The answer comes in the form of narratives provided by our personally internalized cultural worldviews and the stories we tell ourselves about why our lives matter. As Chiyo (Tao Okamoto) tells Will, "All sorrows can be borne if you put them in a story" ("Secondo"). Even the sorrow inherent in the awareness of the inevitability of death can be borne if contextualized in a cultural narrative that imbues existence with meaning and purpose.

One potential lesson to be absorbed from Hannibal is the danger inherent in our own death-denying stories. There is little possibility that watching a series like *Hannibal* will permanently undermine our culturally constructed sense of meaning. There is an equally minuscule probability that we will be influenced to experiment with serial murder or dabble in cannibalism. It is the very absurdity of such possibilities that may hinder our ability to absorb a valuable lesson. Any capacity for violence in ourselves that enjoyment of a show like *Hannibal* and fascination with a character like Hannibal might reveal is made less threatening by the assurance that because Hannibal is so aberrant, so extreme, so *Other* we do not have to worry because we can never be like him. In one sense this is true because we will never attain the power, self-reliance, aesthetic taste, or the artistic talent of Hannibal. But, in another sense we are him, and he is us. The symbiotic relationship between Will and Hannibal, their psychological merger, and the blurring of the boundaries of their identities symbolizes the way in which audiences share many of the same motives as Hannibal (even if the outlets for their expression differ drastically). Hannibal strives to be the author of his own sense of purpose in a finite life and to assert a value to his existence that transcends the physical plane of animal existence through the cultivated enjoyment of refined sensory experiences and the skillful expression of meaning through acts of artistic creativity. Any concerns about the rights of other people, their pain and suffering, even the deprivation of their lives are subservient to his own goals and therefore, he views other people as expendable in the pursuit of his quest for transcendence. A sobering but valuable insight is to realize not just as Hannibal instructs that "every human being is capable of committing acts of great cruelty" ("Su-zakana") but that these acts are often presented in the guise of heroism and motivated by a defense of culturally condoned death-denying ideologies.

After his family had narrowly escaped their encounter with the Red Dragon, Will goes to confront Hannibal about his role in orchestrating the attack. Will tells Hannibal that he is about worn out with crazy sons of bitches. Hannibal corrects him that true ugliness is found in the faces of the crowds ("And the Beast from the Sea"). Hannibal's point is well founded in that more lives are taken in the culturally sanctioned killings of warfare and executions than in the acts of serial killers deemed aberrant madness. As co-creator of TMT Jeff Greenberg put it in the documentary film *Flight from Death*, "More people have been killed in the name of God and country than all the serial murderers all the Jeffrey Dahmer types put together it's just a drop in the bucket compared to how much killing has gone on out of loyalty, patriotism, love for God and country."

In the movie *The Silence of The Lambs* (1991) Clarice Starling says to Hannibal, "You see a lot, don't you, doctor? Why don't you turn that high-powered perception at yourself, and tell us what you see, or, maybe you're afraid to." This raises the question of just how much insight renowned psychiatrist Dr. Hannibal Lecter has into his own motives. The television series addresses this issue somewhat by suggesting that Hannibal has not fully processed his childhood traumas and that there are rooms in his memory palace where it is not safe for him to go. When Will suggests that there are rooms in Hannibal's memory palace that Hannibal cannot bring himself to enter because nothing escapes from them that causes him any comfort and that screams fill some of those places, Hannibal replies that the corridors do not echo screaming because he hears music instead ("Secondo"). Hannibal acknowledges here that artistic and cultural refinement, in this case in the form of music, is the way that he deals with disturbing aspects of existence.

This same pattern of defense was evidenced in season two, when after the trauma of surviving the attempts on his life by Matthew Brown, Hannibal tells Jack that he does not want to continue working for the FBI because he cannot dwell on death anymore and must now focus on putting his energies and efforts into life-enhancing events, which he does by composing an arrangement for the harpsichord and by planning a dinner party featuring his special ingredients ("Futamono"). This clearly shows how Hannibal responds to existential threat by seeking artistic expression both in conventional forms and in the form of murder and cannibalism (activities that for him are the highest modality of artistry). Hannibal may not only avoid conscious reflection on the traumas locked in the seldom visited rooms of his memory palace, but he may also avoid conscious deliberation on how his efforts at cultural refinement and artistic expression especially in the form of murder and cannibalism are at least in part motivated by psychological defenses.

Just as Hannibal resists being the focus of his own keen perceptions, we may resist insights about what the appeal of the character and our fascination with him reveal about us. Many fans (including me) may have a reflexive aversion to reductive explanations that attempt to adequately account for Hannibal by using psychological principles. We want Hannibal to be mysterious. We resist reducing him to a simple psychological backstory. Will Graham states that the trauma Hannibal experienced surrounding the death of his sister Mischa cannot explain and quantify Hannibal and what he does ("Secondo"). Series creator Bryan Fuller shares this sentiment, saying in an interview, "I didn't want to over-explain why he became a cannibal and suggest that his nature is as a result of Nazis eating his sister, which feels like a demystification of the character" (Van Der Werff, 2015).

We do not want Hannibal to suffer from the same foibles of mundane irrationality that afflict people everywhere. While such explanations humanize him, they also demystify him and that which is mysterious is transcendent because it defies explanation by the reductive materialistic worldview of empirical scientific investigation. We want Hannibal's power and refinement to elevate him above the fray of the fragility of the human condition because affording him such status facilitates our own defenses against our own vulnerability. But this very resistance reveals the veracity of the argument that the motives for Hannibal's behavior are the same as the reasons we find him so captivating—namely the all too human desire to deny mortality and transcended corporeality. While recognizing that the appeal of a character like Hannibal Lecter is derived from our flight from death does potentially reduce the ability of fascination with such characters to dampen existential anxiety, it also makes us less vulnerable to habitual defensive responses, such as reflexive justifications of our own cultural worldviews and the potential violence they support or condone, and that is empowering in its own way.

Final Thoughts

Goldstein (1998) claimed that "for the majority of consumers of violent imagery, the violence is a means to an end, an acceptable device valued more for what it does than for what it is" (p. 213). I have presented the case that one such end is the management of death-related anxieties and that one important function of what consuming fictional violence does is that it facilitates and augments a set of terror management defenses that make concerns about personal mortality less worrisome. In contrast to the reality of death, which continues to be a taboo topic, fictional death offers people a means of gaining a sense of mastery over the fear surrounding an otherwise mysterious and uncomfortable issue. However, the fictional depictions of death in popular entertainment tend to be overwhelmingly violent rather than focusing on death as something that inevitably happens with age and deterioration. Rather than promoting an acceptance of the reality of death, fictional depictions of violent death tend to promote a denial of the inevitability of personal death, thereby contributing to the notion that death can be overcome or avoided.

One way that fictional violence encourages a denial of personal vulnerability to death is by promoting an identification with the perpetrator of the violence. By identifying with the powerful killer rather than the powerless victim, viewers can gain a vicarious sense of mastery over death. Just as the inability to imagine the cessation of consciousness gives intuitive credulity to the possibility of immortality, so too does the killer's continued presence on screen give visual confirmation to the irrational hope that death is something that happens to others and not to the self. In some instances, the characters in violent fictions attempt to identify as instruments of death to bolster their convictions that they can avoid being its victim. In these instances, the fictional world becomes a mirror reflecting viewers' own motivations. In *The Punisher*, Frank Castle prepares for battle by donning his black body armor emblazoned with the iconic skull. In *SOA*, members of SAMCRO embrace the iconography of death and come to personify death, as the image of the grim reaper is ubiquitously

171

displayed on the clubhouse, their clothing, and their bodies. Just as these characters identify with death as a source of courage for potentially lethal confrontations, viewers might identify with the fictional killers as a symbolic attempt to avoid fears of powerlessness against the inevitability of personal death.

Another way in which fictional violence perpetuates death denial is through the presentation of exceptionally resilient characters who prove impossible to kill by surviving repeated attempts on their lives against seemingly insurmountable odds. In *Hannibal*, Dr. Lecter avoids attacks on his life by FBI agents and other serial killers and even possibly a fall off a cliff. In *The Punisher*, Frank Castle consistently single-handedly defeats dozens of armed combatants at a time. He is frequently beaten, stabbed, and shot beyond the limits of human endurance, but he can never be killed. In *GoT*, great warriors like Bronn, Arya, and Brienne survive encounters against not only other human warriors but also dragons and zombies.

These fictions convey an illusory message of immortality to those who survive violent confrontations. It is only the losers of such encounters who perish; the winners endure on screen and in viewers' imaginations. Such endurance can be perceived as permanent. One of the more memorable lines from *GoT* occurs in season one when Cersei warns Ned, "When you play the game of thrones, you either win or you die" ("You Win or You Die"). While Cersei is correct that those who compete for power in a violent world run the risk of a premature death at the hands of a rival, her message seems to imply more than that. It seems to imply that when you win the game of thrones, you will not die. The reality is that regardless of whether one succeeds or fails in their attempts to gain political power, they will die. The same deep-seated need to deny mortality underlies the fact that people rarely balk at news reports that talk about how the latest medical breakthrough reduces the chance of death or how a particular vice increases the risk of death. Such statements should strike us as patently absurd because the chance of death for all living creatures remains constant at an unwavering 100 percent. In the final episode of *GoT*, Sansa is seated on her throne ruling as queen in the North, and Arya is sailing off for more adventures in parts unknown. Our experience with the characters ends there, allowing viewers to feel some sense of gratification that Arya and Sansa won out over adversity and survived numerous perils and threats. The inevitability that the journey for these characters, as with all journeys, must end in death is never displayed.

Yet another death-denying mechanism involves the depiction of characters or events that defy the scientific laws assumed to govern the physical world. Of course, such depictions are not present in all types of violent entertainment but are common in the fantasy, horror, and super-hero genres. In a show like *GoT*, the existence in its diegetic world of crea-tures, such as dragons, giants, and white walkers, that seem fantastical to viewers imply that there may be aspects about the world that exceed current scientific understanding, and if such mysteries do remain, then the empirical assumptions that insists on the inevitability of death may be limited as well. Similarly, the flaming sword of Beric Dondarrion and the magical spells of the Red Priestess Melisandre (Carice van Houten) suggest the possibility that there are ways to defy or change the assumed laws of physical causation and therefore that the reality of death presum-ably imposed by those laws is not immutable. The most death denying of such supernatural acts is, of course, the resurrection of Jon Snow, which provides viewers with visual confirmation of the possibility for literal immortality.

Bassett (2011) argued that the vampire is the paragon of death-denying fictional characters and that the appeal of vampires in movies, television, and literature stems from their ability to assuage existential anxiety by providing viewers with a more vivid means of contemplating the details of an immortal existence than typically provided in traditional religious texts.

> The majority of human cultures have speculated about some type of life after death. However, most of these religious notions of immortality seem to vio-late the rules of the physical world people encounter in their day-to-day expe-rience. Consequently, without constant consensual validation, visions of immortality may lose their anxiety-abating power, as nagging doubts persist that these visions may be merely cultural fabrications. Thinking about super-natural creatures such as vampires, even if one does not literally believe in their existence, makes it easier to entertain the idea that there may be a tran-scendent dimension to reality beyond our ordinary understanding of the material world [Bassett, 2011, pp. 17–18].

The superhero genre is another area where viewers are offered pow-erful images seemingly refuting the inevitability of death. The abilities of powered characters like Jessica Jones to drag moving buses to a halt and to jump to the tops of buildings implies that the assumed limits of the phys-ical world can be transcended. Although *Jessica Jones*, like most contem-porary depictions of superheroes, offers scientific rather than supernatural explanations for the origin of these powers, such explanations still provide symbolic validation of hopes that science and medicine can conquer the problem of death.

Perdigao (2016) described another way in which superheroes symbol-ize immortality. Although comic superheroes may die in a particular issue or storyline, readers expect that the character will return in subsequent issues or be reanimated in new instantiations. Similarly, the comic super-hero is constantly reborn in new screen adaptations and reboots of those adaptations. Perdigao asserts that "comics and their adaptations are per-petually poised for returns, new beginnings, and re-readings" because "superheroes are granted a new kind of afterlife when reanimated on big and small screens" (p. 81). She offers an analysis of the CW series *Arrow* (2012–2020) in which the visual and narrative depictions of rebirth "pres-ents a meta-commentary on how resurrection is central to the hero's sur-vival on network television" (p. 82).

Arrow depicts both figurative and literal returns from the dead. Fig-urative rebirths occur when characters presumed dead return in later epi-sodes. The series begins with Oliver Queen (Stephen Amell) rescued from the Island of Lian Yu after being presumed dead at sea five years earlier. There are also numerous instances of literal rebirth, as when Oliver is resuscitated after being killed by Ra's al Ghul (Matthew Nable) and when Thea Queen (Willa Holland) and Sara Lance (Caity Lotz) are brought back to life by the mystical regenerative powers of the Lazarus Pit. From a TMT perspective, not only the specific depictions of resurrection in a given superhero text but also the staying power of superheroes to return across multiple mediums and numerous re-imaginings validate consum-ers' hopes for immortality.

While the vampire and the superhero symbolize immortality, the zombie facilitates denial of mortality by signifying the possibility of con-quering death. Much has been made of the protean ability of the zom-bie to come to symbolize whatever societal fear or cultural malady is most salient during a specific place and time (e.g., Clasen, 2012). Similar amounts of scholarly attention have been devoted to the ways in which the dehumanized target of the zombie offers viewers a guilt-free enjoy-ment of gratuitous violent spectacle. For example, Desilet (2014) asserted that "the dramatic trope of the faceless enemy is a bit too convenient for good drama" (p. 173) and expressed concern that the ease of the dehuman-ized target of zombies and their malleability to signify any type of enemy Other normalizes and facilitates support for hostile attitudes and aggres-sion against whichever outgroup target happens to be in the specific indi-vidual prejudices of the viewer.

Less attention has been given to the fact that zombies are first and foremost a representation of death. For centuries, people have tried to come to terms with the abstract concept of death by personifying it in con-crete forms; the most frequent of which has been an animated corpse or skeleton in varying states of decay (Kastenbaum, 2000). As with the dance of death motif in visual arts, the depiction of zombies from all walks of life across different genders, ages, ethnicities, and social statuses expresses the universality of death as a shared human fate. Further, the slow pace of the zombies as they trudge and creep towards their victims symbolizes the gradual approach of death as the wear and tear of each passing day brings all living people closer to extinction. If the horror of zombies is derived from their ability to remind us of our mortality, then the appeal of watching thousands of zombies be shot, stabbed, bludgeoned, clubbed, eviscerated, and boot stomped on a show like AMC's *The Walking Dead* (2010–2022), should be interpreted as stemming from the symbolic conquest over death such displays convey (for a more extensive TMT analysis of *The Walking Dead*, see Tenga & Bassett, 2016). Similarly, the defeat of the Night King and his army of the dead in the final season of *GoT*, offers viewers comforting reassurance that death itself is an enemy that can be overcome.

TMT (Pyszczynski, Solomon, & Greenberg, 2015) has revealed that psychological protection from death anxiety comes not just in the forms of denying personal vulnerability to death and hoping for a literal victory over death but also in the symbolic realm where the sting of death is made less troubling by the imagining of the enduring posthumous impact one's existence will continue to have on the world after the death of the physical body. Viewing fictional violence augments TMT defenses not just in the literal but also in the symbolic arena by validating the quest for symbolic immortality as heroic and something worth killing and dying for. The motives for fictional violence are frequently depicted as based in the quest for symbolic immortality. For example, in *GoT* we see the desire for legacy as a paramount motivation for Tywin Lannister in his focus on protecting the family name and in Jaime Lannister's longing to have some heroic deeds recorded in *The Book of Brothers*. Similarly, in *SOA* we see the collective identity of the MC as more important than any individual and as something that must be defended at all costs. These death-transcending motives are sometimes glorified as in the martyrdom of Jax Teller in *SOA*. At other times, quests for symbolic immortality are problematized as misguided, such as in the tragic story lines of Jeri Hogarth and Trish Walker in *Jessica Jones* and the Daenerys story arc in *GoT*.

I have laid out the argument that consumption of fictional violence provides some viewers with a means of achieving the necessary psychological function of managing death terror. Effective terror management requires some degree of denial and the adequate operation of psychological defenses such as self-esteem striving and cultural worldview defense that buffer people from the conscious experience of concerns about death. Terror management defenses can be suboptimal when they are not providing enough protection from death anxiety (Yetzer & Pyszczynski, 2019). Such disruptions to the anxiety buffer can be transient, as when traumatic or stressful events shatter confidence in the meaning of one's belief system, or when a rejection or failure lead to the temporary assessment that one is not living up to the standards of their worldview required to maintain self-esteem. Such disruptions in the anxiety buffer leave people vulnerable to the experience of death anxiety when confronted with reminders of mortality. Suboptimal functioning of the death anxiety buffer can also be chronic, as when nihilism, alienation, and low trait levels of self-esteem prevent people from establishing a secure sense of meaning and value in life, leaving them habitually prone to anxiety and depression.

While the consumption of violent entertainment can facilitate terror management processes to avert or repair disruptions to the psychological systems that operate as an anxiety buffer, it is by no means essential to the maintenance of psychological defenses against death anxiety because there are certainly other mechanisms by which people can engage in proximal and distal defenses. Violent films and television programs are just one type of cultural product; but, like most aspects of culture, one important (but certainly not the only) function they serve is to manage existential concerns. So, while people can look to aspects of culture other than violent media to offer the sense of meaning needed to abate existential terror, fictional violence may be more appealing than less violent media because of the greater intensity with which it satisfies the cultural need for perceived value and purpose.

In his journalistic analysis of the cultural appeal of war, Hedges (2002) argued that war is addictive because of the increased sense of urgency, vitality, and importance it affords to people who buy into the justness of its cause and that war perhaps like no other human activity has the power to imbue existence with perceived meaning. Veteran characters in the diegetic world of a show like *The Punisher* give voice to this perspective. Many of the veteran characters lament the decreased sense of meaning and purpose in their civilian lives compared to what they felt in their combat roles. The confrontation with death and the ideological justifications of killing they experienced while on active duty gave these characters an enhanced sense of meaning they feel is now lacking in their peaceful lives as ordinary citizens. In a similar way, consumption of violent media may give viewers a greater vicarious sense of purpose compared to watching other types of non-violent content.

If as Becker (1975) and TMT (Solomon, Greenberg, & Pyszczynski, 2000) assert, the allure of real-world violence can be conceptualized as a balm against existential anxiety by offering people a heroic sense of meaning and purpose that promises immortality via expunging the evil threat posed by an enemy, then the same psychological dynamics can be extended to explain the appeal of fictional violence. Watching fictional violence is potentially addictive not just because of the ways it allows viewers to feel immune to death, but also because the existential threat engendered by the violence makes the concomitant cultural narratives seem all the more meaningful.

But, as TMT theorists have noted (Pyszczynski et al., 2003), cultural worldviews should not be evaluated merely on the criteria of how well they provide adherents with a sense of meaning and value sufficient to buffer death anxiety. Worldviews should also be assessed in terms of the extent to which they maximize the freedom to explore alternative belief systems and allow individuals autonomy to form their own opinions, as well as on how well they minimize hostility towards those with different beliefs (Pyszczynski et al., 2003). Rigid and dogmatic worldviews tend to be the most effective at minimizing anxiety but tend to be the most restrictive of individual autonomy and the most incendiary in promoting hostility and aggression towards different Others.

These same criteria can be applied to analyzing the potential effects watching fictional violence has on its viewers. Any psychological payoff in terms of augmented protection from existential worries must be balanced against any potential increased animosity towards others or increased indifference to the suffering or injustices experienced by others. Previous approaches to violent entertainment have documented the ways in which it can justify violence as an acceptable means of conflict resolution and as a means for reestablishing a sense of justice by righting perceived wrongs (Gerbner et al., 1986). Such glorifications that omit the often tragic, messy, and unintended consequences of violence on all sides of conflict can potentially promote a greater acceptance of real-life aggression. Similarly, other approaches have established that violence is more appealing when victims are presented as deserving of their fate, when the violence of the protagonist is presented as retribution for previous unjustified violence on the part of the villain, or when violence on the part of the protagonist eliminates the threat posed by a purely-evil Other (Zillmann, 1998).

A TMT perspective is compatible with these existing approaches but adds an additional explanatory element. Violence is most evocative in eliciting the need for beliefs about the fairness of the world when it has lethal consequences, or the threat of lethal consequences and mortality has been made salient to viewers. It is when the threat of mortality has been raised that viewers are most strongly motivated to bolster their psychological defenses in the form of validating the comforting beliefs of their worldview. The threat posed by the existence of Others with different belief systems undermines confidence in the validity of cultural worldviews thereby reducing certainty in the comforting assurances of immortality those worldviews offer. Accordingly, onscreen antagonists can be undermining to terror management defenses because they make mortality salient in terms of the physical threat they pose to protagonists but also symbolically when they are presented as ideologically different. Thus, the ultimate defeat and destruction of the antagonists is especially gratifying because it promotes a sense of justice and validates the superiority of the protagonist's and presumably the viewer's cultural worldview.

Depictions of violence as an effective solution to threats posed by alien Others, even if they do not promote actual violence on the part of viewers, can promote a greater animosity towards outgroups perceived as threatening and a greater acceptance of systemic violence and injustices against those groups. In some cases, fictional violence may promote hostility towards specific targets. For example, in *SOA* the conflict between SAMCRO and rival ethnic gangs the Mayans and the One-Niners might elicit or validate, among some viewers, white supremacist ideology and racial animosity. Similarly, in *GoT* the menace of the wildlings on the wrong side of the wall might stoke xenophobia and anxieties about the threat posed by immigrants. However, the effects of violence in such fictions typically have the power to generalize beyond the specific *Other* depicted and can come to validate the need to eliminate any perceived threat to viewers' cultural worldviews. Supernatural enemies like the White Walkers in *GoT* might be the most protean in their ability to signify whatever group a particular viewer might be prejudiced against, but any threat that is eliminated via violent means has the capacity to validate any idiosyncratic animosity held by a specific viewer.

In addition to promoting potential animosity towards Others and acceptance of violence against those Others, there is another possible negative consequence of consuming fictional violence not as directly tied to the violence. Mortality salience intensifies people's needs for confidence in their belief systems. Therefore, the narrative messages conveyed in shows featuring extreme violence can become more persuasive and influential to viewers because the mortality salience elicited by the violence has made them more amenable to embracing such messages. Consequently, messages that reinforce traditional and conventional ideologies that justify the status quo will become more appealing when presented in the context of lethal violence. For example, viewers may be more influenced by the sexism and toxic masculinity conveyed in a series like *SOA* and by the objectification and demeaning of women seen in a show like *GoT* because of the ways in which the extreme violence of the shows makes death salient.

In addition to the potentially harmful effects of increasing hostility towards outgroups, validating support for violence as the best way for dealing with ideological conflict, and justifying systems and beliefs that perpetuate inequality and injustice, exposure to violent fictions that are too palliative in their augmentation of TMT defenses can also have the further undesirable consequence of preventing viewers from ever experiencing the level of death awareness necessary to foster authentic growth. Cultural worldviews are operating optimally when they allow the right balance between denial and acceptance of the reality of death. Terror management defenses can be hyper-optimal when they do not allow for any confrontation with the limits of existence. The awareness of the finitude of existence is an important motivating factor that drives people to prioritize the things that are important in life, to enjoy the poignancy of life's pleasures because they are fleeting, and to seek intrinsic rather than extrinsic sources of meaning and purpose. If people constantly avoid thoughts of death through suppression or via the habitual activation of routinized cultural defenses, they may be comfortable in the absence of anxiety but at the cost of a safe, boring, and conventional life lived without examination or urgency.

TMT research (Solomon, Greenberg, & Pyszczynski, 2015) has shown that the most common reactions to reminders of death are to engage in cultural worldview defenses, strivings for self-esteem, and the quest for symbolic immortality, all of which can have potentially negative consequences in the form of increased greedy materialism, a preference for rigid and inflexible thinking, and greater prejudice, bias, and animosity towards Others. Although less frequent, there are also times when for some people under some circumstances confronting the reality of personal mortality can have beneficial consequences in the forms of more prosocial attitudes and behaviors, enhanced creativity, a greater interest in exploring new ideas and perspectives, and a shift to prioritize intrinsic over extrinsic goals (Rogers, Sanders, & Vess, 2019). If we apply the suboptimal versus hyper-optimal distinction made in the operation of terror management defenses specifically to audience engagement with violent television, it seems likely that the majority of onscreen depictions of fictional killing will be more palliative than provocative regarding existential issues and that the most common response from viewers of these fictions will be reflexive denial and routinized cultural worldview defense. However, it is possible that some types of screen violence may actually promote a more thoughtful engagement with existential issues and potentially spark a serious evaluation of social and moral beliefs. The content of screen violence can be critiqued in terms of the extent to which it is likely to promote defensive or growth-oriented responses.

As analyzed in chapters five and six, even programming created by the same provider in the same genre can differ dramatically in the type of reaction it is likely to elicit in response to the issue of mortality made salient by its violent content. While *The Punisher* and *Jessica Jones* both present viewers with questions about existential and social issues, the former is more comforting and the latter is more challenging regarding those issues. In *The Punisher*, several characters give voice to ethical concerns about the excessive use of lethal force in warfare and law enforcement, express guilt over taking human life, and experience moral turmoil over the morality of taking the law into their own hands. However, none of these concerns are there to prompt a sincere and genuine moral questioning in the minds of viewers but rather to offer plausible deniability for viewers' enjoyment of the violent spectacle of Frank Castle's punishing and the buttressing of death-denying defenses it provides.

Frank's moments of self-doubt are never really about the possibility that he might be wrong or the serious contemplation of a non-violent solution but are simply there to promote the message that, in order to be heroic and accomplish unpleasant but necessary ends, one must cast off societal and moral constraints and embrace violence with unwavering confidence and fury. Watching a show like *The Punisher* reinforces viewers' defenses against death anxiety and enhances their sense of mastery over death by facilitating the belief that violent threats can be overcome by more severe violence and that such violence is always unmistakably dispensed in a just world.

In contrast, *Jessica Jones* offers an example of how a violent television series can provide viewers with an opportunity to grapple constructively with serious existential issues. The show presents viewers with depictions of the dangers of living a defended lifestyle, of trying to avoid pain by numbing it with alcohol and drugs, or by holding back affection and concern for others out of fear of being hurt. Similarly, it also highlights the limits of conventional cultural aspirations such as fame, power, and financial success as failing to offer the death transcendence that motivates their pursuit. Further, *Jessica Jones* encourages viewers not only to experience vicariously the trauma suffered by its titular character and to recognize the importance of working through rather than denying trauma as an impetus for personal growth and authentic meaning in life, but also depicts the difficulty inherent in the process. Whether the consumption of violent programming facilitates the denial of death or prompts existential questioning depends on the narrative structure and context in which the violence is presented.

How violent media affects us is a consequence of the amount of exposure and the types of violence that we consume. Do we hide from, deny, or remain oblivious to possible deleterious effects by insisting it is just entertainment? While an occasional contemplation of the reality of death can jolt us out of habitual and unexamined behaviors and move us to more passionate and self-determined living, a chronic awareness of our vulnerability to death can be overwhelming and leave us overly anxious. From a TMT standpoint, the way a person approaches life must involve finding the right balance of utilizing psychological defenses that minimize death anxiety and contemplating mortality as an impetus towards authenticity and self-actualization. Similarly, the optimal amount of exposure to violent television might also be conceptualized as a balancing act. Watching violent television can provide viewers with some level of denial needed to keep existential concerns at bay. However, the numbing effects of such viewing might be kept in check by regulating viewing habits to include exposure to non-violent depictions of death. Watching dramatic content that offers more realistic confrontations with the inevitability of death and loss (for example, depictions of important characters dying from old age or illness) can potentially moderate the stultifying effect of programming in which death is always presented as due to violent causes.

Engagement with television programming can be a means of exploring other important existential issues beyond just death, such as meaning, isolation, guilt, and identity. However, all of these existential issues are closely related to the problem of death, and people deal with death anxiety by seeking the sense of meaning, identity, and belonging afforded by their cultural belief systems. Many existential thinkers have posited that human beings are meaning-hungry creatures (Frankl, 1963; Heine, Proulx, & Vohs, 2006). Storytelling is one powerful way that people have always attempted to makes sense of the universe and their place in it. While it is certainly possible for people to seek answers to these existential questions in many different ways, one possible mechanism for grappling with existential issues is through the cultural narratives we consume in popular media. This is not to imply that such existential quest is the main motive for the majority of viewers, but it is a possible result at least among some highly engaged viewers. Viewers can come to value the experience of serious intellectual contemplation of important questions of meaning raised by the engagement with fictional media even if the original motive for that engagement was entertainment. The possibility that dramatic television can elicit thoughtful reflection is not limited to any specific type of format or content. However, as previously noted, TMT reveals how people are more strongly motivated to seek answers to questions of meaning when they have been reminded of their mortality.

Viewers' reactions in response to mortality made salient via onscreen violence is a function not only of the amount and type of exposure but can also vary based on individual differences in viewers' personalities, beliefs, and mindset. According to TMT, reminders of death should polarize ideological differences as each side gravitates towards a more extreme version of their pre-existing beliefs (Greenberg & Jonas, 2003). Empirical research supports this position by showing that mortality salience exacerbates political (Castano et al., 2011) and moral differences (Bassett et al., 2015) among participants. If we assume that viewers find gratification in television narratives that confirm and validate their pre-existing worldviews, it stands to reason then that differences in reactions to the events depicted in the diegetic world of a television series would be intensified in response to programming that made mortality salient to viewers. Consequently, the more lethal violence and gore depicted on screen, the more controversial a show may be, because the existential threats of mortality and corporeality elicited by the violence gives rise to increased urgency for worldview validation in the minds of viewers. Whether viewers find the narrative messages of the series comforting or threatening will depend on the extent to which these messages are resonant or dissonant with their pre-existing belief system, but the intensity of their reaction whether praise or criticism will be more vehement in response to the existential anxiety produced by the violent content.

This process is seen in reactions to *GoT* that tend to vary more in valence than intensity, with opinions being passionate on both the positive and negative side. TMT promotes a tendency to objectify women as sexual objects and a misogyny towards women for eliciting lustful impulses that evoke male vulnerability to concerns about creatureliness (Goldenberg, Morris, & Boyd, 2019). Consequently, TMT defenses might result in satisfaction among some male viewers in response to misogynistic aspects of the series. Alternatively, TMT also predicts that mortality salience will promote a greater commitment to valued moral standards (Pyszczynski, 2016). Consequently, among more progressive and egalitarian viewers who reject sexism and patriarchy on grounds that if violates the moral virtue of fairness, existential motives made more pressing by the show's violence may prompt disgust and revulsion in response to perceived misogyny and yield a reaction of frustration with perceived sexism in the series.

While the existential threat produced by the death and gore depicted in violent programing can potentially amplify the magnitude of viewers' cognitive and emotional reactions, the precise nature of those reactions will likely vary as a function of the extent to which the concomitant narrative messages resonate with the pre-existing ideological, political, and moral leanings of viewers' worldviews, as well as the extent to which dispositional and situational factors promote a growth versus defensive mindset. Shows like *The Punisher* and *SOA* can promote among some viewers admiration or enhanced validation of traditional masculine roles and the violence required to execute such roles. Alternatively, other viewers might see in such shows a critique of the flaws of traditional masculine roles, the impossibility of trying to live up to them, and the unfortunate personal and societal consequences stemming from the violence they produce.

Given the power of the psychological need to manage existential anxiety and given the alacrity with which violent television can channel that need into various psychological processes with both beneficial and harmful consequences, what conclusions should be reached about the future of violent television, the societies that create it, and the individuals who consume it? Goldstein (1998) asserted that "violent entertainment may be as inevitable as violence in society" but also claimed that "the manner we consume it, and the ways we respond to it help to define a culture" (pp. 225–226). The idea that the future of fictional and real violence are linked and that both will probably continue as defining characteristics of human activity makes sense when contextualized in the TMT arguments reviewed in this book. The persistence of fictional and real violence can be understood as equally likely to the extent that they are both driven by the same essential death-denying motive.

Becker (1973) was rather dubious about any calls for psychological revolution or social utopias that involved overcoming death anxiety by living fully in the moment with an unadulterated awareness of the transience of existence. He viewed some level of repression as a necessary part of the human condition and doubted that people would ever be able to live without the comfort provided by their culturally constructed belief systems. Further, to the extent that different groups adhere to conflicting or contradictory death-denying ideologies, Becker saw culturally condoned violence in the name of heroism as an intractable problem. Extending this perspective to the issue of fictional violence, it seems unreasonable then to expect any radical cultural transformation in which violence on television becomes substantially less prevalent or diminishes significantly in popularity.

In contrast, not all scholars share Becker's pessimism. For example, Keen (2006) viewed Becker's analysis as only partially correct and skewed by an overly narrow focus on the terror of existence to the neglect of the equally important aspects of awe and wonder. Keen regarded intellectual humility as the anecdote to death-denying violence. More recently, TMT theorists have begun to advance a similarly more optimistic perspective, in which death anxiety can be managed in more positive ways that do not necessarily lead to prejudice, hostility, and violence (Vail & Juhl, 2015). The need to overcome death anxiety motivates people to live up to the standards of their cultural belief system. So, to the extent that cultural narratives focus on a shared sense of humanity and present tolerance, cooperation, and kindness as heroic values, prosocial behaviors can be as effective as antisocial ones in managing existential terror (Pyszczynski et al., 2008).

Therefore, given the potential for more positive terror management mechanisms, there seems a hopeful possibility that even if the prevalence of fictional violence remains unabated, the deleterious impact of consumption can be attenuated. Knowledge of TMT defenses and how watching on-screen violence can tap into them, as well as a general sense of mindfulness and self-awareness, can act as potential protective factors that reduce the negative impact on viewers. Such awareness serves as a deterrent to habitual defensive responses to mortality salience that tend to occur automatically when we are in an intuitive mode of thinking. Tolerance of ambiguity, an ability to live with some level of anxiety, and adopting a deliberate and rational mindset can all potentially inoculate viewers against the ability of violent media to promote hostility and the acceptance of a culture of violence.

Further, viewers could potentially benefit from adopting a sense of skepticism towards their own intuitive and emotional reactions to fictional violence. The sense of satisfaction, gratification, and pleasure felt is not necessarily a metric of the value of consumption. Viewers would be wise to challenge and interrogate their feelings and the motives underlying them. Those screen fictions that bolster denial of death and validate the transcendent immortality ideologies of cultural worldviews will likely elicit the greatest sense of pleasure but also potentially bear the most negative consequences.

Hopefully, the arguments reviewed in this book have provided readers with a fresh theoretical lens through which to think about and interpret personal and societal reactions to violent television. For fans of the television series examined in the preceding pages, I hope this perspective will enhance appreciation for the shows and facilitate contemplation of the many possible social and existential lessons to be gleaned from engagement with them. Lastly, I hope this work will have heuristic value in stimulating others to integrate terror management ideas with other theoretical perspectives and to apply them to explanations of fictional violence in the analysis of cultural products across a diverse array of times, contexts, and mediums.

References

Abad-Santos, A. (2019). Why the second season of Punisher feels like such a drag. *Vox*. January 18. https://www.vox.com/culture/2019/1/18/18187117/punisher-season-2-review.

Abbott and Costello Meet Frankenstein. (1948). Charles Barton (Director). United States. Universal.

AKA A Lotta Worms. (2019). *Jessica Jones.* Sarah Boyd (Director); Netflix. Release date June 14.

AKA Everything. (2019). *Jessica Jones.* Neasa Hardiman (Director); Netflix. Release date June 14.

AKA Freak Accident. (2018). *Jessica Jones.* Minkie Spiro (Director); Netflix. Release date March 8.

AKA Hellcat. (2019). *Jessica Jones.* Jennifer Getzinger (Director); Netflix. Release date June 14.

AKA I Have No Spleen. (2019). *Jessica Jones.* Anton Cropper (Director); Netflix. Release date June 14.

AKA I Wish. (2019). *Jessica Jones.* Mairzee Almas (Director); Netflix. Release date June 14.

AKA. Playland. (2018). *Jessica Jones.* Uta Briesewitz (Director); Netflix. Release date March 8.

AKA Shark in the Bathtub, Monster in the Bed. (2018). *Jessica Jones.* Rosemary Rodriguez (Director); Netflix. Release date March 8.

AKA Smile. (2015). *Jessica Jones.* Michael Rymer (Director); Netflix. Release date November 20.

AKA Sole Survivor. (2018). *Jessica Jones.* Mairzee Almas (Director); Netflix. Release date March 8.

AKA Sorry Face (2019). *Jessica Jones.* Tim Iacofano (Director); Netflix. Release date June 14.

AKA Start at the Beginning. (2018). *Jessica Jones.* Anna Foerster (Director); release date March 8.

AKA Take a Bloody Number. (2015). *Jessica Jones.* Billy Gierhart (Director); Netflix. Release date November 20.

AKA The Double Half-Wappinger. (2019). *Jessica Jones.* Larry Teng (Director); Netflix. Release date June 14.

AKA The Sandwich Saved Me. (2015). *Jessica Jones.* Stephen Surjik (Director); Netflix. Release date November 20.

AKA Three Lives and Counting. (2018). *Jessica Jones.* Jennifer Lynch (Director); Netflix. Release date March 8.

AKA You're a Winner. (2015). *Jessica Jones.* Stephen Surjik (Director); Netflix. Release date November 20.

AKA You're Welcome. (2019. *Jessica Jones.* Krysten Ritter (Director); Netflix. Release date June 14.

Alford, C.F. (1997). *What Evil Means to Us.* Ithaca: Cornell University Press.

American Sniper. (2014). Clint Eastwood (Director). United States. Warner Brothers.

185

Amuse-Bouche. (2013). *Hannibal*. Michael Rymer (Director); NBC. Air date April 11.

And the Beast from the Sea. (2015). *Hannibal*. Michael Rymer (Director); NBC. Air date August 15.

And the Woman Clothed with the Sun. (2015). *Hannibal*. John Dahl (Director); NBC. Air date August 1.

Anderson, C.A., Berkowitz, L., Donnerstein, E., Huesmann, L.R., Johnson, J.D., Linz, D., ... & Wartella, E. (2003). The influence of media violence on youth. *Psychological Science in the Public Interest, 4*(3), 81–110.

Antipasto. (2015). *Hannibal*. Vincenzo Natali (Director); NBC. Air date June 4.

Aon Rud Persanta. (2013). *Sons of Anarchy*. Peter Weller (Director); FX Network. Air date November 19.

Aperitivo. (2015). *Hannibal*. Marc Jobst (Director); NBC. Air date June 25.

Appel, M. (2008). Fictional narratives cultivate just-world beliefs. *Journal of Communication, 58*(1), 62–83.

Aries, P. (1981). *The hour of our death: The classic history of western attitudes toward death over the last one thousand years*. New York: Alfred A. Knopf.

Arndt, J., Cook, A., & Routledge, C. (2004). The blueprint of terror management: Understanding the cognitive architecture of psychological defenses against the awareness of death. In J. Greenberg, S.L. Koole, and T. Pyszczynski (Eds.), *Handbook of experimental existential psychology* (pp. 35–53). New York: Guilford.

Arndt, J., Greenberg, J., Pyszczynski, T., & Solomon, S. (1997). Subliminal exposure to death-related stimuli increases defense of the cultural worldview. *Psychological Science, 8*, 379–385.

Arndt, J., Schimel, J., & Goldenberg, J.L. (2003). Death can be good for your health: Fitness intentions as a proximal and distal defense against mortality salience. *Journal of Applied Social Psychology, 33*, 1726–1746.

Askwith, I.D. (2007). *Television 2.0: Reconceptualizing TV as an engagement medium*. Doctoral dissertation, Massachusetts Institute of Technology.

Avengers: Endgame. (2019). Anthony Russo and Joe Russo (Directors). United States. Marvel Studios.

Bacle, A. (2015). Hannibal finale: Hugh Dancy postmortem of the series' shocking conclusion: Interview. *Entertainment Weekly*. August 29, 2015. https://ew.com/article/2015/08/29/hannibal-finale-hugh-dancy-postmortem-interview/.

Baelor. (2011). *Game of Thrones*; Alan Taylor (Director); HBO. Air date June 12.

Bassett, J.F. (2005). Does threatening valued components of cultural worldview alter explicit and implicit attitudes about death? *Individual Differences Research, 3*, 260–268.

Bassett, J.F. (2011). Ambivalence about immortality: Vampires reveal and assuage existential anxiety. In G. Schott and K. Moffat (Eds.) *Fanpires: Audience consumption of the modern vampire* (pp. 15–30). Washington, D.C.: New Academia Press.

Bassett, J.F. (2014). Every day is a box for the reaper crew: The quest for death transcendence and conflicting moral virtues in *Sons of Anarchy*. *PSYART: A Hyperlink Journal for the Psychological Study of the Arts*. Available at http://psyartjournal.com/article/show/f_bassett-every_day_is_a_box_for_the_reaper_crew_t.

Bassett, J.F. (2016). Man on the run: Ambivalence about masculinity and tensions between individuation versus participation as seen in the male protagonists of selected television shows from the 1970's and 1980's. Paper presented at The Popular Culture Association in the South conference, Nashville, TN, October.

Bassett, J.F., Van Tongeren, D.R., Green, J.D., Sonntag, M.E., & Kilpatrick, H. (2015). The interactive effects of mortality salience and political orientation on moral judgments. *British Journal of Social Psychology, 54*(2), 306–323.

Bastien, A.J. (2018). What Jessica Jones understands about female rage. *Vulture.com*. March 19. https://www.vulture.com/2018/03/jessica-jones-season-2-female-rage.html.

Baumeister, R.F. (1999). *Evil: Inside human violence and cruelty*. New York. W.H. Freeman and Company.

The Bear and the Maiden Fair. (2013). *Game of Thrones*. Michelle MacLauren (Director). HBO. Air date May 12.

Beauchamp, S. (2016). What Daredevil's depiction of the Punisher gets right about war vets. *Vulture.* March 23 http://www.vulture.com/2016/03/what-daredevils-punisher-gets-right-about-vets.html.

Beck, R., McGregor, D., Woodrow, B., Haugen, A., & Killion, K. (2010). Death, art and the fall: A Terror Management view of Christian aesthetic judgments. *Journal of Psychology & Christianity, 29*(4), 301–307.

Becker, E. (1962). *The birth and death of meaning: A perspective in psychiatry and anthropology.* New York: Free Press.

Becker, E. (1973). *The denial of death.* New York: Free Press.

Becker, E. (1975). *Escape from evil.* New York: Free Press.

The Bells. *Game of Thrones*; Miguel Sapochnik (Director); HBO. Air date May 12.

Bering, J.M. (2002). Intuitive concepts of dead agents' minds: the natural foundations of afterlife beliefs as phenomenological boundary. *Journal of Cognition and Culture, 2*, 263–308.

Bibel, S. (2013). *Sons of Anarchy* season 6 finale was the most watched finale in the history of the show. Retrieved from http://tvbythenembers.xap2it.com/2013/12/11/sons-of-anarchy-season-6-finale-was-the-most-watched-finale-in-the-history-of-the-show/222063/.

Bisson, T. (1991). They're made out of meat. *Omni.* April.

Blackwater. (2012) *Game of Thrones.* Neil Marchall (Director). HBO. Air date May 27.

Breaker of Chains. (2014). *Game of Thrones.* Alex Graver (Director). HBO. Air date April 20.

Brehm, J.W. (1966). *A theory of psychological reactance.* New York: Academic Press.

Breikss, S.K.L. (2015). A rare gift. In J. Westfall (Ed). *Hannibal Lecter and philosophy: The heart of the matter,* pp. 135–146, Chicago, Illinois: Open Court.

Brinker, F. (2015). NBC's *Hannibal* and the politics of audience engagement. *Transgressive Television: Politics and Crime in 21st-Century American TV Series,* 303–328.

Brown, N.O. (1959). *Life against death: The psychoanalytic meaning of history.* Hanover, NH: Wesleyan University Press.

Buffet Froid. (2013). *Hannibal.* John Dahl (Director); NBC. Air date May 30.

Bushman, B.J., & Huesmann, L.R. (2006). Short-term and long-term effects of violent media on aggression in children and adults. *Archives of Pediatrics & Adolescent Medicine, 160*(4), 348–352.

Cain, S. (2015). Hannibal: farewell to the best bloody show on TV. *The Guardian,* August 28, https://www.theguardian.com/tv-and-radio/2015/aug/27/hannibal-finale-bryan-fuller-best-show-on-tv.

Captain Marvel. (2019). Anna Boden and Ryan Fleck (Directors). United States. Walt Disney Productions.

Castano, E., Leidner, B., Bonacossa, A., Nikkah, J., Perrulli, R., Spencer, B., & Humphrey, N. (2011). Ideology, fear of death, and death anxiety. *Political Psychology, 32,* 601–621. doi: 10.1111/j.1467-9221.2011.00822.x .

Cave, S. (2012). *Immortality: The quest to live forever and how it drives civilization.* New York: Random House.

Change.org (2019). Remake Game of Thrones season 8 with competent writers. https://www.change.org/p/hbo-remake-game-of-thrones-season-8-with-competent-writers.

Chau, J., & Vanderwees, C. (2019). Introduction—high fantasy, political dreams, and the mainstream: Reflections on *Game of Thrones. Canadian Review of American Studies, 49,* 1–6.

Clasen, M. (2012). Monsters evolve: A biocultural approach to horror stories. *Review of General Psychology, 16,* 222–229.

The Coat Hanger. (2012). *American Horror Story Asylum*; Jeremy Podeswa (Director). 20th Century Fox Television. Air date December 12.

Cohen, F., Sullivan, D., Solomon, S., Greenberg, J., & Ogilvie, D.M. (2011). Finding everland: Flight fantasies and the desire to transcend mortality. *Journal of Experimental Social Psychology, 47*(1), 88–102.

Conn, R., Schrader, M.P., Wann, D.L., & Mruz, B. (1996). Reduction of anxiety about death: Need for beliefs about immortality. *Psychological Reports, 79,* 1315–1318.

Contorno. (2015). *Hannibal.* Guillermo Navarro (Director); NBC. Air date July 2.

Coquilles. (2013). *Hannibal.* Guillermo Navarro (Director); NBC. Air date April 25.

Corn, K. (2013). The faith of our Sons and the tragic quest. In George A. Dunn and Jason T. Eberl (Eds). *Sons of anarchy and philosophy: Brains before bullets* (Kindle version). Retrieved from Amazon.com.

Cox, N.B., & DeCarvalho, L.J. (2016). "Ride free or die" Trying: Hypermasculinity on FX's *Sons of Anarchy. The Journal of Popular Culture, 49(4),* 818–838.

Cox, C.R., Goldenberg J.L.,Pyszczynski T., & Weise, D. (2007). Disgust, creatureliness, and the accessibility of death-related thoughts. *European Journal of Social Psychology, 37,* 494–507.

Cozzolino, P.J., Staples, A.D., Meyers, L.S., & Samboceti, J. (2004). Greed, death, and values: From terror management to transcendence management theory. *Personality and Social Psychology Bulletin, 30(3),* 278–292.

Cripples, Bastards, and Broken Things. (2011). *Game of Thrones.* Brian Kirk (Director). HBO. Air date May 8.

Crosshairs. (2017). *The Punisher.* Andy Goddard (Director); Netflix. Release date November 17.

The Culling. (2009). *Sons of Anarchy.* Gwyneth Horder-Payton (Director); FX Network. Air date November 24.

Danger Close. (2017). *The Punisher.* Kevin Hooks (Director); Netflix. Release date November 17.

Dechesne, M., Pyszczynski, T., Arndt, J., Ransom, S., Sheldon, K.M., van Knippenberg, A., & Janssen, J. (2003). Literal and symbolic immortality: The effects of evidence of literal immortality on self-esteem strivings in response to mortality salience. *Journal of Personality and Social Psychology, 84,* 722–737.

DeFrain, M., Landua, M.J., & Greenberg, J. (2019). A harrowing journey into the heart of motherhood: *Tully. The Ernest Becker Foundation Newsletter, 26(3),* 5–6.

Deggans, E. (2018). 'Jessica Jones' Season 2 is full of (politically inspired) rage. NPR. March 7. https://www.npr.org/2018/03/07/591648179/jessica-jones-season-2-is-full-of-politically-inspired-rage.

DeLillo, D. (1985). *White Noise.* New York: Viking Penguin.

Desilet, G. (2014). *Screens of blood: A critical approach to film and television violence.* Jefferson, North Carolina: McFarland.

DeSpelder, L.A., & Strickland, A.L. (2015). *The last dance: Encountering death and dying (10th edition).* Boston: McGraw-Hill.

Digestivo. (2015). *Hannibal.* Adam Kane (Director); NBC. Air date July 18.

DiPaolo, M. (2011). *War, politics and superheroes: Ethics and propaganda in comics and film.* Jefferson, North Carolina: McFarland.

Dockterman, E. (2019). How Daenerys finally turned into the mad queen of *Game of Thrones.* Time.com. https://time.com/5587311/daenerys-mad-queen-game-of-thrones/.

Dolce. (2015). *Hannibal.* Vincenzo Natali (Director); NBC. Air date July 9.

Dorylus. (2011). *Sons of Anarchy.* Peter Weller (Director); FX Network. Air date September 20.

Doyle, A.C. (1894). *The Memoirs of Sherlock Holmes.* London, England: George Newnes.

Dracula Dead and Loving It. (1995). Mel Brooks (Director). United States. Castle Rock Entertainment.

The Dragon and the Wolf. (2017). *Game of Thrones.* Jeremy Podeswa (Director). HBO. Air date August 27.

Dragonstone. (2017). *Game of Thrones.* Jeremy Podeswa (Director). HBO. Air date July 16.

Durkin, K. (2003). Death, dying and the dead in popular culture. In C.D. Bryant (Ed.) *Handbook of Death and Dying,* pp. 43–49, Thousand Oaks, CA: Sage.

Eastwatch. (2017). *Game of Thrones;* Matt Shakman (Director). HBO. Air date August 13.

Eberl, J.T. (2013) Virtues and vice in the SAMCROpolis: Aristotle views *Sons of Anarchy.* In G.A. Dunn and J.T. Eberl (Eds). *Sons of anarchy and philosophy: Brains before bullets.* (Kindle version). Retrieved from Amazon.com.

Elias, N., & Dunning, E. (1970). The quest for excitement in unexciting societies. In G. Luschen (Ed.), *Cross-cultural analysis of sport and games.* Champaign, Illinois: Stripes.

Ellis, K.M. (2014). Cripples, bastards and broken things: Disability in *Game of Thrones. M/C Journal: A Journal of Media and Culture, 17*(5). http://www.journal.media-culture.org.au/index.php/mcjournal/article/view/895.

Elsby, C. (2013). SAMCRO's ink and personal identity. In G.A. Dunn and J.T. Eberl (Eds). *Sons of anarchy and philosophy: Brains before bullets.* (Kindle version). Retrieved from Amazon.com.

Felson, R.B. (1996). Mass media effects of violent behavior. In S. Prince (Ed) *Screening Violence,* pp. 237–266. New Brunswick, New Jersey: Rutgers University Press.

Ferreday, D. (2015). Game of thrones, rape culture, and feminist fandom. *Australian Feminist Studies, 30,* 21–36.

Fire and Blood. (2011) *Game of Thrones*; Alan Taylor (Director); HBO. Air date June 19.

Firestone, R.W. (1993). Individual defenses against death anxiety. *Death Studies, 17,* 497–515.

Firestone, R.W., & Catlett, J. (2009). *Beyond death anxiety: Achieving life-affirming death awareness.* New York: Springer Publishing Co.

Firestone, R.W., & Firestone, L. (1998). Voices in suicide: The relationship between self-destructive thought processes, maladaptive behavior, and self-destructive manifestations. *Death Studies, 22*(5), 411–443.

Firestone, R.W., Firestone, L., & Catlett, J. (2013). *The self under siege: A therapeutic model for differentiation.* New York: Routledge.

Fischoff, S., Dimopoulus, A., Nguyen, F., & Gordon, A. (2005). The psychological appeal of movie monsters. *Journal of Media Psychology, 10*(3), 1–33.

Flight from Death. (2003). Patrick Shen (Director). Transcendental Media.

Florian, V., & Mikulincer, M. (1997). Fear of death and the judgment of social transgressions: A multidimensional test of terror management theory. *Journal of Personality and Social Psychology, 73,* 369–380.

Flusterluck. (2019). *The Punisher.* Salli Richardson-Whitfield (Director); Netflix. Release date January 18.

Flynn, C.P. (1984). Meanings and implications of near-death experiencer transformations. In B. Greyson and C.P. Flynn (Eds.). *The near-death experience: Problems, prospects, perspectives,* pp. 278–289. Springfield, IL: Charles C. Thomas.

Foltyn, J.L. (2008). Dead famous and dead sexy: Popular culture, forensics, and the rise of the corpse. *Mortality, 13,* 153–173.

Fonagy, P., Gergely, G., Jurist, E., and Traget, M. (2002). *Affect regularization, mentalization, and the development of the self.* New York, NY: Other Press.

Fosl, P.S. (2013). Anarchism and authenticity, or why SAMCRO shouldn't fight history. In George A. Dunn and Jason T. Eberl (Eds). *Sons of anarchy and philosophy: Brains before bullets.* (Kindle version). Retrieved from Amazon.com.

Foutch, H. (2019). The Punisher season 2 review: Bullets for brains. *Collider.com.* January 18. https://collider.com/the-punisher-season-2-review/.

Frankl, V.E. (1963). *Man's search for meaning: An introduction to logotherapy.* New York: Washington Square Press.

Freud, S. (1913/1953). Thoughts for the times on love and death. In *Collected Works, vol. IV,* pp. 288–317. London: Hogarth Press.

Freud, S. (1919/1959). The uncanny. In J. Riviere (Trans), *Sigmund Freud: Collected Papers,* vol IV, pp. 368–407. London: Hogarth Press.

Fritsche, I., Jonas, E., Fischer, P., Koranyi, N., Berger, N., & Fleischmann, B. (2007). Mortality salience and the desire for offspring. *Journal of Experimental Social Psychology, 43*(5), 753–762.

Fromage. (2013). *Hannibal.* Tim Hunter (Director); NBC. Air date May 16.

Fromm, E. (1941). *Escape from freedom.* New York: Holt, Rinehart, and Winston.

Front toward Enemy. (2017). *The Punisher.* Marc Jobst (Director); Netflix. Release date November 17.

Fun Town. (2008). *Sons of Anarchy.* Stephen Kay (Director); FX Network. Air date September 17.

Futamono. (2014). *Hannibal.* Tim Hunter (Director); NBC. Air date April 4.

Genter, R. (2007). "With great power comes great responsibility": Cold war culture and the Birth of Marvel Comics. *The Journal of Popular Culture* 40, 953–978.

Gerbner, G. (1969a). Toward "cultural indicators": The analysis of mass mediated public message systems. *AV Communication Review, 17*(2), 137–148.

Gerbner, G. (1969b). Dimensions of Violence in Television Drama: Violence Profile no. 1. https://web.asc.upenn.edu/gerbner/archive.aspx?sectionID=155&packageID=766.

Gerbner, G., & Gross, L. (1976). Living with television: The violence profile. *Journal of Communication, 26*(2), 172–199.

Gerbner, G., Gross, L., Morgan, M., & Signorielli, N. (1986). Living with television: The dynamics of the cultivation process. In J. Bryant and D. Zillmann (Eds.) *Perspectives on media effects,* pp. 17–40. Hillsdale, NJ: Lawrence Erlbaum and Associates.

Gilbert, S. (2017). *The Punisher* is rooted in American trauma. *The Atlantic.* November 19. https://www.theatlantic.com/entertainment/archive/2017/11/the-punisher-review-netflix/546182/.

Gilbert, S. (2018). The villainous women of 'Jessica Jones.' *The Atlantic.* March 15. https://www.theatlantic.com/entertainment/archive/2018/03/jessica-jones-season-2-review-netflix/555395/.

Giving Back. (2008). *Sons of Anarchy.* Tim Hunter (Director); FX Network. Air date October 1.

Goldberg, V. (1998). Death takes a holiday, sort of. In J.H. Goldstein (Ed) *Why we watch: The attractions of violent entertainment,* pp. 27–52. New York: Oxford University Press.

Goldenberg, J. L, & Roberts, T.A. (2004). The beast within the beauty: An existential perspective on the objectification and condemnation of women. In J. Greenberg, S.L. Koole, and T. Pyszczynski (eds.) *Handbook of experimental existential psychology,* pp. 71–85. New York: Guilford Press.

Goldenberg, J.L. (2012). A body of terror: Denial of death and the creaturely body. In P.R. Shaver and M. Mikulincer (eds.), *Meaning, Mortality, and Choice: The Social Psychology of Existential Concerns,* pp. 93–110. Washington, D.C.: APA.

Goldenberg, J.L., McCoy, S.K., Pyszczynski, T., Greenberg, J., & Solomon, S. (2000). The body as a source of self-esteem: The effects of mortality salience on identification with one's body, interest in sex, and appearance monitoring. *Journal of Personality and Social Psychology, 79,* 118–130.

Goldenberg, J.L., Morris, K.L., & Boyd, P. (2019). Terror management is for the birds and the bees: An existential perspective on the threat associated with human corporeality. In C. Routledge and M. Vess (eds.) *Handbook of terror management theory,* pp. 227–242, San Diego, California: Academic Press.

Goldenberg, J.L., Pyszczynski, T., Johnson, K.D., Greenberg, J., & Solomon, S. (1999). The appeal of tragedy: A terror management perspective. *Media Psychology, 1*(4), 313–329.

Goldstein, J.H. (1998). Why we watch. In J.H. Goldstein (Ed) *Why we watch: The attractions of violent entertainment,* pp. 212–226. New York: Oxford University Press.

Gorer, G. (1955). The pornography of death. *Encounter, 5*(4), 49–52.

Graham, J., Haidt, J., Koleva, S., Motyl, M., Iyer, R., Wojok, S.P., & Ditto, P.H. (2013). Moral foundations theory: The pragmatic validity of moral pluralism. In P. Devine & A. Plant (Eds.), *Advances in Experimental Social Psychology* (Vol. 47, pp. 55–130). San Diego, CA: Academic Press.

Gravett, S. (2017). The Christian imagery of *Sons of Anarchy. The Journal of Religion and Popular Culture, 29,* 190–206.

Greenberg, H. (2001). Heimlich maneuvers: On a certain tendency of horror and speculative cinema. *PsyArt: An Online Journal for the Psychological Study of the Arts.* http://psyartjournal.com/article/show/greenbergheimlich_maneuvers_on_a_certain_ tendency.

Greenberg, J. (2012). Terror management theory: From Genesis to Revelations. In P.R. Shaver and M. Mikulincer (Eds.) *Meaning, mortality, and choice: The social psychology of existential concerns* (pp. 17–35). Washington, D.C.: APA.

Greenberg, J. (2019). *American Animals. The Ernest Becker Foundation Newsletter, 26(3),* 2–3.

Greenberg, J., & Ayars, A. (2013). A terror management analysis of films from four genres: *The Matrix, Life Is Beautiful, Iron Man 2,* and *Ikiru*. In D. Sullivan and J. Greenberg (Eds.), *Fade to black: Death in classic and contemporary film*, pp. 19–36. New York: Palgrave Macmillan.

Greenberg, J., & Jonas, E. (2003). Psychological motives and political orientation—The left, right, and the rigid: Comment on Jost et al. (2003). *Psychological Bulletin, 129,* 376–382. doi: 10.1037/0033–2909.129.3.376.

Greenberg, J., Kosloff, S., Solomon, S., Cohen, F., & Landau, M.J. (2010). Toward understanding the fame game: The effect of mortality salience on the appeal of fame. *Self and Identity, 9,* 1–18.

Greenberg, J., Pyszczynski, T., & Solomon, S. (1986). The causes and consequences of a need for self-esteem: A terror management theory. In R.F. Baumeister (Ed.), *Public self and private self*. New York: Springer-Verlag.

Greenberg, J., Pyszczynski, T., Solomon, S., Rosenblatt, A., Veeder, M., Kirkland, S., & Lyon, D. (1990). Evidence for terror management theory II: The effects of mortality salience on reactions to those who threaten or bolster the cultural worldview. *Journal of Personality and Social Psychology, 58,* 308–318.

Greenberg, J., Pyszczynski, T., Solomon, S., Pinel, E., Simon, L., & Jordan, K. (1993). Effect of self-esteem on vulnerability-denying defensive distortions: Further evidence of an anxiety-buffering function of self-esteem. *Journal of Experimental Social Psychology, 29,* 229–251.

Greenberg, J., Pyszczynski, T., Solomon, S., Simon, L., & Breus, M. (1994). Role of consciousness and accessibility of death-related thoughts in mortality salience effects. *Journal of Personality and Social Psychology, 67,* 627–637.

Greenberg, J., Simon, L., Pyszczynski, T., Solomon, S., & Chatel, D. (1992). Terror management and tolerance: Does mortality salience always intensify negative reactions to others who threaten one's worldview? *Journal of Personality and Social Psychology, 63,* 212–220.

Haidt, J. (2012). *The righteous mind: Why good people are divided by politics and religion.* New York: Random House.

Hannibal Rising (2007). *Peter Webber (Director).* Dino De Laurentiis.

Hannibal (2001). Ridley Scott (Director). February 9, MGM.

Hardy, M. (2019). The east is least: The stereotypical imagining of Essos in *Game of Thrones. Canadian Review of American Studies, 49,* 26–45.

Harris, T. (1981). *The red dragon.* New York: Dell Publishing.

Harris, T. (1988). *The silence of the lambs.* New York: St. Martin's Press.

Harris, T. (1999). *Hannibal.* New York: Delacorte Press.

Harris, T. (2006). *Hannibal rising.* New York: Del Publishing.

Harry Potter and the Prisoner of Azkaban. (2004). Alfonso Cuaron (Director). United States. Warner Bros.

Hayes, J., Schimel, J., & Williams, T.J. (2008). Fighting death with death: The buffering effects of learning that worldview violators have died. *Psychological Science, 19,* 501–507.

Hayes, J., Schimel, J., Faucher, E.H., & Williams, T.J. (2008). Evidence for the DTA hypothesis II: Threatening self-esteem increases death-thought accessibility. *Journal of Experimental Social Psychology, 44(3),* 600–613.

Hedges, C. (2002). *War is a force that gives us meaning.* New York: PublicAffairs.

Heidegger, M. (1927/2008). *Being and Time.* New York: Harper Perennial.

Heine, S.J., Proulx, T., & Vohs, K.D. (2006). The meaning maintenance model: On the coherence of social motivations. *Personality and Social Psychology Review, 10,* 88–110.

High Plains Drifter. (1973). Clint Eastwood (Director). United States. Malpaso.

Hofer, M. (2013). Appreciation and enjoyment of meaningful entertainment: The role of mortality salience and search for meaning in life. *Journal of Media Psychology, 25,* 109–117.

Hoffner, C.A., & Levine, K.J. (2005). Enjoyment of mediated fright and violence: A meta-analysis. *Media Psychology, 7*(2), 207–237.

Holt, J. (2015). An aesthete par excellence. The art of killing. In J. Westfall (Ed). *Hannibal Lecter and philosophy: The heart of the matter,* pp. 161–169, Chicago, Illinois: Open Court.

Home. (2016). *Game of Thrones;* Jeremy Podeswa (Director); HBO. Air date May 1.

Home from Sea. (1983). *Magnum PI;* Harvey S. Laidman (Director); CBS. Air date September 29.

Hoyt, C.L., Simon, S., & Reid, L. (2009). Choosing the best (wo) man for the job: The effects of mortality salience, sex, and gender stereotypes on leader evaluations. *The Leadership Quarterly, 20*(2), 233–246.

Huston, A.C., Donnerstein, E., Fairchild, H., Feshbach, N.D., Katz, P.A., Murray, J.P., Rubinstein, E.A., Wilcox, B.L., & Zuckerman, D.M. (1992). *Big world, small screen: The role of television in American society.* Lincoln: University of Nebraska Press.

International Movie Database. https://www.imdb.com/title/tt0944947/awards.

The Iron Throne. (2019). *Game of Thrones;* David Benioff and D.B. Weiss (Directors); HBO. Air date May 19.

J'ai Obtenu Cette. (2012). *Sons of Anarchy.* Kurt Sutter (Director); FX Network. Air date December 4.

James, W. (1917). *The varieties of religious experience; A study in human nature; being the Gifford Lectures on natural religion delivered at Edinburgh in 1901–1902.* New York: Longmans, Green, and Co.

Johnston, D.D. (1995). Adolescents' motivations for viewing graphic horror. *Human Communication Research, 21,* 522–552.

Jonas, E., Martens, A., Niesta Kayser, D., Fritsche, I., Sullivan, D., & Greenberg, J. (2008). Focus theory of normative conduct and terror-management theory: The interactive impact of mortality salience and norm salience on social judgment. *Journal of Personality and Social Psychology, 95,* 1239–1251.

Jonas, E., Schimel, J., Greenberg, J., & Pyszczynski, T. (2002). The Scrooge effect: Evidence that mortality salience increases prosocial attitudes and behavior. *Personality and Social Psychology Bulletin, 28*(10), 1342–1353.

Jones, T. (2015). A little empathy for Hannibal is a dangerous thing. In J. Westfall (Ed). *Hannibal Lecter and philosophy: The heart of the matter,* pp. 147–157, Chicago, Illinois: Open Court.

The Judas Goat. (2017). *The Punisher.* Jeremy Webb (Director); Netflix, release date November 17.

Kasser, T., & Sheldon, K.M. (2000). Of wealth and death: Materialism, mortality salience, and consumption behavior. *Psychological Science, 11,* 348–351.

Kastenbaum, R. (2000). *The Psychology of Death.* New York: Springer.

Keen, S. (2006). *The future of evil.* New York: The Becker Press.

Kesiber, P., & Pyszczynski, T. (2011). A moral-existential account of the psychological factors fostering intergroup conflict. *Social and Personality Psychology Compass, 5*(11), 878–890.

King, S. (1981). Why we crave horror movies. In A. Ross and P. Eschholz (Eds.) *Models for writers: Short essays for composition,* pp. 524–527. Boston: Bedford.

Kissed by Fire. (2013). *Game of Thrones;* Alex Graves (Director); HBO. Air date April 28.

A Knight of the Seven Kingdoms. (2019). *Game of Thrones.* David Nutter (Director). HBO. Air date April 21.

Ko No Mono. (2014). *Hannibal.* David Slade (Director); NBC. Air date May 9.

Koole, S.L., Fockenberg, D., Tops, M., & Schneider, I.K. (2013). The birth and death of the superhero film. In D. Sullivan and J. Greenberg (Eds), *Death in classic and contemporary film: Fade to black* (pp. 135–152). New York: Palgrave.

Kottler, J.A. (2011). *The lust for blood: Why we are fascinated by death, murder, horror, and violence.* Amherst, New York: Prometheus Books.

Kozlovic, A.K. (2006). Spider-man, Superman—What's the difference? *Kritikos: An*

International and Interdisciplinary Journal of Postmodern Cultural Sound, Text and Image, 3, http://intertheory.org/spiderman-superman.htm.

Krahe, B. (2012). Report of the Media Violence Commission. *Aggressive Behavior, 38,* 335–341.

Kundera, M. (1984). *The unbearable lightness of being.* New York: Harper & Row.

La Rochefoucauld, F.D.D. (1678/1827). *Reflections; or Sentences and moral maxims.* London: Simpson Low, Son, and Marston.

Landau, M.J., Goldenberg, J.L., Greenberg, J., Gillath, O., Solomon, S., Cox, C., Martens, A., & Pyszczynski, T. (2006). The siren's call: Terror management and the threat of men's sexual attraction to women. *Journal of Personality and Social Psychology, 90,* 129–146.

Landau, M.J., Greenberg, J., Solomon, S., Pyszczynski, T., & Martens, A. (2006). Windows into nothingness: Terror management, meaninglessness, and negative reactions to modern art. *Journal of Personality and Social Psychology, 90*(6), 879–892.

The Last of the Starks. (2019). *Game of Thrones.* David Nutter (Director). HBO. Air date May 5.

The Last Supper (1995). Stacy Title (Director). United States. Columbia Pictures.

Laying Pipe. (2012). *Sons of Anarchy.* Adam Arkin. (Director); FX Network. Air date September 25.

Leah. R. (2019). Arya Stark is how old now? Why her "Game of Thrones" scene with Gendry is so controversial. *Salon,* April 22. https://www.salon.com/2019/04/22/arya-stark-is-how-old-now-why-her-game-of-thrones-scene-with-gendry-is-so-controversial/.

Leon, M. (2019). The penultimate episode of the HBO epic failed to service its main characters—several of whom met shocking demises. *The Daily Beast.* https://www.thedailybeast.com/game-of-thrones-the-bells-baffling-decision-to-turn-daenerys-into-a-crazy-murderous-ex-girlfriend.

Li, S. (2019). The Marvel-Netflix Universe's final hero. *The Atlantic,* June 14. https://www.theatlantic.com/entertainment/archive/2019/06/jessica-jones-krysten-ritter-marvel-netflix-universe-ends/591556/.

Lifton, R.J. (1976). *The Life of the Self: Towards a New Psychology.* New York: Simon & Schuster.

Lifton, R.J. (2000). *Destroying the world to save it: Aum Shinrikyo and the new global terrorism.* New York: Holt.

The Lion and the Rose. (2014). *Game of Thrones.* Alex Graves (Director). HBO. Air date April 13.

Logan. (2017). James Mangold (Director). United States. Twentieth Century Fox.

The Long Night. (2019). *Game of Thrones;* Miguel Sapochnik (Director); HBO. Air date April 28.

Love at First Bite. (1978). Stan Dragoti (Director). United States. American International Pictures.

MacDonald, S. (2019). Refusing to smile for the patriarchy: Jessica Jones as feminist killjoy. *Journal of the Fantastic in the Arts, 30*(1), 68–84.

Madison, I. III. (2017). Marvel's *The Punisher* offers a damming critic of America's gun fetish. *The Daily Beast.* November 17. https://www.thedailybeast.com/marvels-the-punisher-offers-a-damning-critique-of-americas-gun-fetish.

Mahon, J.E. (2013). Tig needs and escort home: Is loyalty a virtue? In George A. Dunn and Jason T. Eberl (Eds). *Sons of anarchy and philosophy: Brains before bullets* (Kindle version). Retrieved from Amazon.com.

A Man Without Honor. (2012). *Game of Thrones.* David Nutter (Director). HBO. Air date May 13.

Mancuso, V. (2019). 'Jessica Jones' season 3 review: netflix's MCU goes out on a dark, satisfying note. Collider, June 7. https://collider.com/jessica-jones-season-3-review/.

Manhunter. (1986). Mann, M. (Director). United States: De Laurentis Entertainment Group.

Marcotte, A. (2019). Arya Stark is an adult woman "Game of Thrones" sex shock is rooted in hypocritical purity culture. *Salon,* April 23. https://www.salon.

com/2019/04/23/arya-stark-is-an-adult-woman-game-of-thrones-sex-shock-is-rooted-in-hypocritical-purity-culture/.

Marques, D. (2019). Power and denial of femininity in *Game of Thrones. Canadian Review of American Studies, 49*, 46–65.

Martin, L.L., Campbell, W.K., & Henry, C.D. (2004). The roar of awakening: Mortality acknowledgment as a call to authentic living. In J. Greenberg, S.L. Koole, and T. Pyszczynski (Eds). *Handbook of experimental existential psychology*, pp. 431–448, New York: The Guilford Press.

McAteer, J. (2015). Consuming homicidal art. In J. Westfall (Ed). *Hannibal Lecter and philosophy: The heart of the matter*, pp. 99–107, Chicago, Illinois: Open Court.

McCauley, C. (1998). When screen violence is not attractive. In J.H. Goldstein (Ed.) *Why We Watch: The attraction of violent entertainment*, pp. 144–162. New York: Oxford University Press.

McGregor, H.A., Lieberman, J.D., Greenberg, J., Solomon, S., Arndt, J., Simon, L., & Pyszczynski, T. (1998). Terror management and aggression: Evidence that mortality salience motivates aggression against worldview-threatening others. *Journal of Personality and Social Psychology, 74*, 590–605.

McMahon, J.L. (2008). The existential Frankenstein. In S.M. Sanders (Ed.), *The philosophy of science fiction film*, pp. 73–88. Lexington, Kentucky: The University Press of Kentucky.

McMahon, J.L. (2019). Death, *The Rider,* and a Pale Horse. *Ernest Becker Foundation Newsletter, 26(3)*, 3–4.

Mikulincer, M., & Florian, V. (2002). The effects of mortality salience on self-serving attributions—evidence for the function of self-esteem as a terror management mechanism. *Basic and Applied Social Psychology, 24*, 261–271.

Mikulincer, M., Florian, V., & Hirschberger, G. (2004). The terror of death and the quest for love: An existential perspective on close relationships. In J. Greenberg, S.L. Koole, and T. Pyszczynski (eds.) *Handbook of experimental existential psychology*, pp 287–304. New York: Guilford Press.

Milgram, S. (1963). Behavioral study of obedience. *Journal of Abnormal and Social Psychology, 67*, 371–378.

Milgram, S. (1974). *Obedience to Authority*. New York: Harper.

Miller, L. (2019). *The Punisher* season 2 review: Marvel's most violent hero finds more humanity. *IndieWire*. January 18, https://www.indiewire.com/2019/01/punisher-season-2-review-marvel-netflix-spoilers-1202036634/.

Mittell, J. (2006). Narrative complexity in contemporary American television. *The Velvet Light Trap, 58*, 29–40.

Mizumono. (2014). *Hannibal*. David Slade (Director); NBC. Air date May 23.

A Mother's Work. (2013). *Sons of Anarchy*. Kurt Sutter (Director); FX Network. Air date December 10.

Motyl, M., Hart, J., Cooper, D.P., Heflick, N., Goldenberg, J., & Pyszczynski, T. (2013). Creatureliness priming reduces aggression and support for war. *British Journal of Social Psychology, 52*(4), 648–666.

Mukozuke. (2014). *Hannibal*. Michael Rymer (Director); NBC. Air date March 28.

My Brother's Keeper. (2019). *The Punisher*. Michael Offer (Director); Netflix. Release date January 18.

Na Trioblóidi. (2009). *Sons of Anarchy*. Kurt Sutter (Director); FX Network. Air date December 1.

Nagy, M. (1948). The child's theories concerning death. *The Pedagogical Seminary and Journal of Genetic Psychology, 73*(1), 3–27.

Naka-Choko. (2014). *Hannibal*. Vincenzo Natali (Director); NBC. Air date May 2.

Needham, J.K. (2017). Visual misogyny: An analysis of female sexual objectification in *Game of Thrones. Femspec, 17*, 3–19.

Nell, V. (2006). Cruelty's rewards: The gratifications of perpetrators and spectators. *Behavioral and Brain Sciences, 29*(3), 211–224.

Nelson, L., Moore, D.L., Olivetti, J., & Scott, T. (1997). General and personal mortality salience and nationalistic bias. *Personality and Social Psychology Bulletin, 23*, 884–892.

Nelson, S. (2019). In season 2, the punisher feels like he's trapped in the past. *The Verge.* January 16. https://www.theverge.com/2019/1/16/18184408/the-punisher-review-netflix-season-2-jon-bernthal-jigsaw-billy-russo-ben-barnes.

Norenzayan, A., & Hansen, I.G. (2006). Belief in supernatural agents in the face of death. *Personality and Social Psychology Bulletin, 32*(2), 174–187.

NS. (2010). *Sons of Anarchy.* Kurt Sutter (Director); FX Network. Air date November 30.

Nussbaum, E. (2015a). Marvel's Jessica Jones and the superhero survivor. *The New Yorker.* December 21, https://www.newyorker.com/magazine/2015/12/21/graphic-novel-on-television-emily-nussbaum.

Nussbaum, E. (2015b). To serve man: The savory spectacle of *Hannibal. The New Yorker,* June 22. https://www.newyorker.com/magazine/2015/06/29/to-serve-man.

Oathkeeper. (2014). *Game of Thrones.* Michelle MacLauren (Director). HBO. Air date April 27.

Old Bones. *(2008). Sons of Anarchy.* Gwyneth Horder-Payton (Director); FX network. October 15.

Oleson, J.C. (2005). King of killers: The criminological theories of Hannibal Lecter, part one. *Journal of Criminal justice and Popular Culture, 12,* 186–210.

Oliver, M.B., & Bartsch, A. (2011). Appreciation of entertainment: The importance of meaningfulness via virtue and wisdom. *Journal of Media Psychology, 23,* 29–33.

One-eyed Jacks. (2019). *The Punisher.* Stacie Passon (Director); Netflix. Release date January 18.

Orca Shrugged. (2012). *Sons of Anarchy.* Gwyndeth Horder-Payton (Director); FX network. Air date October 9.

Otterson, J. (2019). 'Game of Thrones' finale sets new series high with staggering 19.3 million viewers. *Variety.com,* May 20, 2019. https://variety.com/2019/tv/ratings/game-of-thrones-series-finale-draws-19-3-million-viewers-sets-new-series-high-1203220928/.

Otto, R. (1923). *The Idea of the Holy.* New York: Oxford University Press.

Ouellette, J. (2019). *Jessica Jones* Season 3 is flawed but packs a powerful payoff in the end: Our hero's journey comes to a fitting end in series finale. Arstechnica.com. https://arstechnica.com/gaming/2019/06/review-jessica-jones-s3-is-flawed-but-packs-a-powerful-payoff-in-the-end/.

Palumbo, D. (1983). The Marvel Comics Group's Spider-Man is an existentialist superhero; or Life has no meaning without my latest marvels! *The Journal of Popular Culture,* 17, 67–82.

Pang Chieh Ho, B.J. (2019). The best takes on Daenerys' controversial decision on 'Game of Thrones.' Digg.com. http://digg.com/2019/game-of-thrones-the-bells-daenerys-review.

Papa's Goods. (2014*). Sons of Anarchy.* Kurt Sutter (Director); FX Network. Air date December 9.

Parent Television Council (2013). An examination of violence, graphic violence, and gun violence in the media. Retrieved from http://w2.parentstv.org/main/Research/ Studies/CableViolence/vstudy_dec2013.pdf.

The Passion of the Christ. (2004). Mel Gibson (Director). United States. Icon Productions.

Patch Over (2008). *Sons of Anarchy.* Paris Barclay (Director); FX Network. Air date September 24.

Patten, D. (2014). 'Sons of Anarchy' final season ratings hit all-time high for FX. Deadline.com. December 15. https://deadline.com/2014/12/sons-of-anarchy-final-season-ratings-record-high-fx-1201326118/.

Paxton, R. (2015). Top 10 Most Gruesomely Violent TV Shows. Screen Rant. July 14. https://screenrant.com/most-violent-tv-shows-bloodiest/.

Payne, J. (2004). *A history of force: Exploring the worldwide movement against habits of coercion, bloodshed, and mayhem.* Sandpoint, Idaho. Lytton Publishing Co.

Perdigao, L. (2016). The Lazarus Phenomenon: Resurrecting the Green Arrow. *Studies in Popular Culture,* 39(1), 81–99.

Peters, H.J., Greenberg, J., Williams, J.M., & Schneider, N.R. (2005). Applying terror management theory to performance: Can reminding individuals of their mortality increase strength output. *Journal of Sport and Exercise Psychology, 27,* 111–116.

Pilot. (2008). *Sons of Anarchy.* Allen Coulter & Michael Dinner (Directors); FX Network. Air date September 3.

Piñeiro-Otero, T. (2016). Intentions and intersections of classical music in Bryan Fuller's *Hannibal* (NBC). *L'Atalante,* 21, 177–189.

Pinker, S. (2011). *The better angels of our nature: Why violence has declined.* New York: Penguin.

Piven, J.S. (2004). *Death and delusion: A Freudian analysis of mortal terror.* Greenwich, Connecticut: Information Age Publishing.

Pizzato, M. (2005). Theatres of human sacrifice: From ancient ritual to screen violence. Albany, New York: State University of New York Press.

The Pointy End. (2011). *Game of Thrones*; Daniel Minahan (Director); HBO. Air date June 5.

Pope, A. (1734/1891). *An essay on man. Moral essays and satires.* London: Cassell & Co.

Poscheschnik, G. (2018). *Game of Thrones*—A psychoanalytic interpretation including some remarks on the psychosocial function of modern TV series. *The International Journal of Psychoanalysis,* 99 (4), 1004–1016. doi: 10.1080/00207578.2018.1425092.

Potlach. (2009). *Sons of Anarchy.* Paul Maibaum (Director); FX Network. Air date October 27.

Primavera. (2015). *Hannibal.* Vincenzo Natali (Director); NBC. Air date June 11.

Prudom, L. (2015). 'Hannibal' finale postmortem: Bryan Fuller breaks down that bloody ending and talks revival chances. *Variety,* August 29, 2015. https://variety.com/2015/tv/news/ hannibal-finale-season-4-movie-revival-ending-spoilers-1201581424/.

Pyszczynski, T. (2016). God save us: A terror management perspective on morality. In J.P. Forgas, L. Jussim, & P. A.M. van Lange (Eds.), *The social psychology of morality* (pp. 21–39). New York, NY: Routledge.

Pyszczynski, T., Abdollahi, A., Solomon, S., Greenberg, J., Cohen, F., & Weise, D. (2006). Mortality salience, martyrdom, and military might: The great Satan versus the axis of evil. *Personality and Social psychology Bulletin, 32,* 525–537.

Pyszczynski, T., Greenberg, J., & Solomon, S. (1997). Why do we need what we need? A terror management perspective on the roots of human social motivation. *Psychological Inquiry, 8,* 1–20.

Pyszczynski, T., Greenberg, J., & Solomon, S. (1999). A dual-process model of defense against conscious and unconscious death-related thoughts: An extension of terror management theory. *Psychological Review, 106,* 835–845.

Pyszczynski, T., Rothschild, Z., & Abdollahi, A. (2008). Terrorism, violence, and hope for peace: A terror management perspective. *Current Directions in Psychological Science,* 17(5), 318–322.

Pyszczynski, T., Solomon, S., & Greenberg, J. (2003). *In the wake of 9/11: The psychology of terror.* Washington, D.C.: American Psychological Association.

Pyszczynski, T., Solomon, S., & Greenberg, J. (2015). Thirty years of terror management theory: From genesis to revelation. In *Advances in experimental social psychology* (Vol. 52, pp. 1–70). Waltham, MA: Academic Press.

The Rains of Castamere. (2013). *Game of Thrones.* David Nutter (Director). HBO. Air date June 2.

Rank, O. (1941). *Beyond psychology.* New York: Dover Publications.

Rautiainen, I. (2017). Punching, kickin,' drinkin' and talkin' shit: The four essentials of being a superheroine: Representation of female characters in Marvel's *Jessica Jones.* Master's Thesis: University of Jyväskylä.

Red Dragon. Release date October 4, 2002. Universal Pictures. Directed by Brett Ratner.

Red Rose. (2014). *Sons of Anarchy.* Paris Barclay (Director); FX Network. Air date December 2.

Richardson, N. (2004). The gospel according to Spider-Man. *The Journal of Popular Culture,* 37, 694–703.

Rieger, D., & Hofer, M. (2017). How movies can ease the fear of death: The survival or death of the protagonists in meaningful movies. *Mass Communication and Society, 20* (5), 710–733.

Rieger, D., Frischlich, L., Högden, F., Kauf, R., Schramm, K., & Tappe, E. (2015). Appreciation in the face of death: Meaningful films buffer against death-related anxiety. *Journal of Communication, 65*(2), 351–372.

Riesman, A. (2017). Why cops and soldiers love the Punisher. *Vulture.* November 16. http://www.vulture.com/2017/11/marvel-punisher-police-military-fandom.html.

Ring, K. (1984). *Heading toward omega: In search of the meaning of the near-death experience.* New York: William Morrow & Co.

Rivera, J. (2015). The 10 most disturbingly gorgeous dishes from NBC's 'Hannibal.' Business Insider.com, June 5, https://www.businessinsider.com/hannibal-food-2015-6.

Roadhouse Blues. (2019). *The Punisher.* Jim O'Hanlon (Director); Netflix. Release date January 18.

Rodrick, S. (2018). Jon Bernthal is learning to keep his demons at bay. *Esquire.* January 3. https://www.esquire.com/entertainment/movies/a14443788/jon-bernthal-the-punisher-cover/.

Rogers, R., Sanders, C., & Vess, M. (2019). The terror management of meaning and growth: How mortality salience affects growth-oriented processes and the meaningfulness of life. In C. Routledge and M. Vess (Eds). *Handbook of Terror Management Theory,* pp. 325–345. London: Academic Press.

Romano, J. (2019).The *Game of Thrones* finale had a chance to break the wheel. It upheld the status quo. Vox.com, May 19. https://www.vox.com/2019/5/19/18629699/game-of-thrones-finale-reaction-who-won-the-iron-throne.

Rosenberg, B.D., & Siegel, J.T. (2018). A 50-year review of psychological reactance theory: Do not read this article. *Motivation Science, 4*(4), 281–300.

Rosenblatt, A., Greenberg, J., Solomon, S., Pyszczynski, T., & Lyon, D. (1989). Evidence for terror management theory I: The effects of mortality salience on reactions to those who violate or uphold cultural values. *Journal of Personality and Social Psychology, 57,* 681–690.

Roti. (2013). *Hannibal.* Guillermo Navarro (Director); NBC. Air date June 6.

Routledge, C., & Arndt, J. (2008). Self-sacrifice as self-defense: Mortality salience increases efforts to affirm a symbolic immortal self at the expense of the physical self. *European Journal of Social Psychology, 38,* 531–541.

Routledge, C., Arndt, J., & Goldenberg, J.L. (2004). A time to tan: Proximal and distal effects of mortality salience on sun exposure intentions. *Personality and Social Psychology Bulletin, 30,* 1347–1358.

Rubin, M. (2018). Fear of self-annihilation and existential uncertainty as predictors of worldview defense: Comparing terror management and uncertainty theories. *The Journal of Social Psychology, 158*(3), 298–308.

Sakizuke. (2014). *Hannibal.* Tim Hunter (Director); NBC. Air date March 7.

Savoureux. (2013). *Hannibal.* David Slade (Director); NBC. Air date June 20.

Scar Tissue. (2019). *The Punisher.* Iain B. MacDonald (Director); Netflix. Release date January 18.

Schedeen, J. (2019). Marvel's *The Punisher*: Will season 2 be Frank's last fight? January 18, IGN. https://www.ign.com/articles/2019/01/18/marvels-the-punisher-season-2-review.

Schimel, J., Hayes, J., Williams, T., & Jahrig, J. (2007). Is death really the worm at the core? Converging evidence that worldview threat increases death-thought accessibility. *Journal of Personality and Social Psychology, 92,* 789–803.

Schimel, J., Simon, L., Greenberg, J., Pyszczynski, T., Solomon, S., Waxmonsky, J., & Arndt, J. (1999). Stereotypes and terror management: Evidence that mortality salience enhances stereotypic thinking and preferences. *Journal of Personality and Social Psychology, 77*(5), 905–925.

Schindler, S., Reinhard, M.A., Dobiosch, S., Steffan-Fauseweh, I., Özdemir, G., & Greenberg, J. (2019). The attenuating effect of mortality salience on dishonest behavior. *Motivation and Emotion, 43,* 52–62.

Schmeichel, B.J., & Martens, A. (2005). Self-affirmation and mortality salience: Affirming values reduces worldview defense and death-thought accessibility. *Personality and Social Psychology Bulletin, 31*(5), 658–667.

Schmid, D. (2005). *Natural Born Celebrities: Serial Killers in American Culture.* Chicago: The University of Chicago Press.

Schmitt, H., Sullivan, D., & Young, I.F. (2019). Colonized immortality striving and racial dehumanization in *Sorry to Bother You*. *Ernest Becker Foundation Newsletter, 26(3)*, 6–7.

Schneider, K.J. (1993). *Horror and the holy: Wisdom-teachings of the monster tale*. Chicago, Illinois: Open Court.

Schneider, K.J. (2019). From despair and fanaticism to awe: A posttraumatic growth perspective on cinematic horror. In D. Sullivan and J. Greenberg (Eds.), *Fade to black: Death in classic and contemporary film*, pp. 217–230. New York: Palgrave Macmillan.

Second Sons. (2013). *Game of Thrones*; Michelle MacLaren (Director); HBO. Air date May 19.

Secondo. (2015). *Hannibal*. Vincenzo Natali (Director); NBC. Air date June 18.

Seeds. (2008). *Sons of Anarchy*. Charles Haid (Director); FX Network. Air date September 10.

Seneca. *Moral Essays, Volume II: De Consolatione ad Marciam. De Vita Beata. De Otio. De Tranquillitate Animi. De Brevitate Vitae. De Consolatione ad Polybium. De Consolatione ad Helviam*. Translated by John W. Basore. Loeb Classical Library 254. Cambridge, MA: Harvard University Press, 1932.

Sepinwall, A. (2008). *Sons of Anarchy*: Kurt Sutter Q&A. NJ.COM. November 26. Retrieved from http://www.nj.com/entertainment/tv/index.ssf/2008/11/sons_of_anarchy_kurt_ sutter_qa.html.

Seven. (1995) David Fincher (Director). New Line Cinemas.

Shaw, D. (2003). The mastery of Hannibal Lecter. In S.J. Schneider and D. Shaw (Eds.), *Dark thoughts: Philosophical reflections on cinematic horror* (pp. 10–24). Lanham, MD: Scarecrow Press.

Shaw, D. (2015). Empathy for the devil. In J. Westfall (Ed). *Hannibal Lecter and philosophy: The heart of the matter*, pp. 199–216, Chicago, Illinois: Open Court.

Shaw, R.L. (2004). Making sense of violence: A study of narrative meaning. *Qualitative Research in Psychology, 1*(2), 131–151.

Sheffield, R. (2012). 'Sons of Anarchy' is Hamlet in black leather. *Rolling Stone*. November 22. Retrieved from http://www.rollingstone.com/movies/news/sons-of-anarchy-is-hamlet-in-black-leather-20121113.

Shiizakana. (2014). *Hannibal*. Michael Rymer (Director); NBC. Air date April 25.

Shrum, L.J. (2001). Processing strategy moderates the cultivation effect. *Human Communication Research, 27*(1), 94–120.

The Silence of the Lambs (1991). Demme, J. (Director). United States: Orion Pictures Corporation.

Sims, D. (2015). The sublime darkness of *Jessica Jones*. *The Atlantic*. November 19. https:// www.theatlantic.com/entertainment/archive/2015/11/jessica-jones-marvel-netflix/ 416685/.

Sims, J. (2018). George R.R. Martin answers *Times* staffers' burning questions. *New York Times*, October 16. https://www.nytimes.com/2018/10/16/t-magazine/george-rr-martin-qanda-game-of-thrones.html.

Sinclair, M. (1984). Whispered issues: Hormones and women's stability. *Washington Post*. https://www.washingtonpost.com/archive/opinions/1984/09/02/whispered-issue-hormones-and-womens-stability/f338997b-4597-43c2-b273-43dbb96e048a/?utm_term =.873b29df664e.

Sleep of Babies. *(2008). Sons of Anarchy*. Terrence O'Hara (Director); FX Network. Air date November 19.

Sloboda, N. (2012). Hamlet in (and off) stages: Television, serialization, and Shakespeare in *Sons of Anarchy. Journal of the Wooden O Symposium, 12*, 85–99.

So. (2010). *Sons of Anarchy*. Stephen Kay (Director); FX Network. Air date September 7.

Solomon, S., Greenberg, J., & Pyszczynski, T. (2000). Pride and prejudice: Fear of death and social behavior. *Current Directions in Psychological Science, 9*(6), 200–204.

Solomon, S., Greenberg, J., & Pyszczynski, T. (2004). The cultural animal: Twenty years of terror management theory and research. In J. Greenberg, S.L. Koole, and T. Pyszczynski (Eds.). *Handbook of experimental existential psychology* (pp. 13–34). New York: Guilford.

Solomon, S., Greenberg, J., & Pyszczynski, T. (2015). *The worm at the core: On the role of death in life.* New York: Random House.

Solomon, S., Greenberg, J., & Pyszczynski, T. (1991). Terror management theory of self-esteem. In C.R. Snyder & D. Forsyth (Eds.), *Handbook of social and clinical Psychology: The health perspective* (pp. 21–40). New York: Pergamon Press.

Sorbet (2013). *Hannibal.* James Foly (Director); NBC. Air date May 9.

Speece, M.W., & Brent, S.B. (1992). The acquisition of a mature understanding of three components of the concept of death. *Death Studies, 16*(3), 211–229.

Spider-Man: Homecoming. (2017). Jon Watts (Director). United States. Columbia Pictures.

Stadler, J. (2017). The empath and the psychopath: Ethics, imagination, and intercorporeality in Bryan Fuller's *Hannibal. Film-Philosophy, 21(3),* 410–427.

Stephenson, C. (2013). A taste for killing. Hannibal: Season 1 (commentary). Lions Gate Films.

Straw. (2013). *Sons of Anarchy.* Paris Barclay (Director); FX Network. Air date September 10.

Su-zakana. (2014). *Hannibal.* Vincenzo Natali (Director); NBC. Air date April 18.

Sullivan, D., & Greenberg, J. (2013a). Introduction: when the lights go down. In D. Sullivan and J. Greenberg (Eds.), *Fade to black: Death in classic and contemporary film,* pp. 1–18. New York: Palgrave Macmillan.

Sullivan, D., & Greenberg, J. (2013b). Conclusion: Cinematic death benefits. In D. Sullivan and J. Greenberg (Eds.), *Fade to black: Death in classic and contemporary film,* pp. 231–246. New York: Palgrave Macmillan.

Sullivan, D., Greenberg, J., & Landau, M.J. (2009). Toward a new understanding of two films from the dark side: Utilizing terror management theory to analyze *Rosemary's Baby* and *Straw Dogs. Journal of Popular Film and Television, 37*(4), 189–198.

Sutherland, C. (1990). Changes in religious beliefs, attitudes, and practices following near-death experiences: An Australian study. *Journal of Near-Death Studies, 9*(1), 21–31.

Sweet and Vaded (2013). *Sons of Anarchy.* Paris Barclay (Director); FX Network. Air date October 22.

Takiawase. (2014). *Hannibal.* David Semel (Director); NBC. Air date March 21.

Tamborini, R. (2011). Moral intuition and media entertainment. *Journal of Media Psychology, 23,* 39–45.

Tan, S. (2019). An illustrated guide to all 6,887 deaths in 'Game of Thrones.' https://www.washingtonpost.com/graphics/entertainment/game-of-thrones/?noredirect=on&utm_term=.57a9ade141dc.

Tassi, P. (2019). The Punisher tries, and fails, to do a Trump storyline in a disappointing season 2. January 20, Forbes.com. https://www.forbes.com/sites/insertcoin/2019/01/20/the-punisher-tries-and-fails-to-do-a-trump-storyline-in-a-disappointing-season-2/#273cf40f7058.

Taylor, L.D. (2012). Death and television: Terror management theory and themes of law and justice on television. *Death Studies, 36,* 340–359.

Taylor, S.E., & Brown, J.D. (1988). Illusion and well-being: a social psychological perspective on mental health. *Psychological Bulletin, 103*(2), 193–210.

Tenga, A., & Bassett, J.F. (2016). You kill or you die, or you die and you kill: Meaning and violence in AMC's *The Walking Dead. The Journal of Popular Culture, 49,* 1280–1300.

Thomas, D. (2000). Death and its details. In S. Prince (Ed.) *Screening violence,* pp. 86–98. New Brunswick, New Jersey: Rutgers University Press.

3 Am. (2017). *The Punisher.* Tom Shankland (Director); Netflix. Release date November 17.

To Be Act 2. (2011). *Sons of Anarchy.* Kurt Sutter (Director); FX Network. Air date December 6.

Tolstoy, L. (1921). A confession. Translated by Louise and Aylmer Maude. http://web.mnstate.edu/gracyk/courses/web%20publishing/TolstoyConfession.htm#:~:text=Differently%20expressed%2C%20the%20question%20is,not%20destroy%3F%22%20...&text=It%20consists%20in%20not%20knowing,an%20evil%20and%20an%20 absurdity.

Tome-wan. (2014). *Hannibal.* Michael Rymer (Director); NBC. Air date May 16.

Trouble the Waters. (2019). *The Punisher.* Jeremy Webb (Director); Netflix. Release date January 18.

Two Dead Men. (2017). *The Punisher.* Tom Shankland (Director); Netflix. Release date November 17.

Two Swords. (2014). *Game of Thrones*; David Benioff and D.B. Weiss (Directors); HBO. Air date April 6.

Uhlich, K. (2015). Hannibal: The TV show that went too far. BBC, Aug 28, http://www.bbc.com/culture/story/20150828-hannibal-the-tv-show-that-went-too-far.

Unholy Night. (2012). *American Horror Story Asylum.* Lehmann, M. (Director); FX. Air date December 5.

United States. Surgeon General's Scientific Advisory Committee on Television, Social Behavior, & United States. Public Health Service. Office of the Surgeon General. (1972). *Television and Growing Up: the Impact of Television Violence: Report to the Surgeon General.* US Government Printing Office.

Vail, K.E., & Juhl, J. (2015). An appreciative view of the brighter side of terror management processes. *Social Sciences, 4*(4), 1020–1045.

Vail, K.E., Arndt, J., & Abdollahi, A. (2012). Exploring the existential function of religion and supernatural agent beliefs among Christians, Muslims, Atheists, and Agnostics. *Personality and Social Psychology Bulletin, 38*(10), 1288–1300.

Vail, K.E., Juhl, J., Arndt, J., Vess, M., Routledge, C., & Rutjens, B.T. (2012). When death is good for life: Considering the positive trajectories of terror management. *Personality and Social Psychology Review, 16*(4), 303–329.

van den Bos, K., Poortvliet, P.M., Maas, M., Miedema, J., & van den Ham, E.J. (2005). An enquiry concerning the principles of cultural norms and values: The impact of uncertainty and mortality salience on reactions to violations and bolstering of cultural worldviews. *Journal of Experimental Social Psychology, 41*(2), 91–113. doi: 10.1016/j.jesp.2004.06.001.

Van Der Werff, E.T. (2015). Cannibalism isn't that big of a deal. Vox.com. June 4, https://www.vox.com/2015/6/4/8729679/hannibal-season-3-interview-bryan-fuller.

Vess, M., Routledge, C., Landau, M.J., & Arndt, J. (2009). The dynamics of death and meaning: The effects of death-relevant cognitions and personal need for structure on perceptions of meaning in life. *Journal of Personality and Social Psychology, 97*(4), 728–744.

Virtue, G. (2019). Farewell, Jessica Jones: The last woman standing in the Marvel-Netflix era. *The Guardian*, Jun, 14. https://www.theguardian.com/tv-and-radio/2019/jun/14/jessica-jones-netflix-marvel-season-threeVirtue,%20G.%20(2019).%20Farewell,%20Jessica%20Jones:%20The%20last%20woman%20standing%20in%20the%20Marvel-Netflix%20era.%20The%20Guardian,%20Jun,%2014.

Virtue of Vicious (2017). *The Punisher.* Jim O'Hanlon (Director); Netflix. Release date November 17.

Walk of Punishment. *(2013). Game of Thrones.* David Benioff (Director). HBO. Air date April 14.

Walton, P.L. (2019). "You win or you die": The royal flush of power in *Game of Thrones. Canadian Review of American Studies, 49,* 99–114.

Wattercutter, A. (2018). Season 2 of *Jessica Jones* proves she's ahead of her time. Wired.com. March 18. https://www.wired.com/story/jessica-jones-season-2/.

Wegner, D.M. (1994). Ironic processes of mental control. *Psychological Review, 101,* 34–52.

Wegner, D.M., Schneider, D.J., Carter, S.R., & White, T.L. (1987). Paradoxical effects of thought suppression. *Journal of Personality and Social Psychology, 53,* 5–13.

Westfall, J. (2015). Hello Dr. Lecter. In J. Westfall (Ed). *Hannibal Lecter and philosophy: The heart of the matter,* pp. xi-xx, Chicago, Illinois: Open Court.

The Whirlwind. (2019). *The Punisher.* Jeremy Webb (Director); Netflix. Release date January 18.

Wilson, B.J., Kunkel, D., Linz, D., Potter, J., Donnerstein, E., Smith, S.L., ... & Gray, T. (1997). Violence in television programming overall: University of California, Santa Barbara study. *National Television Violence Study, 1,* 3–184.

Wilson, B.J., Kunkel, D., Linz, D., Potter, W.J., Donnerstein, E., Smith, S.L., Blumenthal, E.,

& Berry, M. (1998). Violence in television programming overall: University of California, Santa Barbara study. In *National television violence study* (Vol. 2, pp. 3–204). Thousand Oaks, CA: Sage.

Winter Is Coming. (2011). *Game of Thrones*. Timothy Van Patten (Director). HBO. Air date April 17.

Wisman, A., & Goldenberg, J.L. (2005). From the grave to the cradle: Evidence that mortality salience engenders a desire for offspring. *Journal of Personality and Social Psychology, 89*, 46–61.

With an X. (2011). *Sons of Anarchy*. Guy Ferland (Director); FX Network. Air date October 11.

Withers, J.M. (2010). Lady Macbeth as Hamlet's Mother: *Sons of Anarchy*, Season One. *International Journal of Motorcycle Studies*, 6 (1). http://ijms.nova.edu/Fall2010/ IJMS_Rvw.Withers.html.

Wolpe, D. (2003). The real meaning of the Adam and Eve story. Presentation at the Rabbinical Assemblies Convention. Los Angeles, CA. April.

Wonder Woman. (2017). Patty Jenkins (Director). United States. Warner Brothers.

Wong, M.S. (2015). Cosmopolitan Hannibal. In J. Westfall (Ed). *Hannibal Lecter and philosophy: The heart of the matter*, pp. 3–14, Chicago, Illinois: Open Court.

Worcester, K. (2012). The punisher and the politics of retributive justice. *Law Text Culture, 16*, 329–352.

The Wrath of the Lamb. (2015). *Hannibal*. Michael Rymer (Director); NBC. Release date August 29.

Wren-Lewis, J. (1988). The darkness of God: A personal report on consciousness transformation through an encounter with death. *Journal of Humanistic Psychology, 28*(2), 105–122.

Yalom, I.D. (1980). *Existential psychotherapy*. New York: Basic Books.

Yalom, I.D. (2009*). Staring at the sun: Overcoming the terror of death*. San Francisco, California: Wiley.

Yetzer, A.M., & Pyszczynski, T. (2019). Terror management theory and psychological disorder: Ineffective anxiety-buffer functioning as a transdiagnostic vulnerability factor for psychopathology. In C. Routledge and M. Vess (Eds). *Handbook of Terror Management Theory* (pp. 417–448). London: Academic Press.

You Win or You Die. (2011). *Game of Thrones*. Daniel Minaham (Director). HBO. Air date May 29.

Young, I.E., Sullivan, D., & Palitsky, R. (2018). Applying Terror Management Theory to art, film, and media: A theoretical and empirical review. In C. Routledge and M. Vess (Eds). *Handbook of Terror Management Theory*, pp. 535–558. London: Academic Press.

Young Frankenstein. (1974). Mel Brooks (Director). United States. 20th Century Fox.

Zanin, A. (2013). Sometimes a motorcycle is just a motorcycle: Freud and Hamlet come to Charming. In George A. Dunn and Jason T. Eberl (Eds). *Sons of anarchy and philosophy: Brains before bullets*. (Kindle version). Retrieved from Amazon.com.

Zanin, A. (2015). The art of killing. In J. Westfall (Ed). *Hannibal Lecter and philosophy: The heart of the matter*, pp. 185–195, Chicago, Illinois: Open Court.

Zilboorg, G. (1943). The fear of death. *Psychoanalytic Quarterly, 12*, 465–475.

Zillmann, D. (1998). The psychology of the appeal of portrayals of violence. In J.H. Goldstein (Ed.) *Why We Watch: The attraction of violent entertainment*, pp. 179–211. New York: Oxford University Press.

Zillmann, D., & Gibson, R. (1996). Evolution of the horror genre. In J. Weaver and R. Tamborini (Eds.), *Horror films: Current research in audience preferences and reactions*, pp. 15–31. Hillsdale, New Jersey: Lawrence Erlbaum Associates.

Zuckerman, M. (1994). Behavioral expressions and biosocial bases of sensation seeking. New York: Cambridge University Press.

Zuckerman, M., & Litle, P. (1986). Personality and curiosity about morbid and sexual events. *Personality and Individual Differences, 2*, 49–65.

Index